Springwood Avenue Harmony

Best Wishes

Pamela Horner

Charlie Horner

Springwood Avenue Harmony Series

Volume 1 (1871 - 1945)

Springwood Avenue Harmony

The Unique Musical Legacy of Asbury Park's West Side
Volume 1 (1871 - 1945)

Charles J. Horner Jr.
Pamela Horner

Edited by Don Stine and Douglas E. Friedman

Classic Urban Harmony® Press, Somerset, NJ

Cover photo Credits: Vivian Eley record from the Classic Urban Harmony
Archives; Photo of Vivian Eley courtesy of Clifford Johnson; Ad for the
Smile-A-While Inn from the *Asbury Park Press;* Photo of Clifford Johnson
by Joseph A. Carter Sr., courtesy of Madonna Carter Jackson;
Photo of the Dickerson Band, courtesy of Anita Clark; Photo of
Leroy Vanderveer, courtesy of Rhonda Ladaye

Library of Congress Control Number: 2020900159

Published by Classic Urban Harmony Press
210 Sherwood Court
Somerset, NJ 08873
www.ClassicUrbanHarmony.net

Printed in the United States

First Edition

This book is dedicated to the memory of
Rhythm & Blues pioneer and friend, Bobby Thomas,
and to the hundreds of unsung and long forgotten music heroes
from the West Side of Asbury Park, New Jersey.
After years of silence, we've again given you voice.

"A people without the knowledge of their past history, origin and culture is like a tree without roots."

- Marcus Garvey

Contents

Preface

Writing this book has been a journey. When we embarked on it we had no idea where it would take us or how we might be changed by it. Oh, at first we thought we knew where we were going. We were experienced music historians specializing in black music. When our friend, Bobby Thomas, implored us to help preserve the legacy of music from Asbury Park's Springwood Avenue, we thought it would be straightforward. Then we read Daniel Wolff's intriguing book, *4th of July, Asbury Park,* and realized there was more here than met the eye. Continuing on was like opening a hundred-year-old locked safe. Would we find buried treasure or be opening Pandora's Box? Or maybe both?

We rode off into uncharted territory. We started with interviews of area singers and musicians, basically anyone who would talk to us. We learned of a music's evolution, shaped by the social, economic, racial and political divides of a ten-block area struggling to survive. There were tales of good times and bad, cases of against-all-odds glorious success mixed with tragedy and despair.

We started with a multimedia presentation on our findings for the Asbury Park Historical Society, followed by a historic gospel concert to honor the Missionary Jubilaires. With the help of the Society and photos from noted area photographer Joseph A. Carter Sr. (courtesy of daughter Madonna Carter Jackson), we assembled a huge exhibit on Asbury Park's West Side music that ran for a week at the Heaven Gallery on Cookman Avenue, followed by a month at Monmouth University. From there, the exhibit was greatly expanded and moved to the Monmouth County Historical Association Museum in Freehold, New Jersey, where it stayed for five months.

Each step led to more contacts and more information. Yet, the more we learned, the more we realized how little we knew. Still, we plodded on, letting the road take us where it would. Through the journey, we brought to life the stories of some amazing musicians and singers whose accomplishments had been buried for many years.

One more thought. Researching and writing this book has changed us. We are not the same people who embarked on this trip several years ago. We've grown in knowledge and perception. We now understand that music isn't a by-product of communities like the West Side - it's the heart and soul of those communities. That may be changing as increased mobility makes close-knit communities a thing of the past. We hope not. They say it's not the destination but the journey that counts. This is the first of two volumes of Asbury Park's West Side music history. With the completion of the second volume, we'll have reached our destination. We can never go back . It's a one way trip!

Charlie & Pamela Horner, October 21, 2019.

ACKNOWLEDGMENTS

The authors want to express our sincere gratitude to the following people for their help with this monumental two volume work: Lynn Abbott, Nicky Addeo, Ernest Boynton Jr., Billy Brown, Virginia Brown, Stan Cain, Dennis Carroll. Ellen Carroll, Bill Carter, Ryan Celli, Eileen Chapman, Tom Chesek, Frank Cicerale, Marian Cicerale, Anita D. Clark, David Clayton, Yvonne Clayton, Ellen Coleman, Ron Coleman, Al Covington, Ray Dahrouge, Ben Dinkins, Milton Edelman, William Farley, Douglas E. Friedman, Linda Friedman, Denise Gardner, Claire Garland, Rick Geffken, Kay Harris, Madonna Carter Jackson, Stoney Jackson, Cliff Johnson, Jake Jones, Ted Jones, Edna Jones-Farley, Chris Jordan, Melissa Keeling. Jayme Klein, Ira Kreizman, Rhonda Ladaye, Karen Pugh Lascaris, Herman Latimore, Christine Lutz, Tony Maples Jr, Kathleen Melgar, Jean Mikle, Karen Mindingall, Curtis Moreland, Caleb Morris, Willie Morris, Evelyn Murphy, Sam Murphy, David Parreott, Dorian Parreott, Joe Peterson, Helen Chantel-Pike, Carol Price, Vaune Peck, Gilda Rogers, Susan Rosenberg, **Gary D. Saretzky**, Norman Seldin, Doug Seroff, George Severini, Sam Siciliano, Robert Skank, Jennifer Ward Souder, Darryl Stewart, Robert Stewart, Don Stine, Lorraine Stone, Billy Terrell, Bobby Thomas, Randy Thomas, Leon Trent, Charles Trott, Lenny Welch, Rev. Randy Wilson, Richard Witcher, Daniel Wolff and Roger Young.

In addition, we'd like to thank the following organizations and institutions for their unwavering support and assistance: Asbury Angels Foundation, Asbury Park African American Music Project, Asbury Park Historical Society, Asbury Park Library, Asbury Park Music Foundation, Asbury Park Museum, Bruce Springsteen Archives and Center for American Music at Monmouth University, Institute For Jazz Studies at Rutgers University, Monmouth County Archives, Monmouth County Historical Association Museum & Library, Monmouth University's Center For The Arts, Ocean Township Historical Museum, Rutgers University Libraries New Jersey Regional Studies Special Collections, and the T. Thomas Fortune Foundation.

Special thanks goes to Madonna Carter Jackson for her tireless efforts to preserve and publish the photos taken by her father, Joseph A Carter Sr., the West Side's premiere photographer. We credit and thank Madonna for permission to use many of those photos in this two volume work.

Every effort has been made to obtain rights to and credit the many photos used. As the photos in this volume are 75 to 150 years old, locating some copyright owners was not possible. With most of the photos, copyrights have expired. Publicity photos fall under the category of "Fair Use," especially in context of a scholarly work such as this.

A portion of the proceeds from these works will be donated to the Asbury Park Historical Society for their dedication to the history of Asbury Park and their belief in our work.

Unidentified Asbury Park musician, ca. 1906.
Property of the Classic Urban Harmony Archives.

INTRODUCTION

The year was 1906. It was most likely summertime when this young, twenty-something African American musician (pictured on the opposite page) nervously walked into the Sunbeam Photography Studio to have this portrait taken.

Sunbeam was a small outfit, located at 1 Main Street in Asbury Park, New Jersey. It was not the biggest photography studio in the shore resort city. No, that honor belonged to Knowlton Company on Cookman Avenue in the "white" section of town. Sunbeam was most likely housed in a small wood frame building between Wesley Lake and the railroad depot. The railroad brought in hundreds of thousands of vacationers each summer to bask in the sun and frolic in the surf. Sunbeam was on the border of Asbury Park proper, with its grand hotels, fine restaurants, bathing pavilions and its electric lit boardwalk. Directly behind Sunbeam was the beginning of the shadow city west of the tracks, called West Park. Just a couple months earlier, Asbury Park had annexed West Park but that didn't make a difference. West Park was a collection of wood framed buildings, some large but most just small shanties on unpaved streets with a serious lack of water and sewer lines. You see, Asbury Park was a segregated city. West Park was home to the African Americans, Native Americans and Southern European immigrants who built the beachfront resort and labored in its hotels and restaurants, but were largely excluded from enjoying it. Sunbeam Studios catered to people of all races and religions, so long as they could afford to sit for a portrait. Time has erased all evidence of Sunbeam Studios except for this one photograph and a 1906 newspaper help wanted ad that read, "WANTED. Photographer, out-door operator. Must be sober."[1]

So, who was this young musician. The photograph gives no clue as to his name or place of origin. Remember, 1906 was still the dawn of American popular music. Jazz, blues and gospel music had not yet been born. Ragtime was replacing waltzes and marches in popularity. Back then, when music wasn't experienced live, it was distributed by sheet music, piano roll or gramophone wax cylinders. Radios, motion pictures with sound, and even 78 rpm records were still in the future.

Even then, cutting edge "hot" music streamed from the night clubs, bars and restaurants along Asbury Park's Springwood Avenue. Located on the West Side (still called West Park, then), Springwood Avenue would soon give rise to some of the most influential musicians and singers in American popular music. Yet, you won't find the

African American section of Asbury Park mentioned in any encyclopedic books on jazz, blues or rhythm & blues. There are jazz history books galore on New Orleans's Storyville, New York's Harlem, Chicago's South Side and even South Central Los Angeles. But until now, there are no books on Asbury Park's West Side, in spite of the area's influences on Count Basie, Duke Ellington, Sonny Greer, Claude Hopkins, Erskine Hawkins, Cozy Cole, Fats Waller, Donald Lambert, Willie Gant and many more. Think that Asbury Park had nothing to do with the blues? The first country blues record by a black male vocalist accompanied by a guitar was by a West Side artist.

All of this may cause the reader to think that the rich musical legacy of Springwood Avenue was somehow unique. It was not. Asbury Park's West Side was but a microcosm of what went on in countless inner city areas across the country. Whenever a group of people is restricted to a small geographic area and cut off from the rest of a city, those people develop their own society, their own culture, their own music. The evolution of music in Asbury Park's West Side is not so different from that of other African American neighborhoods across the country like Baltimore's Pennsylvania Avenue, Philadelphia's North or West Philly, Newark's Third Ward, Memphis' Beale Street, Indianapolis' Indiana Avenue and countless others.

If Asbury Park's West Side was at all unique, it was partly because of its location. Asbury Park was a resort town with hundreds of thousands of vacationers every year. Many frequented the after hours clubs on the West Side for the music. Big name black entertainers played Asbury Park, as it was a nice stop between Atlantic City and New York. Asbury Park High School, one of the few integrated institutions in the city, had a strong emphasis on music education. Black youth saw their older family members playing the Springwood Avenue venues and wanted to follow in their footsteps.

So, who is the young musician in the 1906 portrait? Perhaps he was performing at a Springwood Avenue night spot. Or maybe he was a touring musician, just there to work at one of the "whites only" grand hotel ballrooms. We'll probably never really know. But to us, he represents part of Asbury Park's music legacy that began shortly after the city's founding in 1871 and continued through the eras of jazz, blues, r&b, soul and rock music. Would the 1970's and 1980's rock music of Bruce Springsteen, Southside Johnny, and others have still happened without the West Side musicians that came before them? Probably. But we do know that in music, as in life, everything seems connected. Take away one link in a continuum and everything could turn out quite differently.

- Charlie and Pamela Horner

Notes to the Introduction

[1] "Photographer," *Asbury Park Press*, 15 Aug, 1906, p. 5..

Chapter One

Asbury Park's West Side Beginnings: 1871 - 1900

F. W. Beers Monmouth County Atlas, 1873, showing Ocean Grove and the beginnings of Asbury Park.

Since just after its founding, Asbury Park, New Jersey has been a "music city." As a seaside resort it attracted vacationers, and vacationers wanted to be entertained. The musicians of the beachfront venues, from Arthur Pryor to Bruce Springsteen, are well known. Less recognized, yet just as important, are the musicians and singers of the shadow city west of Asbury Park's railroad tracks. Music from that area, known first as "West Park" and then as the "West Side," is what this book is all about.

The city of Asbury Park, New Jersey was founded in 1871 by James A. Bradley. Prior to that the land that was to become one of New Jersey's premier shore resorts had been just a distressed and desolate stretch of oceanfront. Along the shore, extending back some five hundred yards, was only shifting sand with scarcely any vegetation. Giant sand dunes, some ten to fifteen feet high, littered the beach. Further inland, pine trees, scrub oaks and dense impenetrable undergrowth formed an almost uninhabitable wilderness.[1]

The first inhabitants of the land that would become Asbury Park were undoubtedly members of the Lenni-Lenape tribe of Native Americans. By the early 1800's, members of an extended family of Cherokees, surnamed the Richardsons, migrated from Georgia to central New Jersey where they intermarried with their Lenape cousins, the Reevey family. That was the origin of the "Sand Hill" tribe that would make their home west

James Revey · Jonathan Richardson · Isaac R. Richardson · Chief Ryers Crummal · Robert Richardson · Robert Revey

Theodora Richardson Bell · Edith Richardson Gardner · Christina Richardson Dickerson · Adeline Richardson Thomas · Restella Richardson Fox · Charlotte Richardson Gaines

Descendants of the Sand Hill Indians, ca. 1962. Jonathan Richardson
(top, second from left) led his own orchestra and the popular
Knights of Pythias Brass Band. Christina Richardson Dickerson
(front, third from the left) played piano in the James Dickerson Band.

Both were important Asbury Park ensembles in the early 20th Century.
[*See Chapters Three and Six*].
Photo courtesy of Christina Richardson's great nephew, musician Bill Carter.

and northwest of current day Asbury Park.[2] "Sand Hill Indians" would be employed by James Bradley to build many of Asbury Park's Victorian-style homes. In time, the Sand Hill Indians would intermarry with African American residents of West Park and contribute much to the culture of the area. In particular, their contributions to music will be covered in *Chapter Three*.

But, in the entire stretch between the established town of Long Branch to the north and the Shark River to the south, there was only a scattering of inhabitants. In 1868, there were no residents at all in what would become Asbury Park. One of the closest inhabitants to this area was Britton White, whose farm lay a few hundred yards west of what is now downtown Asbury Park, in the area that would become West Park.[3]

Britton White was the great-grandson of a Revolutionary War loyalist of the same name who originally owned much of the land that now makes up Asbury Park. In 1779, the New Jersey legislature seized that land, along with that of many other loyalists and offered it for sale. Either the sale never took place, or the purchaser never took possession, for the White family continued to farm the area long after that.[4] In their farmhouse, on January 16, 1807, Britton White was born.[5]

In 1868, Rev. W. B. Osborne and Rev. George Neal, pastors from nearby Long Branch, visited the area looking for an isolated enclave to hold religious camp meetings. This led to the formation of the Methodist Camp Meeting Association. Osborne and Neal selected the shore area just south of Long Pond (now Wesley Lake). They purchased land from Britton White and others and in 1870, divided it into lots for their members to form Ocean Grove. The first

James A. Bradley
Founder of Asbury Park
Courtesy of the Asbury Park Museum

lot was purchased by James A. Bradley.[6] Bradley was a wealthy New York City businessman, co-owner of the Bradley & Smith brush manufacturing company.

Ocean Grove's original charter prohibited most popular music (except religious music) dance, liquor, tobacco, card playing, theatre, Sunday bathing and much more. In 1871, James Bradley eventually wandered north of Long Pond, purchased 658 acres from Luther Elting for close to $100,000 and began building Asbury Park.[7] While still holding to Methodist beliefs, Asbury Park was to be a city, as opposed to the permanent Christian camp meeting community of Ocean Grove. Furthermore, Asbury Park was to serve as a buffer between the strictly religious Ocean Grove and the wide-open town of Long Branch, just ten miles up the coast. Long Branch had a reputation for drinking, gambling and all sorts of debauchery since its beginnings in the late 1700's. [In fact, Dodge City's infamous Long Branch Saloon of American "Wild West" lore, was named by its first owner after his prior hometown in New Jersey.][8]

James A. Bradley laid out plans for Asbury Park's streets and sold building lots to encourage settlement. As early as January 1872, advertisements could be seen in the New York City newspapers offering lots 33 by 100 feet for $50 to $400. The ads described the "Park" as "a frontage of one mile on the Atlantic Ocean and a roadway of a half a mile on the banks of Wesley Lake [the new name for Long Pond].[9]

In its early years, Asbury Park experienced phenomenal growth. From the undeveloped wilderness of sand dunes, stunted trees and briars, Asbury Park soon took shape. Initially, Bradley had arrived by horse-drawn carriage with a black servant, John Baker. Baker, a former slave from Virginia, became arguably Asbury Park's first African American resident.[10] But, by the summer of 1874, New York City residents, anxious to escape the sweltering summer heat, began arriving at Asbury Park by the boatloads.

In the summer of 1875, a rail line of the New Jersey Central was finished, connecting Long Branch with Ocean Beach to the south. The line included a shared depot stop at the western edge of Asbury Park and Ocean Grove.[11] Now, Asbury Park and Ocean Grove could be easily accessed by train from New York City in an hour and a half, and from Philadelphia in two hours and ten minutes. By 1900, Bradley's city had become a bustling summer resort with two hundred hotels and boarding houses offering some eleven thousand rooms for rent. The summer population topped fifty thousand but also included three thousand year-round residents. The train excursions from New York City and Philadelphia brought as many as six hundred thousand summer vacationers. [Of course, Ocean Grove's charter prohibited the train from stopping at the station on Sundays, but that didn't seem to deter people.]

Asbury Park's streets were paved and fifteen miles of storm drains and pipes were added to make Asbury Park the first American seaside city to have a "perfect" drainage system. Streetlights were added. A wide permanent boardwalk was built, connecting wooden piers. Now, refined, well-dressed vacationers could view the ocean without

Asbury Park & Ocean Grove Railroad Depot. From a 1906 post card.

The Coleman House and surrounding beachfront area, ca. 1878.
From T. F. Rose, *Historical and Biographical Atlas of the New Jersey Coast*, 1878.
Courtesy of the Asbury Park Historical Society.

getting sand-covered or wet. Sandy beaches welcomed bathers and sun lovers from Wesley Lake to Deal Lake, about a mile in distance.

As the vacation crowds grew bigger, so did the hotels. One of the earliest and grandest was the Coleman House which opened around 1877. On any summer night, it housed more than three hundred vacationers. It had all the amenities, including a fine dining hall, a bowling alley, a billiard room and a pharmacy. By 1900, numerous other grand hotels had opened across from the beach, including Hotel Brunswick, the Hotel Columbia and the Hotel Plaza.

Asbury Park was only designed to be a small city between the railroad tracks and the ocean. In that area, by 1900, there were already seven churches, numerous restaurants, grand hotels, bathing pavilions, a roller skating rink, an opera house, a downtown shopping and business district and a large brick school with seven hundred children.[12]

Educational Hall, Asbury Park, NJ, ca. 1878.
T. F. Rose, *Historical and Biographical Atlas of the New Jersey Coast*, 1878.
Courtesy of the Asbury Park Historical Society.

In 1876, Bradley even purchased the magnificent Educational Hall building, left over from that year's Philadelphia Centennial Exposition. He had it moved, literally piece by piece, and reassembled in Asbury Park on Grand Avenue near First Avenue. The building originally cost $12,000 to build but Bradley bought it for $900. Of course, moving it must have added greatly to its cost![13] The venue was capable of holding 1500 people. In 1905, the building was moved again, to the southwest corner of Asbury Avenue and Main Street.[14] Educational Hall would be used for major concerts, including one by the African American spiritual group, the Fisk Jubilee Singers in 1891. [*See Chapter Two*].

Among the other African American entertainers to play Asbury Park's Educational Hall were those in the companies of various productions of *Uncle Tom's Cabin*. In the fifty years that followed its first publishing, stage interpretations of Harriet Beecher Stowe's influential pre-Civil War novel had been a mainstay of minstrel entertainment. Though most of these hugely popular minstrel interpretations of *Uncle Tom's Cabin* were filled with demeaning racial stereotypes, the larger productions required huge casts. At first, the entertainers were whites in black-face. As time went on, the competition to be more "authentic" led to hiring black entertainers. Notable musically among these entertainers were black vocal quartets and octets. An unidentified production of *Uncle Tom's Cabin* first played Asbury Park's Educational Hall in August of 1880.[15] We don't know anything of the cast of that show. But in 1902, the Hall was visited by Stetson's Uncle Tom's Cabin Company. Stetson's show was huge, with numerous singers both white and black, a full orchestra and even bloodhounds. Stetson's company first formed in 1889. The 1902 version of the show featured the Creole Lady Quartet singing ragtime tunes when they played Asbury Park.[16] Though not stated in references from that time, it is likely the Educational Hall show audiences were segregated. African Americans did on occasion use Education Hall for special events including a memorial service for a beloved pastor in 1882.[17]

1903 Songbook from Stetson's
Uncle Tom's Cabin Production.
Classic Urban Harmony Archives

Asbury Park electric trolleys, ca. 1900
Courtesy of the Asbury Park Museum

In an era before the automobile, Asbury Park was relatively easy for vacationers to get to. Train excursions for the eighty-mile trip from Philadelphia began at 7 a.m. from the North Philadelphia depot and cost $1.50 per person.[18] Arriving at the Asbury Park - Ocean Grove station, vacationers could grab a carriage ride or walk along Wesley Lake to the beach. They'd often find Wesley Lake filled with close to 400 pleasure boats, each with fancy awnings and cushions. At the beach, there were three principal bathing areas from which ropes were stretched into the water and securely fastened to posts driven into the sand. That way, bathers could go quite a distance into the surf, safely.[19]

4 — The Casino—Asbury Park.
Copyright 1905 by J. Murray Jordan.

1905 Postcard showing the grandeur of Asbury Park's beach resort.

In 1888, Asbury Park became the first city in New Jersey, and the second city in the United States to have an electric trolley. Boats still competed with railways to bring vacationers to Asbury Park, but large boats could not dock in either Asbury Park or Long Branch. Thus, the Atlantic Coast Electric Railroad built a system of tracks to carry passengers from a dock at the Shark River inlet to the south, through and around Asbury Park, across a bridge over Deal Lake and up to Long Branch.[20]

But the railroad tracks that brought such prosperity to Asbury Park also symbolized something more sinister. West of Main Street, beyond the initial boundary of Asbury Park which ended at the railroad tracks, was a completely different scene. That area, referred to at first as "West (Asbury) Park" and later as "The West Side," housed the workforce that had been brought in to build the resort area of Asbury Park and work in the hotel and other business service jobs. These workers were a mix of Native Americans and African Americans who fled the Reign of Terror of the Ku Klux Klan in the southern states, along with members of the Jewish faith and recent immigrants from southern Italy (Sicily), Germany, Turkey.[21] Asbury Park was expanding so rapidly that Bradley could ill afford to pay workers on public work projects. For years, he paid them in store credit instead of dollars, an illegal labor practice for which he was cited in 1879.[22]

The Beginnings of
West [Asbury] Park

Before 1882, the area just west of Asbury Park was still pretty much the domain of Britton White and his family, whose farmhouse was one of the few residences there. In March of 1882, White gave in to the relentless offers to purchase his land. He sold all 75 acres to Frederick G. Burnham of Newark for $75,000, a huge sum at that time. Like Bradley had done to the east, Burnham laid out streets and partitioned the area into building lots of 50 by 150 feet, offering them for sale at $1,200 to $2,500 per lot.[23] Many lots sold for much less, depending on location.

"The streets of 'West Park' radiated erratically from the main artery of Springwood Avenue in marked contrast to the geometric regularity of the Asbury Park core. Whereas Bradley envisioned his development as a haven for the elite, Burnham sought instead to capitalize on the housing demand generated by the scores of workers who staffed the beachfront hotels. West Park was thus a hastily assembled space, lacking both the grandeur and long term vision that had structured the early growth of the Asbury Park core."[24]

Frederick G. Burnham
Courtesy of the Asbury Park Museum

Lots sold swiftly as the demand for land in Asbury Park proper exceeded demand. Within a year, West Park was dotted with cottages. Burnham profited handsomely. That was until 1886, when sales were stifled by what became known as the Charter Oak Scandal.

Sometime prior to 1886, George R. Lord also invested heavily in West Park real estate. Lord would later be called the "Founder of the West Side." Lord apparently sold a couple of plots of land to George M. Bartholomew, president of the Charter Oaks Insurance Company of Hartford, Connecticut. Bartholomew paid with two promissory notes, essentially legal IOU's. Bartholomew had a habit of borrowing money through Charter Oaks, eventually totaling $1,000,000 of debt. When payment came due, Bartholomew disappeared to Canada, bankrupting Charter Oaks. In the meantime, Lord sold the two notes to the First National Bank of Asbury Park at a discounted rate. When the bank realized Bartholomew had defaulted on the loans, they mistakenly thought that he'd invested in Burnham's land and put a lien on Burnham's property. People stopped purchasing West Park lots from Burnham due to the bank lien on them. Burnham then sued the bank and its officers for $100,000.[25] It was never reported as to whether or not Burnham won his case, but from that point on, George Lord became the primary real estate developer of West Park land.

By 1894, West Park had grown to a population of 2500, including what newspapers referred to as the "colored settlement." The area had thirty-five stores and a number of churches. [26]

Before 1900, the West Park streets were unpaved and without a sewage system or garbage pickup. While electricity was provided for the beach promenade, people in West Park used kerosene lamps. From the beginning, each of West Park's ethnic groups settled into their own little enclaves. But since West Park was only ten blocks long and even less wide, interaction was necessary and cordial. People of West Park were united by one common plight. They were all looked upon as second class citizens by the white Methodist ruling class of Asbury Park proper. As the years went by, the population of the West Side would become more and more African American and Italian American. Italian immigrants and their descendants would settle into the area closest to Asbury Park and just west of the tracks, that was called "Little Italy." African Americans would settle farther west, along Springwood Avenue. But for now, West Park would remain an ethnically diverse area.

By the mid-1880's it became clear that workers, especially African American and Italian workers, were not to share the same privileges and amenities as Asbury Park's guests and residents. People of color were only allowed on a small section of Asbury Park's beach, at the foot of Wesley Lake,[27] in an area called the "Mud Hole." The Mud Hole was known for its dark water and particularly rough surf. It's said that the Mud Hole is where the city's sewers dumped into the ocean. While some Asbury Park historians dispute this, it was firmly believed by the black community. Whether true or not, perception was in this case as important as reality. In fact, older West Side residents who swam there, swear they saw excrement floating by them in the water.[28]

From the late 1880's on, Asbury Park was a segregated city. Being that the beachfront area was privately owned, it was *legally* segregated through much of the 20th Century. People of color were allowed to work in the grand hotels and serve in the fancy restaurants but were not allowed to frequent them as guests. They couldn't shop in the downtown stores or even walk the length of the boardwalk without being harassed.[29] In 1892, Bradley had a big twenty-five foot placard put up in one of the grand pavilions that read, "Colored persons are requested not to occupy this pavilion." Bradley defended his actions on business grounds. He said hotel and boarding house keepers had requested the policy because their boarders would not "mingle with colored folk." At this point, there had been more than two and a half million dollars invested in Asbury Park, most of it in hotels and boarding houses.[30] Whenever a segment of the population is locked out of the mainstream society, it develops its own city. Such became the West Side.

African American bathers at the "Mud Hole, ca. 1909.
George Grantham Bain Collection.
Library of Congress, Prints & Photographs Division, [LC-B2- 432-8]
Photo in public domain.

The main thoroughfare through West Park was Springwood Avenue. Springwood Avenue was the ten-block extension of Asbury Park's Lake Avenue into West Park. Its beginning was humble. A 1905 newspaper clipping describes West Park residents and businessmen petitioning Neptune Township to improve the street's condition. The gutters on both sides of the street were blocked with rubbish of all kinds and the center of the street had mud several inches deep.[31] But soon, Springwood Avenue became the lifeline of the community. Springwood acquired everything the West Side community needed - stores, businesses, doctor's offices, pharmacies, churches, barbershops, restaurants, theaters, pool halls, dance halls and night clubs. The West Side community developed its own unique culture. And an integral part of any community's culture is its music.

Notes to Chapter 1

1 "History of Asbury Park 1860 To 1876," *Asbury Park Press*, 30 May, 1896, p. 1.

2 http://www.sandhillindianhistory.org/cherokee-indian-book.html, "Chapter 2: History of the Richardson – Revey Clan"

3 "History of Asbury Park 1860 To 1876," *Asbury Park Press*, 30 May, 1896, p. 1.

4 "A Suggestive Relic," *The Monmouth Inquirer*, 31, Jan, 1889, p. 5.

5 "Britton White" (Obit), *The Monmouth Inquirer*, 16 Apr, 1885, p. 3.

6 "Early Days in Ocean Grove," *Asbury Park Press*, 24 Aug, 1891, p. 13.

7 Franklin Ellis, *History of Monmouth County, New Jersey*, (Philadelphia: R. T. Peck & Co, 1885), p. 865.

8 "Kansas Fun Facts and Trivia," http://www.legendsofamerica.com/ks-facts.html .

9 "For Sale - Asbury Park Lots," *Brooklyn Daily Eagle*, 20 Jan, 1872, p. 3.

10 Daniel Wolff, *4th of July, Asbury Park,* (New York: Bloomsbury Publications, 2005), p. 15.

11 *Philadelphia Inquirer*, 14 Jun, 1875, p. 3.

12 Wolff, *4th of July.* p. 26 - 28.

13 "Philadelphia and Suburbs," *Philadelphia Inquirer*, 2 Dec, 1876, p. 2.

14 "Down Memory Lane," *Asbury Park Press*, 2 Oct, 1949, p. 3.

15 "Miscellaneous," *The Monmouth Inquirer,* 12 Aug, 1880, p. 2.

16 "Favorite Play Given," *Asbury Park Morning Press*, 30 Aug, 1902, p. 5.

17 "Miscellaneous," *The Monmouth Inquirer,* 29 Jun, 1882, p. 2.

18 "A Trip to the Seashore," *New York Times*, 27 Jun, 1877, p. 1.

19 "Ocean Grove," *Detroit Free Press*, 3 Sep, 1878, p. 1

20 "The Electric Railway System of the Northern Coast of New Jersey," *Street Railway Journal*, Vol. XII, No. 9, Sep. 1890, p. 505 -509,

21 Wolff, *4th of July,* p. 71.

22 *Buffalo Commercial,* 31 Dec, 1879, p. 1

23 "Seaside Matters," *Courier Post* [NJ], 28 Mar, 1882, p. 1.

24 Placard from the Asbury Park Museum, 2019.

25 "Suing a Bank," *New York Times*, 5 Dec, 1886, p. 10.

26 "West Park and Grove," *Asbury Park Press*, 23 Jul, 1894, p. 6.

27 "Bathing Groups Open Saturday," *Asbury Park Press*, 26 Jun, 1908.

28 The authors' conversations with longtime area resident, Ronald Coleman, 2012.

29 For a detailed account of Jim Crow conditions in Asbury Park during the late 19th Century see David Goldberg, "Greetings From Jim Crow, New Jersey: Contesting the Meaning and Abandonment of Reconstruction in the Public and Commercial Spaces of Asbury Park, 1880-1890," Concept, [S.l.], v. 30, Nov, 2006. Available at: https://concept.journals.villanova.edu/article/view/279

30 "Founder Bradley Explains," *New York Times*, 25 Oct, 1893, p. 5.

31 "Want Street Improved," *Asbury Park Press*, 28 Mar, 1905, p. 1

Chapter Two

West Side Music: Rooted in The Church

Music has always been a central part of African American life, and the center of African American society is the Church. Most black singers got their earliest training singing as youngsters in church choirs and quartets. By the beginning of the 20th Century, West Park's people of color had a number of churches including the A.M.E. Zion Church (founded 1878), the Second Baptist Church (founded 1885), St. Augustine's Episcopal Church (founded 1890), Mt. Moriah Baptist Church, (founded 1896)[1] and the Mt. Pisgah Baptist Church (started as a mission 1901, organized as a church, 1902).[2] In addition, an 1887 church directory lists the African M. E. Church (corner of Second and Main) and the Colored Baptist Mission (Park Hall).[3]

St. Stephen A.M.E. Zion Church

The A.M.E. Zion Church, originally located on Springwood Avenue, was first organized in 1878 by Elder S. J. Berry.[4] It was rebuilt in 1914 at 126 Union Avenue, where it took on the name St. Stephen A.M.E. Zion. From the beginning, music played a role in St. Stephen's services. In fact, there are reports of A.M.E. Zion having an active choir in 1878.[5]

The St. Stephen's choir was so highly regarded by 1921, they were invited to assist legendary contralto Marian Anderson in a sold-out recital in nearby Ocean Grove. The choir sang all African American spirituals that night.[6] At that time, the pastor of St. Stephen's was Reverend William Henry Eley. St. Stephen's musical influence on Rev. Eley's own family would become evident after his passing in 1928.[7] The Reverend's daughter, Vivian Eley would go on to become the West Side's first Broadway star [see Chapter 9]. His other daughter, Alice Eley Johnson, would direct St. Stephen's Junior Choir and sing with the Versatile Glee Club on the radio in the late 1940's. Her son, Clifford Johnson also sang in St. Stephen's Choir before becoming a professional jazz musician [see Chapter 12]. Future West Side music educator and musician Dorian Parreott also got his start in St. Stephen's Choir.[8]

In recent years, St. Stephen A.M.E. Zion Church relocated again to 1001 Springwood Avenue. The church choir is still going strong today.

Second Baptist Church of Asbury Park

The Second Baptist Church of Asbury Park began as a mission in 1880. It was an outgrowth of the (white) First Baptist Church of Asbury Park. Initially, worship services were held in a Salvation Army building on Springwood Avenue. In 1881, the congregation moved to the upper floor of a building at the corner of Springwood and Atkins Avenues, the former site of the West Side Drug Store.

Sceond Baptist Church, ca. 1930.
From Harris & Mossell
Courtesy of Rutgers University Library

Fires were a common danger of the times, with many buildings made of wood. On October 8, 1898, the Second Baptist Church was one of fourteen buildings destroyed when fire swept through the business section of West Park.[9] But in 1901, the congregation purchased and began renovating a building on Atkins Avenue that would become their church for many years.[10]

St. Augustine's Episcopal Church

St. Augustine's Episcopal Church got its start in the Autumn of 1890. Back in 1877, brothers Isaac, Theodore and Richard Richardson of the Sand Hill Indians tribe had purchased fifteen acres of then farmland from James Bradley in West Park. For more than ten years, the Richardson families had worshiped in the primarily white Trinity Church in Asbury Park.[11] Then Reverend A. J. Miller, the rector of Trinity Church

[Left] St. Augustine's Episcopal Church, ca. 1900 From a postcard.
[Right] Interior, Easter Sunday, 1904.
Courtesy of Claire Garland. SandHillIndianHistory.com.

began conducting Episcopal church services in West Park. For three years, services were held at Morrow's Hall on the corner of Lake Avenue and Langford Street, just off of Springwood Avenue.[12] Morrow's Hall was one of West Park's first entertainment venues *[see Chapter 3]*. It was used for African American and Italian American events and was of considerable size. Some dances drew as many as two hundred couples. But Morrow's Hall was also home for important meetings and religious worship. In addition to St. Augustine's Episcopal services, it also was a site for Jewish worship before the first Asbury Park synagogue was built.[13] Jewish residents mostly occupied the area west of the tracks, north of Asbury Avenue.

Meanwhile, the Bishop of the New Jersey Diocese took an interest in Reverend Miller's work and donated $637.43 (the amount of the 1892 Advent offering) for the purchase of property and construction of a chapel in West Park. On All Saint's Day, 1893, Father Miller laid the cornerstone for a permanent St. Augustine Church at 114 Sylvan Avenue.[14] Over the next couple decades, the Richardson men built and then enlarged the church to include the altar for the chancel, a bell tower, and pews for 200 people. Members of the Richardson-Reevey Sand Hill Indian families formed a choir and a brass band *[see the Jonathan Richardson Orchestra, Chapter Three]* to serve the church and the local community. Theodora Richardson served as church organist for many years,[15] as did Christina Richardson Dickerson.[16]

Mt. Pisgah Baptist Church

Mt. Pisgah Baptist Church first formed as a mission in November 1901. Newspapers placed the church at Springwood and what was called Second Avenue in West Park.[17] Second Avenue became Borden Avenue around 1908 so the church is still located today at 1301 Springwood Avenue at Borden Avenue. Within their first months of existence,

Mount Pisgah Baptist Church, 1301 Springwood Avenue (at Borden Avenue) as it looked in 1930 (from Harris & Mossell. Courtesy of Rutgers University Library) and today.

The Fisk University Jubilee Singers, ca. 1886.
Red Bank native and the singers' manager, Charles Mumford,
bottom row, second from the left. Courtesy of Doug Seroff.

Mt. Pisgah was sponsoring music events, including an "Old Folk's Concert" by the Mt. Pisgah Working Club[18] and a free Sunday School concert.[19]

Jubilee Songs

In 1871, a small but talented group of former slaves left Fisk University in Nashville, Tennessee, on a series of singing tours to raise funds for their impoverished school. Along the way, they battled prejudice and oppression, as well as the hardships of the road. Often with no rest or money, they faced hunger, exhaustion and serious illness. But through perseverance they sang their way into the hearts of a nation and the world.

The Fisk University Jubilee Singers sang spirituals, the religious folk songs developed by their parents and grandparents as slaves in the cotton fields of the American South. Calling the songs "jubilee songs," the Fisks introduced African American music and culture to hundreds of thousands of people worldwide, from President Grant to the Queen of England. By the time they returned seven years later, they'd raised hundreds of thousands of dollars for their school, having sung for presidents and royalty.

On April 1, 1884, the Fisk Jubilee Singers sang in nearby Red Bank, New Jersey at the Red Bank Opera House. The booking agent on this occasion was a white man from

Red Bank named Charles Mumford. After this concert the group split into two separate Fisk Jubilee Singers groups. One, led by Frederick Loudin, returned to Europe. The other, then managed by Charles Mumford, continued touring in the United States and occasionally overseas, through the turn of the century.[20]

Over the years, the Fisk Jubilee Singers made numerous Monmouth County, New Jersey appearances including the Atlantic Highlands Temple (1887)[21], Red Bank's Opera House (1884, 1885, 1886)[22], Ocean Grove's Great Auditorium (1923) and Asbury Park, where they sang at the aforementioned Educational Hall in January, 1891[23] and the Park Opera House in February 1897[24]. At one Fisk Jubilee Singers concert, probably the one in Asbury Park's Educational Hall, the city's founder, James A. Bradley, took to the stage and rendered a song at the request of the group's manager who then donated $5 to the Fisk University Building Fund. Bradley would later point to that incident as proof that he was not opposed to "colored men." [His statements were made in 1893 when he was running for state senate and needed the African American vote.][25] Needless to say, the Fisk University Singers sang for white as well as black audiences.

THE

Fisk Jubilee Singers

WILL GIVE THEIR FIRST AND ONLY CONCERT THIS SEASON IN RED BANK AT THE

Red Bank Opera House,

ON

Friday Eve'g, Oct. 8, '86.

THIS IS THE ORIGINAL COMPANY FROM FISK UNIVERSITY, AND INCLUDES THE OLD FAVORITES.

Seats may be secured at Adlem & Colo's at usual prices.

The Fisk Jubilee Singers contained eight vocalists but in the course of a program would often break down into quartets (male, female and mixed). The phenomenal success of the Fisk Jubilee Singers spawned thousands of imitators. Many "jubilee groups" toured to raise money for their own schools. Others tried to capitalize on the popularity of the Fisks without representing any organization. We know of at least one such jubilee group, "the New Orleans Colored Singers" [probably the New Orleans Jubilee Singers] who sang at an Asbury Park ten-day Sunday School Assembly in 1881.[26] Perhaps the most popular form of spiritual or jubilee-style singing was quartet singing.

While we don't know of any professional touring jubilee quartets from Asbury Park's West Side in the late 1800's, it's likely that different churches had their own quartets. A program at St. Stephen's AME Zion Church on May 27, 1923, featured the Second Baptist Church Quartet singing "I Couldn't Hear Nobody Pray".[27] We just don't know how far back that quartet began singing.

The popularity of minstrel shows among white America in the 1890's pushed professional spiritual quartets into the background.[28] Professional black spiritual quartets that joined minstrel shows in order to survive, soon found themselves also singing "plantation songs" as white audiences longed for the days of "the South before the War". Still, some black quartets managed to survive with a mix of spirituals and secular songs. Groups like the celebrated Miller Quartette Concert Company of

Philadelphia played West Park in 1890.[29] The group was composed of William A. Miller (director and accompanist), Miss M. Campbell (soprano), L. W. Parker (tenor), Miss C. B. Webb (contralto), W. F. Miller (basso) and Henri Strange (elocutionist).[30]

The Ross-Fenton Farm

Of the Asbury Park area venues that hired African American vocal quartets as entertainers, none was so well known as the Ross-Fenton Farm. For almost 50 years, Ross-Fenton Farm was the area's vacation spot for the rich and famous, drawing internationally known celebrities and patrons alike. Yes, the Ross-Fenton Farm was a segregated "whites only" resort where people of color could only work or entertain them.

Ross-Fenton Farm was established by husband and wife Charles Ross and Mabel Fenton, two famous vaudeville artists, in 1899. Located on the north bank of picturesque Deal Lake, just north of Asbury Park, the Ross-Fenton farm would become one of the most prestigious and popular vacation spots in the nation. The Ross-Fenton Farm was indeed a working farm with large greenhouses but also included a large lakeside hotel, several guest cottages and two casinos. Some who frequented the Ross-Fenton Farm included John Philip Sousa, Fannie Brice, Sophie Tucker, Irving Berlin, Babe Ruth, Ed Sullivan, Jack Dempsey, Jackie Gleason, Danny Kaye, Eddie Duchin and countless others.[31]

Ross-Fenton Farm: An early Postcard

While it's been reported that Ethel Waters broke the color line when she sang there in 1949,[32] that is far from the truth. At its grand opening in 1899, Ross-Fenton had a "colored quartet" singing there as entertainment.[33] The quartet most likely sang a mix of spirituals and plantations songs. Advertisements show the quartet was still singing there as late as 1909.[34] [The Ross-Fenton Farms burned down in 1950 and is now a housing development.]

Henry T. Burleigh

Harry Thacker Burleigh was perhaps the first African American to gain international recognition as a composer, arranger and concert singer. Burleigh's magnificent arrangements of more than fifty spirituals for concert singers became an important contribution to American music.[35] Concert singers Roland Hayes, Marian Anderson and Paul Robeson would make these spirituals a part of their repertoires. His arrangements of spirituals like "Deep River" are still in use in church hymnals today.

While living in New York City in the late 1800's and early 1900's, Burleigh and his wife would often spend weekends at one of the rented boarding houses in Asbury Park's West Side.[36]

Burleigh would return to perform in Asbury Park a number of times after that, most notably at First M. E. Church in 1924[37] and at the Asbury Park High School in 1927[38] and 1931[39]. His repertoire contained many of his spirituals.

Notes to Chapter Two

1 Clive Davis, "Blacks in Asbury Park, New Jersey: A Brief Social History," Thesis submitted to Rutgers College (1993), p. 52

2 "Church Directory," *Asbury Park Press*, 2 Nov, 1901, p. 3.

3 "Asbury Park Church Directory," *Asbury Park Press*, 28 Jul, 1887, p. 4.

4 Lenora Walker McKay, *The Blacks Of Monmouth County,* (1976), p. 58.

5 Tyron McAllister, "Modern Sounds Of Praise," *Asbury Park Where Music Lives,* ed. Helen Chantel-Pike, (Asbury Park: Clayton Press, 2011), p. 13.

6 "Marian Anderson Delights Audience," *Asbury Park Press*, 11 Aug, 1921, pp. 1-2.

7 "Rev. William H. Eley" [Obit.], *Asbury Park Press,* 30 Jul, 1928, p. 2.

8 Authors' conversations with Clifford Johnson and Dorian Parreott, 2015.

9 "Fire In West Asbury Park," *New York Times*, 8 Oct, 1898, p. 2.

10 McKay, *Blacks Of Monmouth County*, pp. 55 - 56.

11 http://www.sandhillindianhistory.org/cherokee-indian-book.html, "Chapter 5: The Move To Sand Hill," p. 1 - 2.

12 McKay, *Blacks Of Monmouth County,* p. 63.

13 Daniel Wolff, *4th of July, Asbury Park,* (New York: Bloomsbury Publications, 2005), p. 104.

14 Don Stine, "St. Augustine's Episcopal Church Celebrating 125 Years," *The Coaster* [Asbury Park], 3, Jun, 2015.

15 http://www.sandhillindianhistory.org/cherokee-indian-book.html, "Chapter 5: The Move To Sand Hill," p. 2.

16 Authors' correspondences with Claire T. Garland, Director of the Sand Hill Indians Historical Association, 11 Jan, 2019

17 "Begins Pastoral Work," *Asbury Park Press*, 9 Nov, 1901, p. 1.

18 "Press Calendar," *Asbury Park Press,* 25 Nov, 1901, p. 5.

19 "Free Concert Monday Night," *Asbury Park Press,* 28 Nov, 1901, p. 1.

20 Lynn Abbott and Doug Seroff, *Out Of Sight: The Rise of African American Popular Music, 1889 - 1895,* (Jackson, MS: University of MS, 2002), pp. 42-43.

21 "News From Middletown," *Red Bank Register*, 20 Jan, 1897, p. 1

22 "The Jubilee Singers Once More," *Red Bank Register*, 26 Mar, 1884, p. 1; Ad for Fisk Jubilee Singers, *Red Bank Register*, 30 Sep, 1885, p. 2; "At Opera House," *Red Bank Register*, 6 Oct, 1886, p. 2.

23 *Asbury Park Journal*, 10 Jan, 1891, p. 3.

24 *Asbury Park Journal*, 18 Feb, 1897, p. 1.

25 "Founder Bradley Explains," *New York Times*, 25 Oct, 1893, p. 5.

26 "A Sunday-School Congress," *New York Times*, 2 Aug, 1881, p. 5.

27 "Memorial Display," *Asbury Park Press*, 26 May, 1923.

28 Abbott and Seroff, *Out Of Sight*, p. xi.

29 *Asbury Park Journal*, 9 Jul, 1890.

30 Abbott and Seroff, *Out of Sight*, p. 104.

31 Slide show assembled by the Township of Ocean Historical Museum.

[32] "Ethel Waters Crashes Fenton Color Line," *Baltimore Afro American*, 24 Aug, 1940.

[33] "Ross-Fenton Farm Event," *Asbury Park Press*, 15 Jul, 1899, p. 5.

[34] *Casino Theatre Asbury Park Official Beach Program*, (Asbury Park: Seashore Advertising Co, 1909). Courtesy of Don Stine.

[35] Eileen Southern, *The Music of Black Americans*, (New York: W. W. Norton & Co. 1971), pp. 284 - 287.

[36] Jean E. Snyder, *Harry T. Burleigh: From the Spiritual to the Harlem Renaissance*, (Champaign: University of Illinois Press, 2016), p. 134.

[37] "Harry T. Burleigh," *Asbury Park Press*, 23 Feb, 1924, p. 1.

[38] Ad, *Asbury Park Press*, 26 May, 1927, p. 12.

[39] Ad, *Asbury Park Press*, 21 May, 1931, p. 4.

Chapter Three

Ragtime, Stride Piano And the Birth of Jazz

Asbury Park and Segregation

In 1896, United States Supreme Court Decision, *Plessy vs. Ferguson*, made "separate but equal" the law of the land. The landmark constitutional law case upheld state racial segregation laws for public facilities, a practice of discrimination that Asbury Park was already well on its way to implementing.

Rev. J. Frances Robinson
Courtesy of the Asbury Park Museum

Not that the African American population of the West Side didn't protest. Back in 1887, when founder Bradley first proposed that most of the beach and boardwalk be off limits to people of color, Reverend J. Frances Robinson, pastor of the West Park's St. Stephen A.M.E. Zion Church, firmly rebuked Bradley from the pulpit. "We will take no dictation from James A. Bradley or any other white man on the face of the earth," Robinson shouted. "Mr. Bradley and the white people object to the negroes on the beach, where the free air of heaven blows, and yet in the dining room they are willing to have the negro sweat right over them."[1] Waving a copy of the local newspaper, *The Journal,* in his hand, Robinson proclaimed, "Mr Bradley might just as well try to hang his handkerchief on the horns of the moon as to keep out the black man from the beach. We fought for liberty and the salvation of this Union and we are going to enjoy the peace of it."[2]

What Reverend Robinson didn't want to acknowledge was that, though morally wrong, Bradley owned the beach. At that time he had a legal right to exclude anyone he wished. Besides, West Park was not then within the boundaries of Asbury Park. Not one person of color owned any land in Asbury Park proper, and therefore, they had no say in its laws or regulations. By the time West Park became a part of Asbury Park, racial discrimination was too entrenched to reverse.

West Park's Earliest Entertainment Halls
Morrow's Hall

One of the earliest of West Park's large halls, Morrow's Hall, was used for entertainment as well as community gatherings, religious services, social engagements and political rallies. Built somewhere around 1890, the venue was located on the southeast corner of Lake Avenue and Langford.[3] Lake Avenue no longer crosses Langford but the current day location would have been most likely between Prospect and Langford Avenues, just south of Cookman.

A 1908 newspaper article stated, "In the vicinity of Springwood Avenue, there is never lack of entertainment. Morrow's Hall and Lyric Hall are open nearly every night of the week with concerts, balls, receptions, fairs, festivals, etc., which are usually well supported. There's always someone willing to back these secular diversions. The churches also hold many concerts, fairs, festivals and public entertainments."[4]

Indeed, church services and events were held there as early as 1890 by St. Augustine's Episcopal Church and the African Baptist Mission.[5] Morrow's Hall was also a site for Jewish worship before the first Asbury Park synagogue was built.[6] [Although plans were developed in 1893 to build a synagogue at Fifth & Main,[7] the first Asbury Park synagogue we can document was built in West Park at 1211 Springwood Avenue in 1896.[8]]

On August 1, 1894, African American residents of West Park gathered at Morrow's Hall to protest the wave of lynchings in the South and to endorse Ida B. Wells, early Civil Rights and Women's Rights crusader.[9] Wells' investigations and writings helped expose the extent of lynchings that were happening.

Morrow's Hall was frequented by all the residents of West Park, regardless of race or religion. African American brass bands like Wheeler's Band and Richardson's Band (led by Sand Hill Indian, Jonathan Richardson), played there often. So did the 30-piece Young Italian Band, led by Prof. L. Volo and managed by Henry Benvenga.[10]

Lyric Hall and Garden (Bijou Hall)

First opened on July 9, 1903,[11] Lyric Hall and Garden claimed to be the "Largest [African American] Amusement Resort in America" at that time. It could accommodate 1000 people.[12] It was located at 1149 - 1151 Springwood Avenue at Atkins Avenue, within 150 feet of the Second Baptist Church. The building was described as having a shingled front with a rounded hood over double doors. The interior was attractive with hardwood used throughout.[13] In addition to an entertainment hall, the Lyric contained a billiard room and a shaving parlor. The Lyric featured concerts, dances, wrestling matches, political meetings and social events. We don't know what was on the location prior to the Lyric, but the property was purchased in 1903 from Samuel Patterson after he suffered heavy investment losses from the Monmouth Trust Company scandal. [The Monmouth Trust Company of Asbury Park failed in 1903 after two directors embezzled and falsified accounts.][14] The new owner of the property and builder of the Lyric Hall and Garden was Dr. Hugh S. Kinmouth.

Dr. Hugh Sutherland Kinmouth

Virtually unknown to the public today, Dr. Hugh S. Kinmouth was a prominent figure in Asbury Park's early history. Kinmouth was born in 1847 in Delaware County, New York, and spent his formative years working on a farm. When the Civil War broke out, he lied about his age to enlisted as a bugler in Company I, Thirteenth New York Volunteer Cavalry. He served throughout the war with the Twenty-second Army Corps. After the war, Kinmouth resumed his schooling and later attended the Roxbury Academy. In 1867, he moved to New Jersey, settling in Lower Squankum. There he studied medicine in the office of Dr. S. M. Diabrow. Later he attended and graduated from the Columbia University's College of Physicians and Surgery, Class of 1870. In the Spring of 1872, Dr. Kinmouth came to Asbury Park, becoming one of the city's first practicing physicians. He also opened Kinmouth Drugstore on Cookman Avenue near Main.[15] The drugstore soon was advertised to have the "largest and most complete stock of drugs, medicines, druggist sundries, toilet articles, perfumes, trusses, crutches and all surgical supplies in any drug house in the state.[16]

Dr. Hugh S. Kinmouth

Hugh Kinmouth and A. L. Thomas, in 1879, founded a weekly newspaper called the *Shore News*. In 1895, Dr. Kinmouth sold the newspaper to his nephew, J. Lyle Kinmouth, who began publishing the newspaper as a daily under the name of the *Asbury Park Press*.[17] Kinmouth was a major landholder in Bradley Beach, selling lots of land that formed the basis of that community.[18] One of his most notable real estate projects was the building of the multi-story Kinmouth Building at 710 Mattison Avenue, one block east of Main. That building would house the Savoy Theater, an important Asbury Park theater.[19] In 1888, Dr, Kinmouth was elected to the Board of Directors of the Seashore Electric Railway, of which he was a major stock holder.[20] That coincided with the introduction of Asbury Park's trolley system, the first in the state. As a key member of Asbury Park's City Council, Dr Kinmouth unsuccessfully fought Ocean Grove's ordinance against the train stopping at their shared station on Sundays.[21]

Of significance to Asbury Park's entertainment scene, Kinmouth was the one who influenced City Council to have "paid music" at the beach.[22] Prior to that, concerts along the beach were free to attend and musicians were not paid. Paying the bands brought higher quality entertainment and big name bands like Arthur Prior to Asbury Park. Dr. Kinmouth unsuccessfully ran for Asbury Park Mayor and for state senator twice, in 1902 and again in 1905.[23] By 1920, Dr. Kinmouth found himself in failing health and feeling more and more despondent. He'd often said that "elderly persons are beset by ills of increasing severity and that there is no alleviation for them but the grave."

On July 21, 1920, Dr. Kinmouth prescribed himself morphine and took his own life. He was 73.[24] The Kinmouth Building still stands on Mattison Avenue in Asbury Park today, the only monument to one of the city's most important figures. But returning to when Dr. Kinmouth opened the Lyric Hall and Garden on Springwood Avenue in 1903, he looked to an educated businessman to manage it. That man was W. Frank Patterson.

W. Frank Patterson

W. Frank Patterson was another fascinating character in Asbury Park's early history. Patterson was an African American journalist who arrived in Asbury Park around 1892. Frank was born in Indiana around 1862, where his father of the same name worked as a barber. The 1870 and 1880 Censuses list Frank living with his family in Logan, Indiana and then Attica, Indiana. We believe Frank to be the same W. Frank Patterson who in 1890 and 1891 edited the *Indianapolis Freeman*, the first illustrated African American newspaper in the country.[25] The *Indianapolis Freeman* was distributed nationwide and became a major voice for African Americans.

Arriving in New Jersey in 1892, Patterson began publishing his own Democratic newspaper, *W. Frank Patterson's Weekly Chat,* from his home on E Street and Tenth Avenue in Belmar, NJ. He continued publishing the weekly until at least 1899.[26] In 1897, Frank married Katherine "Kate" E. Davis, née Scudder. Kate, who had children from a previous marriage, was performing professionally as a monologist and humorist under the name Te-Wan-Ka. Te-Wan-Ka was at times referred to as a "full-blooded Indian" and was said to be well known on the New York stage.[27] As Te-Wan-Ka, Kate gave dramatic recitals locally and as far away as New Haven, Connecticut.[28] Kate also became editor of the *W. Frank Patterson's Weekly Chat.*

On the night of July 30, 1900, Frank and Kate Patterson were at home with Kate's daughter. Their son-in-law, Richard Lee, burst in the door, reportedly intoxicated. Lee, a coachman, lived with Kate's daughter in the Patterson household. Lee demanded his wife get him a glass of water, but being ill, she refused. At that point, Kate Patterson remarked, "I should think that lazy n***** would get his own water and not make you get it!" A heated argument ensued between the two. Lee drew his razor and slashed Mrs. Patterson two or three times. Her right forearm was cut to the bone and her right hand was almost completely severed from her wrist. Frank Patterson grabbed a hickory club and tried to defend his wife. Unfortunately, he was severely cut in the face, the cut extended through both eyelids and the eyeball of his left eye, down the side of his cheek and through both lips. Neighbors hearing the wife's screams rushed to the scene as Patterson collapsed from loss of blood and Lee ran off.[29] Frank Patterson received 20 stitches[30] and did recover. He lost his left eye and was left with a scar from his forehead to his chin.[31] Richard Lee was arrested and sent to trial.[32]

By January, 1901, W. Frank Patterson had recovered sufficiently to announce that he and William H. Leonard, a printer, would be starting West Park's first newspaper. It was to publish on April 1.[33] Whether it ever came out is unknown to us. A day later, Patterson announced that he was writing a book entitled, "The American Negro in Art, Music, Athletics." It was to be a fully illustrated volume of about 400 pages and would be issued in September.[34] We don't know of this ever coming out either. In February, 1901, W. Frank Patterson started another political newsletter, similar to his previous *W. Frank Patterson Weekly Chat*. This one he called *The Mosquito*.[35]

Throughout this time, W. Frank Patterson was active in a number of political, business and social organizations.[36] Then in the Summer of 1903, Dr. Kinmouth hired Frank to manage Lyric Hall and Garden. In November, Dr. Kinmouth made major renovations to the east wing of Lyric Hall, adding a storeroom on the first floor intended to be a drugstore and adding living apartments on the upper floor.[37] A furnished lodge room was added for West Park's secret organizations.[38] The Pattersons moved into one of the Lyric Hall residential apartments at 1151/1153 Springwood Avenue.[39]

Alas, W. Frank Patterson's tenure as manager of the Lyric lasted only a couple years. It was cut short by another violent incident. On the evening of November 29, 1905, a young carpenter named Daniel D. Franklin went to Lyric Hall to get some music that belonged to him. Franklin, a carpenter who lived on Avenue A in West Park, was the son a former Bethel A.M.E. Church pastor. Patterson, it is said, refused to give up the music, claiming it did not belong to Franklin. Heated words were exchanged and things went from bad to worse. Patterson grabbed a sickle that was hanging on the wall and threw it at Franklin. Franklin tried to avoid the weapon but it struck him in the right calf, passing through the flesh with the point protruding several inches on the other side. Franklin fell to the floor and spectators rushed to his aid, pulling the sickle from his leg. As the sickle was curved, removing it caused further damage. Franklin was rushed to the hospital where he almost died. W. Frank Patterson was arrested and held for a grand jury.[40] Patterson was released on bail until his trial in February 1906.

W. Frank Patterson was tried for atrocious assault and battery. Dr. H. S. Kinmouth, the owner of the Lyric Hall, various businessmen, the pastor of a nearby church, a justice of the peace and even the victim himself (calling Patterson a friend) wrote to the judge asking for leniency. Patterson had an excellent local reputation and was active in the National Negro Businessmen's League that had been founded a few years earlier by Booker T. Washington and other black leaders. Local businessmen wrote that before Patterson managed Lyric Hall, it was "a very disorderly place" and that "it was unsafe for women to pass on that side of the street" but after he took over, they wrote, it had been conducted in a highly respectable manner."[41]

Nevertheless, W. Frank Patterson was found guilty and sentenced to 18 months in prison. His lawyers immediately appealed to the New Jersey Court of Errors and Appeals. Bail was set at $1000 which Frank could not pay. He was confined to the county jail until the money could be raised,[42] which it eventually was. The Appeals Court upheld the sentence when Patterson did not appear on the day of the hearing. Losing the appeal, W. Frank Patterson was sent to state prison.[43] On admission to the state prison, Patterson was described as blind in his left eye and having numerous scars on his face and arms. After incarceration from July 7, 1907, to April 3, 1908, he was paroled.[44]

Returning to Asbury Park's West Side, W. Frank Patterson again began working for Dr. Kinmouth, this time as a painter. By 1910, he and his wife had moved across the street to 1122 ½ Springwood Avenue[45] and a year later to 29/31 Atkins Avenue.[46]

By 1911, the building housing Lyric Hall became the Bijou Dance Hall, though many continued referring to it as the Lyric. It's possible the hall was divided and both venues operated simultaneously until 1920 when the building became a Recreation and Health Center.[47]

In 1915, the new Royal Theatre supplanted the Lyric as the grandest theater on Springwood Avenue. Advertisements listed W. Frank Patterson as the manager of the Royal. Shortly after that, W. Frank Patterson passed away. The 1920 Census shows Kate living as a widow.[48]

Asbury Park Annexes West Park, 1906

On May 16, 1906, after months of debate, the citizens of both Asbury Park and West Park voted to have Asbury Park annex the West Side. This was done out of financial need. Asbury Park needed the tax revenue. Still, the annexation was not without opposition. Asbury Park's founder, James A. Bradley, argued that annexing the Springwood Avenue area would "place Asbury Park in the hands of people of the West Side, many, very many of whom, are not imbued with the old established American ideas, especially as to beer and liquors". Bradley further argued that if Springwood was annexed, "our city will have the largest pro-rata colored voters of any city in New Jersey... leading to a great depreciation of property... The majority of the colored vote of Monmouth County is a purchasable article."[49]

Some proposed annexing only that part of West Park north of Mattison Avenue, thus excluding Springwood Avenue. They argued that the Springwood Avenue area was a crime ridden collection of shanties, speakeasies and "colored houses of questionable character [prostitution]."[50]

Black residents of West Park argued back that "over the past few years, [West Park had only] three murders, six men shot and three badly cut, and not one of the above named crimes was committed by colored people."[51] Besides, West Park was badly in need things Asbury Park could supply, such as a sewage system, paved streets and better fire and police protection.

In the end, people overwhelmingly voted for the annexation of West Park, as far south as the Wesley Lake Brook, which included the Springwood Avenue area. Thereafter, the area of West Park, now called the West Side, became part of Greater Asbury Park. And, though never reaching the opulence of the city east of the tracks, the West Side improved dramatically.

Two years later, in April 1908, a newspaper article detailed the changes that were occurring on the West Side since annexation. "The annexed portion of the city west of the railroad is forging ahead so rapidly on business and building improvement lines that a stroll up Springwood Avenue reveals many new or improved structures every few weeks. Some very substantial buildings are going up and others have sprung into existence since last Fall almost with mushroom rapidity. A number of cement block houses, stores and apartment buildings have been erected, other old buildings have been replaced with new ones and the work is still progressing. There is an almost continuous line of stores and shops from Prospect Avenue to Atkins Avenue on both sides of Springwood and business places are beginning to invade the side streets."[52]

Bradley's fear of giving West Side African Americans more of a say in the running of Asbury Park than he wanted, may have come true to a small degree. Though Bradley didn't have to follow *Plessy vs. Ferguson*, the threat of black voting power apparently forced the city's ruling government to grant people of color limited use of that small stretch of the beach called the Mud Hole.

As a 1911 editorial in *The Afro-American* sarcastically complained, "The white folk down at Asbury Park seem to think that there is not enough salt in the water of the Atlantic Ocean at that point to preserve them from contamination, if colored people bathe in the bosom of old ocean at the same place they bathe. The result was that colored folks had to go without bathing, unless they found a tub big enough to take a dip in. Now Asbury Park has two [political] parties, same as most other places in the North and West [not the South], Republican and Democrat. The colored voters threatened to take the matter into politics and help the Democrats elect their ticket. When the authorities found this out, for the Republicans are in power, they got busy and have provided a suitable place where colored folks may take a dip in old ocean without offending the sensibilities of the white folks..."[53]

But Bradley's comments about West Side residents not being "imbued with American values" were not solely directed against African Americans. America was riding a wave of nationalism that was creating a strong backlash against immigrants - especially Italian immigrants. During the 1880's, 300,000 Italians had immigrated to the United

States. During the 1890's it was 600,000. Between 1900 and 1910, the numbers had swelled to 2,000,000. Most were farmers and laborers from southern Italy and Sicily. Since the point of entry was Ellis Island, many immigrants settled in New York City and New Jersey.[54] In Asbury Park, Italians resided in the West Side neighborhood of Little Italy, easy walking distance from jobs as laborers along the beach. To the Ku Klux Klan, who were on the rise in New Jersey through the 1910's and 1920's, the Italian immigrants were Roman Catholics, "the most dangerous of all invaders".[55] Immigration from southern Italy and Sicily would continue until 1924 when the country's anti-immigration fever would lead to the Immigration Restriction Act. The law restricted the number of annual immigrants admitted from certain countries to 2% of the number of people from that country living in the United States in 1890. It effectively restricted immigration of Southern and Eastern Europeans, particularly Italians and Eastern European Jews. With the Great Migration of African Americans out of the South beginning, the West Side was just beginning to take shape.

Ragtime

Musically, the country was enthusiastically absorbing a new genre of African American derived music called "ragtime." What the general public called ragtime was actually two closely associated genres - "coon shouts" and Scott Joplin-style structured piano rags. It is important to separate the two.

As Abbott and Seroff so elegantly wrote, "When ragtime made its stunning leap from African American underclass culture into mainstream fashion, it provided the first real professional opportunities for a wide range of black performers; however every prospect was mitigated by systemic racism. The era's biggest hits were not Scott Joplin's stately piano rags; "coon songs" were what appealed to the masses. To the popular music industry and the contemporary white audience, ragtime and coon songs were virtually synonymous."[56]

[We hate using the crude and racist term, "coon songs," to describe a music genre, but see no way around it, as it is how the general public labeled the music. It also illustrates the racial prejudice of the era.]

"Coon song" lyrics were often "grounded on crude racial stereotypes and portrayed blacks in either a contemptuous or condescending manner, [but] the music that typically accompanied it

Scott Joplin, ragtime composer.
Modern sheet music from the
Classic Urban Harmony Archives

represented an enlightened rhythmic departure from the straight-laced waltz time of the popular ballad. Most 'coon' songs contained slight syncopation, in both their vocal and accompaniment."[57] Coon shouts would enter black vaudeville and be transformed into original blues. [*See Chapter Four for more on this topic.*]

Simultaneously, real ragtime, as popularized in part by the compositions of Scott Joplin and others, was basically piano music featuring a syncopated rhythm.

"Structurally, ragtime may have grown out of march music, which was often published in piano rolls or sheet music for piano. In ragtime, a march-like rhythm is produced by the left hand which accents the first and third notes of a measure in contrast to the syncopated melody of the right hand. March music was extremely popular in the late 19th Century with the influence of John Philip Sousa's Band. Syncopation, played by the right hand, seems to be of African American origin."[58]

Brass Bands

Brass bands captivated the entire country for the last half of the 19th Century. Virtually every small town in America boasted of at least one. Some towns had several. Brass bands were common to almost every ethnic group.[59] They were formed by and represented businesses, social organizations, churches, labor organizations, fire departments and the like. They performed in halls and the marched the streets in parades to celebrate holidays of all sorts.

Brass bands could be of varying size, and could be broken down depending on the occasion. There is a report of an "Asbury Park Colored Band" marching in the Firemen's Parade as early as 1883.[60] But one of the earliest well-known West Park brass bands grew out of Richardson's Orchestra.

Jonathan Theodore Richardson was born on January 31, 1875. He lost his right arm as a result of polio at the age of six[61] but it never deterred him from doing what he wanted to do. Richardson was a direct descendant of the Sand Hill Indians. Even before Asbury Park was build, members of the Sand Hill clan had taken up musical instruments to entertain in the nightclubs of Long Branch.[62]

The first documented performance of Jonathan Richardson's Orchestra was in 1902, when they played a concert and dance for the Victorian Company No. 2, UR (Uniformed Rank), of the fraternal organization, the Knights of Pythias at Suydam Hall.[63]

The Colored Knights of Pythias

The Order of Knights of Pythias was founded in Washington, DC, in 1864. Like many fraternal organization of that era, its membership was limited to white males only. In fact, the Supreme Lodge conventions of 1869, 1871, 1878 and 1888 all rejected petitions from African American groups to form Pythian Lodges.[64] It is said that some African Americans who were able to "pass," infiltrated the K. of P. long enough to study the system and withdraw to start a "colored" version of the fraternal organization and brotherhood. By the 1880's there were "Colored Knights of Pythias" lodges.[65] One, the Olive Branch Lodge, was formed in West Park. The Colored Knights of Pythias did not discriminate. People of any race could join.

A great many Pythians were Civil War Veterans and some lodges formed their own military drill teams called Uniformed Ranks or UR. The UR was an unofficial reserve force, maintaining a military readiness should the nation need them. In practice, the UR was more of a fancy drill team suitable for parades and other official functions.[66] And parades needed music for marching. At first they just had a fife and drum unit. Eventually they recognized the need for a brass band.

Richardson's Orchestra and the Colored Knights of Pythias Brass Band

Jonathan Richardson's Orchestra had a long association with the local Olive Branch Lodge of the Colored Knights of Pythias. In fact, Richardson, himself, was a member. The Richardson Orchestra was West Park's premiere band in the first ten years of the Twentieth Century. At times as small as four pieces,[67] Richardson's Orchestra could

Richardson Orchestra, ca. 1905. Jonathan T. Richardson, far right.
Courtesy of Richardson's granddaughter, Rhonda Ladaye

Richardson's Orchestra and /or K of P Brass band, possible at a rehearsal. Ca. 1910.
Courtesy of Jonathan T. Richardson's granddaughter, Rhonda Ladaye

expand to many more, depending on the venue and occasion. And Richardson's Orchestra played for everyone.

Many of the functions Richardson's Orchestra played at were held in Morrow's Hall, like the Violet Social Club reception (February, 1903),[68] the Elysian Club reception (November, 1903),[69] the benefit concert for the Free Library & Reading Room in West Park (May, 1906),[70],[71] and the St. Augustine Women's Guild's "Ye Olden Time Concert" (March, 1905).[72] The latter concert drew more than 300 people.[73]

The year 1908 was an eventful one for "Professor" Jonathan T. Richardson. In April the Richardson Orchestra (four pieces) played a coronation reception at Morrow's Hall.[74] Another Morrow's Hall performance of April 28, 1908, was probably typical of concerts of that era. It consisted of Richardson's Orchestra playing a variety of orchestra selections plus solos, recitations and readings by other artists. In addition, the Black Wonders Jubilee Singers sang several songs.[75] [We don't know if they were from Asbury Park.] Richardson's Orchestra also shared the billing at Morrow's Hall

Richardson's Orchestra along with the Olive Branch Lodge
Knights of Pythias Uniformed Rank.
Photo courtesy of Jonathan Richardson's granddaughter, Rhonda Ladaye

with a two-act farce-drama by Bob Johnson and his Jolly Grass Widows Company (May, 1908).[76] Other Morrow's Hall performances by Richardson's Orchestra included the Business Women's May Party (May 20, 1908)[77]

Marrow's Hall was not the only place Richardson's Orchestra played. When the Lyric Hall and Garden first opened in 1903, Richardson's Orchestra supplied the music after a program of comical boxing contests.[78] May of 1908, found them playing at a dance for the Caterers May Reception in the Lyric Hall and Garden. Prizes were given for the best waltz dancers.[79]

Of course, Jonathan Richardson and his orchestra continued to play for and support the St. Augustine church that he and his family built and were members of.[80] In January of 1905, they played a fancy dress Japanese tea party given in the choir room of St. Augustine Chapel,[81] probably one of many appearances the orchestra made for the church.

Early in 1908, Jonathan Richardson formed a brass band from members of the Knights Of Pythias Olive Branch Lodge Uniformed Rank. Initially, 26 members enrolled, many of whom were already experienced musicians. The Knights Of Pythias Brass Band began regular rehearsals with Jonathan Richardson as leader and director.[82] The K of P Brass Band led the Uniformed Rank in numerous street parades around Asbury Park and elsewhere. Professor Richardson's granddaughter, Rhonda Ladaye, said her grandfather was the band leader who wore a white braid around the front of his neck during the parades on the West Side.[83]

Some members of the Knights of Pythias Brass Band were most likely also members of Richardson's Orchestra. Richardson's Orchestra furnished the entertainment for the Knights of Pythias Olive Branch Lodge fifth (1907),[84] sixth (1908),[85] and seventh (1909)[86] anniversary celebrations. Following the seventh anniversary, members of the Olive Branch Lodge honored five recently deceased members by following the brass band and drum corp in a march to the Mount Prospect Cemetery where flowers and wreaths were placed on the graves.[87]

The Richardson Orchestra and the Knights of Pythias Brass Band existed concurrently. An October, 1908, K. of P. Reception for the Ladies of Rebecca Court illustrates the distinction between the two. Prior to the reception, "The Knights of Pythias Brass Band and auxiliary drum corps paraded with the Uniformed Rank of the Order. They made a fine appearance on the street. The Band played several selections in the [Marrow's] Hall and then dancing was the order until a late hour to the music of Richardson's Orchestra."[88] The Knights of Pythias Brass Band played at the ground breaking ceremony of Asbury Park's main post office in 1910.[89]

In 1909, Richardson's Orchestra teamed with Professor Eugene Watson to conduct twice-a-week dance classes in Morrow's Hall. Classes were held every Monday and Friday evening with Richardson's Orchestra supplying the music.[90]

While the names of the individual members of Richardson's musical groups have been obscured by the passing of time, we do know at least one member. William H. Hughes, clarinetist for the Knights of Pythias Brass Band, member of the Zion A. M. E. Church and well-known waiter at the Coleman House Hotel, died of a hemorrhage at the age of 36 in January 1910.[91]

By 1915, Richardson was running ads to get his orchestra work in the beachfront hotels.[92] While these hotels were "whites only" for vacationers, they often hired people of color for entertainment. Richardson's Orchestra, and presumably his Knights of Pythias Brass Band, existed in some form into the 1930's and probably beyond.[93]

Wheelers Brass Band

Richardson's Knights of Pythias Band was not the only brass band on the West Side. Alex F. Wheeler organized the Wheeler Band in May of 1907, several months prior to the formation of the K. of P. Brass Band. Professor Wheeler assembled his band mostly from men who had never before played a musical instrument. The band began with 15 members.

Wheeler's Brass Band was smartly dressed. Their uniforms consisted of light blue fatigue suits and caps. The coats and trousers were trimmed with black mohair braid, the fronts of the coats being each decorated with six gold-lace frogs on each side.[94]

One of Wheeler's Band's first engagements was a hot chicken supper benefit for the Bethel A. M. E. Church.[95] This was followed by a special Easter service at Mt. Moriah Baptist Church in April[96] and an Easter Carnival and dance at the Lyric Hall. Prior to this performance, the band gave a street parade.[97]

On Memorial Day, 1908, Wheeler's Band paraded with West Side veterans from Shockley's Hall (at Adams Street and Atkins Avenue) down Springwood Avenue and Main Street to the Bethel A. M. E. Church (at Second Avenue and Main Street). The marchers attracted considerable attention with their music and colors flying.[98]

When Howe's circus came to town in the Summer of 1908, "Professor Wheeler's Military Band" performed in the street parade and at the fairgrounds.[99] The circus would return annually with Wheeler's Band taking part in it.[100]

Wheeler's Band was not confined to Asbury Park. On May 22, 1908, they opened the Summer season of concerts in Keyport, NJ.[101] In October of that year, they performed at Beech's Hall in Red Bank.[102] In November 1909, they serenaded the new mayor of Belmar.[103] In 1910, Wheeler's Band gave an extended outdoor concert on Main Street as part of Manasquan's July Fourth celebration.[104]

In November 1908, Wheeler's Brass band supplied the music for one of the nights of the A. M. E. Zion Church's annual week-long bazaar. A second night's entertainment was handled by Professor Griffin and his Victor Orchestra, another local music group.[105]

Wheeler's Band and Orchestra started off 1909 by playing an evening concert and supper at Morrow's Hall organized by the Ladies Lincoln Club of the West Side to celebrate the 100th anniversary of Abraham Lincoln's birth.[106] Actually, Lincoln's 100th birthday was a huge celebration throughout Asbury Park and elsewhere. With the day a legal holiday, banks were closed and businesses shuttered at the noon hour. Flags were displayed all over and the celebration was widespread. Asbury Park veterans of the Civil War who'd fought to preserve the Union, donned their uniforms and attended programs of celebration. On the East Side, a mass gathering took place in Liberty Hall. But nowhere was there more jubilation than on the West Side. A

Brass band on the West Side, date unknown. Courtesy of Claire Garland.

morning celebration there in Morrow's Hall lasted well beyond noon. The exercises were presided over by Asbury Park's Mayor T. Frank Appleby. Music was supplied by Richardson's Knights of Pythias Brass band.[107]

Wheeler's Band appeared at a clay pigeon shooting contest in nearby Manasquan in March, playing American and Irish tunes.[108] By May of 1909, Wheeler's band was reportedly giving nightly parades on the West Side for the People's Theatre on Springwood Avenue. The band also played in the theater.[109]

On May 13, the Wheeler Band celebrated their second anniversary with a concert at Lyric Hall. Other local brass bands were joined in the concert, including Richardson's Knights of Pythias Band and black bands from Eatontown and Fair Haven, New Jersey.[110] Reports of the event had Professor Frank Wheeler as the guest of honor with more than 200 people of color attending, many of them musicians. The Wheeler Band was in full regalia and played numerous songs. The Eatontown and Knights of Pythias brass bands performed (no mention of the Fair Haven band). Other entertainment included recitations and readings. A buffet luncheon was served at a late hour.[111]

Wheeler's fifteen-piece band supplied music for the annual Sunset Lake Ice Carnival, in January, 1910. Several thousand skaters donned masks and costumes, heading out onto the colorful illuminated ice of Sunset Lake for a grand time. Wheeler's Band played from the comfort of a grandstand on St. John's Island.[112]

An April 1910 article said Wheeler's Band enlivened Springwood Avenue and then held a sociable in Aberdeen Hall, their meeting place.[113] The exact location of Aberdeen Hall is unknown to us. Later that month, Wheelers Band held a benefit at Mt. Moriah Baptist Church on Springwood Avenue to raise money for new uniforms[114] as well as a Morrow's Hall reception with the Knights of Pythias Band.[115]

In the early decades of Asbury Park's history, the city was patrolled by different private fire fighting companies. On the West Side, one such company was the Eureka Fire Company on Springwood Avenue, established by the Richardson extended family of Sand Hill Indians. As many structures were made of wood, fire companies were kept quite busy. When the Eureka Fire Company acquired a new $900 hose wagon in 1910, the whole West Side turned out to see it. Marking the occasion was a big dance at Morrow's Hall with both Richardson's Orchestra and Wheeler's Band entertaining. After the wagon was exhibited, it was returned to the manufacturer until the fire house could be remodeled to accommodate it.[116]

November 14, 1910, marked bandleader Alex F. Wheeler's 34th birthday and the West Side bands took the opportunity to celebrate. Both Wheeler's Band and Richardson's Knights of Pythias Band marched through a mix of rain and snow from Prospect Avenue all the way to Ridge Avenue and then back again to Morrow's Hall. There they moved indoors and alternated playing songs. Attendance was said to be sparse due to the weather, tending to keep the ladies indoors.[117]

While Wheeler's band received its share of good press coverage, uncovering the names of his band members has been challenging. Sadly, newspapers felt band members names were only newsworthy in cases of crimes or deaths. One negative incident afforded us the name of one of Wheeler's horn players. Musician George Henderson made the news in 1911 when two of his lady friends got into an argument and one threatened the other with a razor. No one was hurt and all charges were dismissed.[118] In 1912, band member G. W. Henson died of heart trouble. He was reported to be well known on the West Side as a plasterer and member of Wheeler's Band.[119]

Like Richardson's Orchestra, Wheeler's Band would last through the 1920's and possibly longer.[120]

Other Early West Side Bands

Though Richardson's Orchestra, the Knights of Pythias Brass Band and Wheeler's Brass Band were the most popular music ensembles on the West Side in the first twenty years of the Twentieth Century, they were by no means the only ones.

An early reference was found for the Victor Orchestra under Professor Griffin performing at an A. M. Z. Zion Church bazaar in 1908.[121] The Victor Orchestra was observed rehearsing several times a week at Burns Villa, 1130 Springwood Avenue, in

1909. Some of the members were said to play regularly at the Sunday services in St. Augustine's Church. F. Leon Harris was the leader. The orchestra was made up of the following members: F. Leon Harris, Samuel King and Alfred Haynes (first violins); William Yeiser and Morgan Jensen (second violins); Fred King and John Sampson (cornet); James Dickerson and Charles Richardson (trombones); Oscar Burns (piano); George Haynes (flute) and Leroy Vanderveer (drums).[122] Any connection between this orchestra and the one that was recording for Victor Records would at this point be speculation. James Dickerson and Leroy Vanderveer would soon rise to greater importance in the music world. *Their story will be covered in Chapter Six.*

In addition, an Italian American brass band was started on the West Side in December, 1908. Thirty participants initially signed up and rehearsals were held at 911 Springwood Avenue. Professor L. M. Vola, a graduate of the Royal Conservatory of Music, Naples, Italy and a musical director in New York, was chosen to instruct the new band. Those individuals who were not acquainted with musical instruments were given individual instruction. Prior to this, when local Italian societies and organizations needed the services of a band for their celebrations, festivals and funerals, they hired one from New York City.[123]

It was reported that the "old city proper" [East Side of Asbury Park] had a brass band of a dozen or more pieces that occasionally appeared in public but that there seemed to be a "lack of interest in maintaining a good city band" there.[124]

Influence of Black Ragtime on Arthur Pryor

Left: Arthur Prior, East Side superstar
Photo in Public Domain.
Above: An Arthur Pryor Band 78 rpm
recording for *Victor Records*. From
the Classic Urban Harmony Archives

By the early 1900's, the syncopation in ragtime was making its way into the brass bands that were immensely popular at the time.

Ragtime music swept the country in the late 1890's. Its popularity would last from the mid-1890's until the end of World War I, though its acceptance was far from universal. Leading white educators called for the teaching classical music in school as "the only possible and certain cure for the abandonment of coon songs and popular ragtime trash, which lower the musical taste of young people in the present generation and it is obvious that children who are accustomed to hearing the best music will grow dissatisfied with the inferior music."[125]

Still, while many were decrying the effects of black "ragtime" music on white youth, Asbury Park's first real shore area superstar, Arthur Pryor, a white musician and bandleader, was quietly incorporating ragtime syncopated rhythms into his marches and drawing huge crowds.[126]

Pryor began playing with John Philip Sousa's popular marching band. After some time, Pryor left to form his own band. Responding to the country's thirst for ragtime music, Pryor's music was heavily influenced by black ragtime, but played by all white musicians. Ragtime songs played and recorded by Pryor included "The St. Louis Rag," "King Of Rags" and "Dill Pickles Rag."

Postcard of a crowd lsitening to Arthur Pryor's Band playing at the Asbury Park Casino, ca. 1910. From the Classic Urban Harmony Archives.

"Asbury Park hired Arthur Pryor and his band for the 1904 season, and he was an instant hit. That first summer, he played 269 concerts and drew more than three hundred thousand listeners. Within a few years, the city was paying him $17,000 a season [a huge amount for 1908]. In five years, Pryor would quit touring elsewhere and buy a house in Asbury."[127]

The phonograph record was still in its infancy but the *Victor* label was rapidly winning the rpm war with their 78's. Had there been any industry "charts" then, Pryor would have had 27 "best sellers" for *Victor* between 1904 and 1916.

The Black Patti Troubadours and Founder Bradley

In 1905, Asbury Park planned to open a magnificent structure on the beachfront called the Casino. It was primarily built to accommodate summer long concert series by Arthur Prior. Admission to his concerts would be 15 cents during the week and 25 cents on Sunday. The Casino would open on July 1. At the planning meeting on June 14, the Beach Commission also "reluctantly decided to contract for the appearance of Nolan's Black Patti Troupe."[128]

The Black Patti Troubadours
play Asbury Park's Casino,
August 2, 1905.

In the late 1890's the public's fascination with ragtime created unique opportunities for black entertainers. The best known were highly financed all-black musical comedy productions known as "big shows." Big shows were elaborately staged and costumed, and played in large mainstream (white) theaters with a cast of 40 or more. Certainly one of the most popular was a troupe called the Black Patti Troubadours.

Proprietors of the Black Patti Troubadours were Voelckel and Nolan, two white men, who exercised complete control of the production. The star of the troupe was Sissieretta Jones, the so called "Black Patti." Jones was universally accepted as "the greatest singer of her race." Black Patti would sing opera along with popular music in her performances.[129] She would eventually

41

sing before four United States presidents and tour world wide.

On August 2, 1905, the Black Patty Troubadours became the first, and for a long time, the only black performers to play the new Asbury Park Casino.

In January, 1906, James Bradley offered to sell the city an auditorium building and surrounding plot of beachfront land known as Auditorium Square, for a little more than $50,000.   It was

Black Patti returns to Asbury Park's
Casino, April 27, 1910.

between Kingsley Street and Ocean Avenue, bounded by Sunset and Sixth Avenues. The city planned heavy use of the auditorium for a convention center.[130] However, before the deal was finalized, Bradley withdrew the offer with no explanation.

Newspapers reported that Bradley's change of heart was due to Black Patti. It seems that a year earlier, the Black Patti Troubadours' managers inquired about leasing the Auditorium for a one night stand and Bradley told them no. His refusal was reportedly based on his fear of the growing "dominance of the colored element on the boardwalk to which he claimed the Black Patti show gave additional encouragement and support."[131]   The show's managers then went to the Public Grounds Commission and the result was the August 2 date at the Casino. The show was successful and the Commission cleared a lot of money from the concert. But at a city council meeting, someone suggested that instead of buying Bradley's Auditorium, the city should just rent it for popular concerts like the one with Black Patti. Bradley found out about the suggestion and immediately canceled his offer.

"Yee God's!" Bradley exclaimed. "Black Patti on the auditorium stage? Never! Not as long as I live!"[132]

While the city of Asbury Park didn't get to purchase Auditorium Square, they did bring Black Patti back to the Casino four years later, on April 27, 1910. The show was another financial success. The ad noted that "the balcony was reserved for colored people."[133]

Other Early West Side Theatres and Dance Halls

At the same time that Arthur Pryor was exciting vacationers along the Boardwalk, the really hot ragtime music was smoking along Springwood Avenue. The West Side was developing quite a nightlife.

Along with a number of smaller night clubs, Springwood Avenue had a couple of theaters and dance halls including the Majestic Theatre at 909 Springwood, the aforementioned Bijou Hall/Lyric Hall at 1151 Springwood and the Royal Theatre at 1206 Springwood.[134]

Black vaudeville star, Lawrence Deas, who played Asbury Park in 1911, was excited about the opportunities along Springwood Avenue. He broke ground for a new theatre on the Avenue in June 1912, with the intent to rush its completion by that July 4, 1912. Will H. Brown, formerly with the *My Friend From Dixie Company*, played there in September of 1912, along with Oma Crosby Brown.[135] The Deas and Deas Theatre is known to exist through May of 1913.[136]

The Royal Theatre

The crown jewel of Springwood Avenue entertainment in the 1910's was the Royal Theatre. The first mention of the Royal Theatre seems to have been in July of 1912, when Zel Bledseaux played there.[137] Bledseaux had been the first tenor with the Jamboo [vocal] Quartet of the Black Patti Troubadours, one of the country's more elaborate, all black productions.[138]

1912 ad for the Royal Theatre at
1209 Springwood Avenue.
"The Cosiest [sic] Playhouse On The Coast"

The Royal Theatre was at first located at 1209 Springwood Avenue and was owned by Albert C. Fletcher. Fletcher was an entrepreneur from Newark who was active in politics and advocated for more recognition of black voters.[139] Fletcher also believed in the future of a new entertainment medium, moving pictures. Sometime prior to the 1912 summer season, Fletcher acquired (or built) the first Royal Theatre to present live vaudeville and motion pictures to the Springwood Avenue audiences. Early motion pictures were still silent pictures in 1912, but a Royal Theatre ad from that year advertised "vaudeville and talking moving pictures."[140] There were attempts to synchronize Gramophone recordings with moving pictures before 1920, but these attempts were rare. Fletcher appears to have been a pioneer in talking motion pictures.

Managing the Royal Theatre in 1912 was Billy Ward, a black comedian who also moonlighted as a performer at the Majestic Theatre the same year.[141] Following the 1912 summer season, Ward announced that the Royal would be open all winter.[142]

As the 1913 summer season began, the *Indianapolis Freeman*, one of the country's leading black newspapers reported on the Royal Theatre's grand opening. [*In shore areas, grand openings refer to start of the summer season.*] Curiously, the newspaper

43

listed Lawrence Deas as the Royal's "proprietor," not A. C. Fletcher. No further references to the Deas Theatre are reported.

The Royal was reported to be "one of the grandest openings of a colored theatre ever recorded... The interior and exterior were elaborately decorated and the Citizens Military Band

rendered some grand selections. Mr. Lawrence Deas, the popular proprietor and Mr. Sam Tolson made addresses of welcome to the patronage assembled that crowded the doors to suffocation." Entertainment included an orchestra directed by Mrs. Dolly Deas [probably Deas' wife] of Boston, an elaborate vaudeville program including McKissick & Shadney, singers and dancers; The Great Costello, Simms and Thompson; and Isoloa Ringgold, queen of song. Other performers at the Royal that summer included popular comedian Cliff Green, the Claybrook singers and musicians, Italian impersonator Charles Bougia and minstrel performers Christie & Palmer.[143] [*The story of Lawrence Deas will be pursued in more detail in Chapter Four*]

Though Lawrence Deas ran the Royal's live vaudeville entertainment throughout the summer, A. C. Fletcher continued showing motion pictures there.[144] After that summer, during the autumn of 1913, the Royal was used by the Woodrow Wilson Colored Democratic Club for political meetings.[145]

On Sunday morning, March 3, 1914, snow began falling in Asbury Park. It was the beginning of a terrible blizzard that blanketed the East Coast from Virginia to Maine. All told, the snow storm caused the deaths of fifty people and caused ten million dollars damage, a huge sum for 1914. Asbury Park was hit pretty badly, with thirty inches of wet snow, blocking railroad traffic, breaking tree limbs and downing poles and wires. It was the worst snow storm Asbury Park had seen since 1888.

Worst off was the mighty Royal! The weight of the wet snow caused the walls to buckle and at 5:30 Sunday afternoon, the entire roof caved in. The building was completely destroyed with only the front of the structure left standing. The loss to owner, A. C. Fletcher, was estimated at $3000.[146]

Undeterred, Albert Fletcher immediately purchased the 30' wide by 100' deep lot across the street at 1206 Springwood Avenue and began construction of a new Royal Theatre. While many of the Springwood Avenue buildings of that time were wood structures, Fletcher had the new two-story Royal Theatre constructed of fire resistant hollow clay tiles. The building was given an inspection by the Asbury Park Board of Health on July 27, 1914[147] and presumably opened soon after. The new Royal Theatre location had the advantage of being right next to the Metropolitan Hotel (1200 Springwood). The Metropolitan, opened in 1900, was one of the classier hotels open to people of color in Asbury Park at that time. Its dining room accommodated 50 to 60 guests.[148]

Other lodging open to African American vacationers at that time included the Hampton Inn, Whitehead Cottage (25 Atkins), Idle Hour Cottage (617 Church) and the Herb Cottage (134 Atkins), all on the West Side..

Managed for A. C. Fletcher by W. Frank Patterson, the Royal presented live vaudeville entertainment during the summers and motion pictures during the off seasons. The Whitman Sisters, major black entertainers and one of the hottest vaudeville acts in the country, played to a sold out audience at the Royal Theatre in September 1915. It was a return engagement.[149] Well-known black vaudeville female impersonator, Andrew Tribble, performed at the Royal along with Charles Gibson and Blondie Robinson as part of a tabloid musical comedy in July 1916.[150]

Right: 1915 Ad for the "new" Royal Theatre
Below left, ad for Andrew Tribble
Below right, Royal manager Leon Williams

To Friends, Acquaintances and Strangers
A Merry Christmas and A Happy New Year

Andrew Tribble
Per. Address: C. V. B. A. Headquarters, New York City

LEON WILLIAMS

In 1918, Leon Williams was brought in to manage the theatre. Williams had once managed the famed Lafayette Theatre in Harlem.[151]

The Royal would continue in its original use until it was acquired by Harry J. Rockafeller, manager of the Shubert Theatre on Main Street. In 1919, Shubert would convert the Royal into an all motion picture theatre.[152] The acquisition must have been a lease, because the Royal was still owned by A. C. Fletcher when it was put up for sheriff's sale in 1923.[153] By 1927, the building at 1206 Springwood Avenue had been turned into a parking garage.[154]

Edward Kennedy "Duke" Ellington and Asbury Park

In 1913, a 14-year-old Edward Kennedy "Duke" Ellington visited Asbury Park for the first time. Ellington was born and raised in Washington, DC. He was exposed to piano playing as a youngster and even took lessons, but never had much interest in it. He preferred playing baseball to music.

"Every summer, my father would send my mother and me on our vacation to visit his sister in Atlantic City, or my mother's brother, John Kennedy in Philadelphia," Ellington wrote. "We'd travel by Pullman parlor car, and they were wonderful times, but one year [my mother] decided to go to Asbury Park. I was about ready for high school then and, although it was a vacation for her, I went looking for a job. There was the big Atlantic Ocean and all those big hotels but it was a rainy season and bellhop jobs were hard to get. A lot of us kids were all crowded around a hotel one day, hoping something would turn up, when the man came out and said, 'Well, we don't have any need of a bellhop because business is so bad, but over on First Avenue they need a dishwasher.' So then there was a race of all the kids to First Avenue to get the dishwashing job, and I got there first."[155]

Edward Kennedy "Duke" Ellington
Publicity photo from the Paul Ressler Archives

Based on the location Ellington described, the hotel he worked at for the summer of 1913 was

46

probably the Coleman House, one of the oldest of the beachfront grand hotels.

Working as a dish washer, young Ellington befriended a head-waiter named Bowser and the two discussed music, especially piano playing.

While in Asbury Park, Ellington heard ragtime piano music for the first time. The catalyst for his awakening was a piano roll of one of the

THE COLEMAN HOUSE, ASBURY PARK, N. J.

Early postcard of the Coleman House,
From his description, this is likely the hotel where
young Duke Ellington worked washing dishes in 1913.

nation's top 1913 ragtime dance tunes, "Junk Man Rag."[156]

"Junk Man Rag" was written by a talented young pianist named Charles Luckeyth "Luckey" Roberts. Roberts was born in Philadelphia but moved to Harlem around 1908 where he started playing rent parties and composing ragtime tunes. Roberts was an extraordinary pianist and was "the man to beat" in Harlem cutting contests. He began publishing his ragtime compositions in 1909, beginning with "The African 400 (An Educated Rag)" that was recorded by Arthur Pryor that same year.[157] Roberts' "Junk Man Rag" was recorded by several artists on piano roll and at least one *Victor* phonograph recording by the Victor Military Band in 1914.[158] By 1913, the song was extremely popular in many vaudeville shows and dance halls.[159]

Ellington recalled the piano roll of "Junk Man Rag" as being recorded by a young Philadelphia musician named Harvey Brooks, though no surviving piano rolls by Brooks are known to exist.[160]

"I cannot tell you what that music did to me," Ellington wrote of hearing "Junk Man Rag." "It was different from the average piano selection. The individuality of the man showed itself in the composition as he played it. I said right then, 'That's how I would like to play a piano, so without being told, everybody would know I was playing.'"[161]

While Ellington never mentioned hearing ragtime pianists perform live on the West Side, it's likely that he did. He and his mother were undoubtedly staying on the West Side, as people of color were generally not given residence in the beachfront area. Working as a dishwasher in a major hotel, he would have stayed into the late evenings and most likely walked home along Springwood Avenue. If so, he would have heard the music filtering out of the nightclubs, even if he was too young to be admitted. In addition, Asbury's grand hotels were known to employ African American musicians for entertainment, even though their restaurants were restricted to white patrons.

By the end of the summer, Ellington's interest in piano playing was piqued to the point that he and Bowser stopped off in Philadelphia on the way home to track down Harvey Brooks, who gave Ellington some tips on playing. "When I got home I had a real yearning to play," recalled the Duke.[162]

Duke Ellington would go on to become one of the world's greatest jazz bandleaders, just one of many whose career was shaped by Asbury Park's West Side music.

Black Entertainers in White Venues

While people of color were largely barred from frequenting beachfront venues, famous African American entertainers were often hired to play them. One such entertainer of national acclaim, Wilbur Sweatman, played the East Side Criterion Theatre and Savoy Theatre in 1912[163] and 1915,[164] respectively. Sweatman, "The Daddy of the Clarinet," pioneered a style of ragtime-jazz clarinet. Sweatman was known for playing two or at times three clarinets simultaneously.

World War I

When the war in Europe began in August 1914, most Americans, including the people of the West Side, did not want the United States to get involved. For residents of Asbury Park, the war in Europe seemed a long way off. But, by April 1917, with Germany conducting unrestricted submarine warfare against American ships, and revelations surfacing that Germany had tried to recruit Mexico into attacking the United States, Americans too found themselves at war.

On the morning that the United States entered World War I, Asbury Park was recovering from the worst fire in the city's history. A fire that started in the Natatorium on the boardwalk had spread westward, consuming four city blocks. Forty-eight buildings from the Boardwalk to Grand Avenue between First and Second Avenues, were completely destroyed. It may have seemed that the city's residents had enough to worry about. Still, it didn't take long for the effects of war to reach Asbury Park.

The United States government mobilized the entire nation for war, and all were expected to do their part. The military instituted a draft in order to create an army capable of winning the war. By then, West Side residents, for the most part, supported the war. President Woodrow Wilson proclaimed "The world must be made safe for democracy" and African Americans reasoned that if they did their part in the war effort, they might be soon be afforded the same democratic rights as the liberated Europeans. Many African American men were eager to join the war effort, viewing the conflict as an opportunity to prove their loyalty, patriotism, and worthiness for equal treatment in the United States.

In 1917, the United States Armed Forces were segregated. African Americans were not allowed in the Marines and the Navy only afforded blacks a few positions. The Army was another story. Entirely black units were formed and trained. While most African American units were in support roles, two all-black outfits had combat roles and fought bravely along side the French. The most famous was the 369th Infantry, who gained fierce reputation as the "Hell Fighters." African American regiments in World War I were usually accompanied by bands. The 369th Infantry band was led by James Reese Europe, a prominent musician whose syncopated style became immensely popular in France, both among American troops and the French public. James Reese Europe is credited with introducing many Europeans to jazz and ragtime rhythms along with African American performance styles. Later vaudeville star Noble Sissle was a key member of Europe's band during the War and just after. While we don't know if Europe's band ever played Asbury Park, he did play the Bridge Water Inn seven miles north, in the Pleasure Bay area of Long Branch, just prior to the War.[165] Europe was murdered by a band member soon after returning from France.

Draftees from Asbury Park were sent first to Camp Dix (later called Fort Dix) in Lakehurst, NJ. The camp was hastily constructed in June, 1917. Draftees from other locations were often sent to camps in the deep South. In August, 1917, West Side residents read with horror, the newspaper descriptions of rioting by black soldiers stationed in Houston, Texas. Unaccustomed to and fed up with Jim Crow policies and brutality by local police, 156 black soldiers marched from their base to Houston, firing on police and civilians. When it was over, five policemen, nine civilians and five soldiers were dead. One hundred soldiers were court marshaled and tried. Ninety-five were found guilty and nineteen were hanged.[166]

When eighteen African American draftees left Asbury Park for Camp Dix, the West Side gave them a big parade as a send-off. The parade started at the Asbury Park Armory and marched down Springwood Avenue to Atkins and back to the railroad station. The drafted men led a procession of a detachment of police, Company D, the Ocean Grove Minute Men, the West Grove Drum Corp, Wheeler's Band, several groups of black fraternal organizations, the Red Cross and members of the Fire Departments of Asbury Park and Ocean Grove.[167]

Then on November 11, 1918, a truce was declared and the war ended. All told, the war cost almost 20 million lives, more than 100,000 of them Americans. That doesn't even count another 20 million more wounded.

Asbury Park's West Side welcomed home its heroes - forty-two of the seventy-seven African American soldiers from Asbury Park who went to war, arrived home on July 11, 1919.[168] The soldiers paraded behind Wheeler's Brass band followed by some of the city's fire trucks. Crowds began to form a full hour before the parade started and by the time the men marched away from the Elks Home on Atkins Avenue, the sidewalks of Springwood Avenue were packed with admiring throngs. Many children were in the parade audience, dressed in their Sunday finest. After making many turns in and out of the side streets off of Springwood Avenue, the parade continued on to Morrow's Hall. At Morrow's Hall, Wheeler's Band and Haynes' Orchestra serenaded the crowd with selections of the newest music - jazz.[169].

But while the war in Europe was winding down, an even more deadly situation was on the minds of Asbury Park residents. The great Influenza Pandemic of 1918 was ravaging the world's population. Worldwide, the "Spanish Flu" had infected 500 million people over a time period of 15 months, killing 50 million. Approximately 675,000 Americans died of the flu, 195,000 in the month of October 1918, alone. Victims died within hours or days of developing symptoms, their skin turning blue and their lungs filling with fluid that caused them to suffocate.[170]

Crowded conditions in military base camps and ships helped spread the illness. More American soldiers died of influenza than were killed in battle. More than 500 soldiers in nearby Camp Dix died of influenza in the Fall of 1918.[171] Of the 77 African American soldiers recruited from Asbury Park's West Side, only two failed to return. Both died of influenza at Camp Dix.[172]

As the pandemic worsened in October 1918, the city of Asbury Park urged citizens to limit contact with others. Schools, theaters and many businesses were closed. Police were ordered to disperse all street gatherings. The disease was particularly widespread on the West Side, due to closer living quarters.[173]

Between the loss of young musicians to the draft and the fear of contracting influenza at public gatherings, the entertainment scene on Springwood Avenue suffered greatly. But, by the Summer of 1919, the pandemic had lessened and the young soldiers were returning home. Springwood Avenue began to rebound.

Harlem Stride On
The West Side

In the first two decades of the Twentieth Century, along Springwood Avenue and in other urban centers, the hot music of ragtime evolved into Stride Piano (sometimes called Stride Ragtime or Harlem Stride). Stride is defined as a style of jazz piano playing in which the right hand plays the melody while the left hand plays a single bass note or octave on the strong beat and a chord on the weak beat. It is closely related to ragtime but is often faster and has more swing.

Stride was "syncopation alternating between the right and left hands and the counter melodies created by a moving bass line. This was putting a new twist on the regular way to play ragtime - alternating the syncopation between both hands made it twice as difficult to perform, thereby enabling the performers to win [cutting] contests."[174] And while ragtime in 1920 was played by many white artists, stride was performed almost exclusively by black pianists.

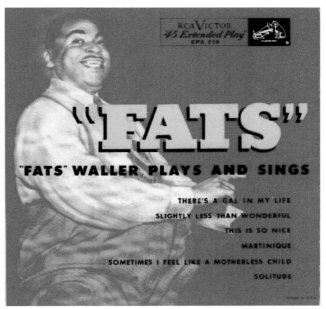

Stride piano great, Fats Waller
EP jacket from the
Classic Urban Harmony Archives

Early pioneers of stride playing included the New Brunswick, NJ, born James P. Johnson, Fats Waller, Willie "The Lion" Smith, Donald "The Lamb" Lambert and Willie Gant.

Fats Waller and Sonny Greer played at the Plaza Hotel in 1919. Vintage post card shows the hotel at that time.

Thomas "Fats" Waller was born in New York City on May 21, 1904, and was taught stride piano by James P. Johnson. In the early years, Fats Waller was known to perform in Asbury Park on several occasions. Waller played the beachfront Plaza Hotel in 1919 as a trio with Long Branch drummer Sonny Greer and violinist Shrimp Jones.[175]

Still living in New York and needing to support a newborn son, Fats Waller spent the summer of 1921 gigging in Asbury Park. His friend and fellow stride pianist, Corky Williams, was living in Asbury Park. Corky secured Fats a place to stay and got him a gig at Scotty's Bar and Cabaret, described in Waller's biography as "a popular night spot that featured swinging music."[176]. In actuality, Scotty's was a huge seafood restaurant located in Avon-by-the-Sea, only two and a half miles south of Asbury Park, on the Shark River.[177] Scotty's was one of the area's most popular dining spots in the early Twentieth Century. Excursion trains used to bring in as many as 2000 people for Scotty's Summer clambakes.[178]

After his gig at Scotty's, Waller stayed in Asbury Park for the summer, often jamming after hours with Corky Williams and a young Bill (Count) Basie.[179] [*More on Basie in Chapter 5.*]

Scotty's Bar and Restaurant, a popular seafood restaurant on the Shark River,

Corky Williams

Gerald Motley "Corky" Williams was born in New Rochelle, New York, on January 15, 1896 to John R. Williams and Carie Motley Williams. Sometime prior to 1915, Corky's father died and the family moved to Harlem in New York City. It is there, presumably, that Corky took up ragtime piano. Corky entered the military in August 1918, toward the end of World War I. While in the service in France, he formed a jazz band with other servicemen. Meanwhile, Corky's mother married William Turpin and moved to Asbury Park.[180] There, at 1109 Springwood Avenue, Carie Williams Turpin ran the Clef Ice Cream Parlor. The Parlor specialized in homemade cakes of all kinds, shortcakes and ice cream.[181] Carie Turpin was also an early activist for women's rights. As chairperson of the Colored Women's Patriotic Business League, she organized a rally of more than 250 women demanding work for women at the Morgan Munitions Plant during World War I.[182] [Ten days later, the Morgan Munitions Depot in Sayreville, NJ, exploded. Over three days of continuing explosions, 100 were killed and hundreds more injured.[183]

Corky returned from the war and moved in with his mother and stepfather in Asbury Park. By then the Clef Ice Cream Parlor had moved around the corner to 124 Sylvan Avenue. In 1919, Corky Williams began entertaining customers there with a ragtime combo, advertised as just in from France.[184]

By 1920, Corky Williams was on his way to becoming a skilled ragtime and stride piano player. Young Bill Basie, who competed against him in talent contests at the time, wrote, "I was certain [Corky] could play more piano than I was playing at that time."[185]

Fats Waller recalled Corky played piano at night and during the day working as a soda jerk at his mother's Clef Ice Cream Parlor. Stride pianists in those days made three to five dollars a night plus tips. Corky had an edge over most stride piano players. He was the only one who sang while he played. Corky specialized in bawdy risque tunes like "The Boy In The Boat."[186]

In 1921, Corky Williams was gigging with stride pianists Fats Waller and Russell Brooks in Harlem.[187] But with summer approaching, jobs were just as plentiful around Asbury Park. Corky advertised his jazz band in the local paper. "Jazz band of three, four or five pieces. Open for one or two nights weekly [sic] engagements. Suitable for hotel and private functions. Corky, The Clef, 124 Sylvan Avenue."[188]

In August of 1921, Corky played a "Monster Jazz Review" at Lafayette Hall on Springwood Avenue. There were two jazz bands. Interestingly, Corky billed himself as the "Piano Hound."[189]

It was 1921 when young Bill Basie first arrived in Asbury Park. [*See Chapter Five.*] Count Basie, Fats Waller and Corky Williams used to jam together almost every night.[190] In October, 1921, Corky Williams married Annie Bernice Roberts, originally from Ithaca, New York.[191] Corky and his wife continued to reside at 124 Sylvan Avenue in Asbury Park's West Side. Corky continued to supply dance music for parties and the like.[192]

Sometime around late 1923, Corky Williams and his wife moved to New York City where Corky led the Orient Cabaret Band.[193] While still living and performing in New York, Corky and his stepfather William Turpin opened a hotel and boarding house called the Clef Country Home at 238 Columbus Avenue, a couple of blocks from Springwood Avenue in Asbury Park. It was advertised as a quiet vacation spot.[194]

HARRY "LIFTY" LEWIS
Master of Ceremonies — Strictly For Laffs

Accompanied By

"CORKY WILLIAMS"
Colored Pianist & Vocalist, Who Reflects The Late
"Fats Waller" Style.

DINE AND DANCE

AMATEUR NIGHT FRIDAY

RICARDO'S
LANSFORD, PA.

One of Corky Williams'
last performances in 1949
near Hazelton, PA.

In New York City, Corky Williams' career was just beginning. In 1927 he began hosting his own weekly half-hour radio program on WCGU, Coney Island. There he entertained radio audiences with his piano playing and singing.[195] He was joined on the air by blues legend Alberta Jones, whom Corky accompanied by piano.[196]   Corky would accompany Alberta Jones on her Gennett label recordings of "Dying Blues" and the risque "Shake A Little Bit" in 1928.[197] That same year Corky also accompanied blues singers Louise Anderson (*Gennett Records*)[198] on record. Later in 1938, Corky would record behind Ruby Smith (*RCA's Bluebird* label). Ruby Smith was the niece of Bessie Smith's husband.[199]

Corky Williams would continue entertaining with stride and boogie woogie piano gigs in New York, New Jersey and Pennsylvania until his death in 1950.

Fats Waller and Andy Razaf

Meanwhile, by the late 1920's. Fats Waller was collaborating songwriting with poet and lyricist, Andy Razaf. Andy Razaf was born as Andriamanantena Paul Razafinkarefo in Washington, DC, in 1895. His father was Grand Duke Paul Henry Razafinkarefo nephew of Queen Ranavalona III, ruler of the Kingdom of Ranavalona (also called Imerina Kingdom), now part of Madagascar. Andy's mother, Jennie Maria Waller (no relation to Fats Waller) was the 15-year old daughter of the United States consul to Ranavalona. Andy's father was killed during the French invasion that made Madagascar a French colony.[200] At that time Andy's mother returned to the United States where he was born. Andy Razaf (name shortened because it was too hard to pronounce) was raised in Harlem and at age 16 quit school and took a job as an elevator operator in Tin Pan Alley to peddle his songs. Andy Razaf would go on to co-write the hit songs, "Ain't Misbehavin'," "Black & Blue," "In The Mood," "The Joint Is Jumpin'," "Stompin' At The Savoy" and many more.[201]

Andy Razaf
Publicity photo

By 1928, Andy's mother had married Albert Coles and moved to 119 Atkins Avenue in Asbury Park.[202] The Coles lived on the second floor, above what had been a tea room. Andy would often spend time there visiting his mother.

That same year, Fats Waller and Andy Razaf were hired to write four songs for a show being produced at Connie's Inn in New York. To avoid any distractions, Andy arranged for the two to write songs at his mother's house in Asbury Park. Andy arranged to rent an upright piano and have it delivered to his mother's home. It was difficult to tie Fats Waller to one location for very long. "My mother used to make the finest food and special cookies just to keep him at our home in Asbury Park," Razaf once told historian Leonard Feather.[203]

Waller only stayed for a day on that occasion, but it was enough to put together three songs and most of the framework for a fourth - a song that contained the lyric, "Every honey bee, fills with jealousy, when they see you out with me." Yes, the hit song "Honeysuckle Rose" was written in Asbury Park's West Side.[204]

Razaf and Waller would collaborate on numerous songs. At least one other of their hits, "My Fate is in Your Hands," also has an Asbury Park connection. As Fats Waller once related, "Andy Razaf, Al Poindexter, violinist, and myself were speeding through Asbury Park on our way to Bradley Beach about 1:30 one morning when a constable stopped us. He soaked a $50 fine on us, and the three of us did not have the necessary dough. Razaf said, 'Give me a break, Mr. Constable. My fate is in your hands, you know.' And whether it was those words or not, the constable softened and accepted the money we had, about $24, in payment of the fine. The next day, Andy, reciting the incident, said, 'Fats, let's write a piece with the title 'My Fate is in Your Hands." We did and you know the rest."[205]

Razaf would later take up residence in Asbury Park and then nearby Belmar. He died in Los Angels in 1973.

Notes to Chapter 3

[1] Daniel Wolff, *4th Of July, Asbury Park: A History of the Promised Land*, (New York: Bloomsbury Publishing, 2005), pp. 42 - 44.

[2] "Colored Men Protest," *Asbury Park Press*, 6 Jul, 1887, p. 1

[3] *Boyd's Directory of Asbury Park, Ocean Grove*, (Philadelphia: C. E. Howe Company, 1916). Courtesy of the Asbury Park Public Library.

[4] "Greater Asbury A Reality," *Asbury Park Press*, 1 May, 1908, p. 3.

[5] "Church Notes," *Asbury Park Press*, 2 Aug, 1890, p. 1.

[6] Daniel Wolff, *4th Of July*, p 104.

[7] "Jewish Synagogue," *Asbury Park Press*, 18 Jul, 1893, p. 1

[8] "Jewish New Year," *Asbury Park Press*, 5 Sep, 1896, p. 1

[9] "Twenty Years Ago Today In Asbury Park," *Asbury Park Press*, 1 Aug, 1914, p. 8

[10] "Italian Band Benefit," *Asbury Park Press*, 9 Apr, 1909, p. 1.

[11] "Local Happenings," *Asbury Park Press*, 8 Jul, 1903, p. 4.

[12] "Local Happenings," *Asbury Park Press*, 17 Aug, 1903, p. 4

[13] "Dr Kinmouth New Enterprise," *The Journal [Asbury Park]*, 24 Jul, 1903, p. 6.

[14] "Windows to the Past: Forty Documents and Photographs from the Monmouth County Archives," Exhibit at the Monmouth County Library Headquarters 125 Symmes Drive Manalapan, New Jersey Oct, 2012. Courtesy of Gary D. Saretzky, Archivist, Monmouth County Archives.

[15] "Dr. Kinmouth Is New City Beach Commissioner," *Asbury Park Press*, 1 Jan, 1913, p. 1.

[16] Ad, *Asbury Park Press*, 29 Jun, 1892, p. 5.

[17] "About Us: Asbury Park Press," http://static.app.com/about/

18 "Bradley Beach," *The Shore Press [Asbury Park]*, 28 Apr, 1893, p. 3.

19 "Ill and Despondent, Physician Ends Life," *Asbury Park Press,* 22 Jul, 1920, pp. 1-2.

20 "Electric Railway Election," *Asbury Park Press*, 18 Jun, 1888, p. 1.

21 "Sunday Trains," *The Shore Press [Asbury Park],* 13 Feb, 1902, p. 4.

22 "Reactionary Policy," *Asbury Park Press,* 8 Nov, 1904, p. 2.

23 "Geran Candidate to Succeed Brown as State Senator," *Asbury Park Press,* 27 Apr, 1911, p. 1

24 "Ill and Despondent, Physician Ends Life," *Asbury Park Press,* 22 Jul, 1920, p. 1-2.

25 *Gibson City Courier (IN),* 29 Aug, 1890, p. 5

26 "Windows to the Past: Forty Documents and Photographs from the Monmouth County Archives," Exhibit at the Monmouth County Library Headquarters 125 Symmes Drive Manalapan, New Jersey Oct, 2012. Courtesy of Gary D. Saretzky, Archivist, Monmouth County Archives.

27 "Colored Democrats Meet," *Asbury Park Press*, 21 Sep, 1899, p. 1

28 *The Shore Press (Asbury Park),* 20 Dec, 1900, p. 4.

29 "Wicked Negro Wields Razor," *Asbury Park Press,* 31 Jul, 1900, p. 1.

30 "Numerous Accidents, *Asbury Park Press,* 16 Aug, 1900, p. 3.

31 "May Lose Sight Of Eye," *Asbury Park Press,* 2 Aug, 1900, p. 1.

32 "Indictments Returned," *Asbury Park Press,* 12 Oct, 1900, p. 1.

33 "West Park To Have A Newspaper," *Asbury Park Press,* 9, Jan, 1901, p. 1.

34 "Book On Famous American Negroes," *Asbury Park Press,* 10 Jan, 1901, p. 1

35 "Local Happenings," *Asbury Park Press,* 25 Feb, 1901, p. 3.

36 "New Clubs Organized," *The Journal [Asbury Park],* 17 Oct, 1902, p. 8.

37 "Local Happenings," *Asbury Park Press,* 27 Nov, 1903, p. 3.

38 "New Lodge Room Ready," *Asbury Park Press,* 23 Dec, 1903, p. 2.

39 "Married This Afternoon," *Asbury Park Press,* 1 Oct, 1908, p. 2.

40 "Leg Is Pierced By Sharp Sickle," *Asbury Park Press,* 1 Dec, 1905, p. 1.

41 "Windows to the Past: Forty Documents and Photographs from the Monmouth County Archives," Exhibit at the Monmouth County Library Headquarters 125 Symmes Drive Manalapan, New Jersey Oct, 2012. Courtesy of Gary D. Saretzky, Archivist, Monmouth County Archives.

42 "Sickle Thrower Gets 18 Months," *Asbury Park Press,* 7 Feb, 1906, p. 1.

43 "Thrower of Sickle Sent To State Prison," *Asbury Park Press,* 3 Jul, 1907, p. 1.

44 "Windows to the Past: Forty Documents and Photographs from the Monmouth County Archives," Exhibit at the Monmouth County Library Headquarters 125 Symmes Drive Manalapan, New Jersey Oct, 2012. Research courtesy of Gary D. Saretzky, Archivist, Monmouth County Archives included [1] Descriptive List of Convicts, New Jersey State Prison, pp. 3396 - 3397, New Jersey state Archives and [2] Minutes, New Jersey Court of errors and Appeals, June 19, 1907, New Jersey State Archives. .

45 1910 Census

46 "Voter Rolls," *Asbury Park Press,* 21 Oct, 1911, p. 5.

47 "Press Calendar," *Asbury Park Press,* 7 Jan, 1920, p. 4.

48 1910 Census

49 Daniel Wolff, *4th Of July*, pp. 85 - 86.

50 James A. Bradley, "Annexation," *Asbury Park Press*, 19 Mar, 1906, p. 3.

51 L. C. Hubbert, "A Righteous Appeal," *Asbury Park Press*, 19 Mar, 1906. p. 4.

52 "West Side Has All-Around Boom," *Asbury Park Press*, 22 Apr, 1908, p. 7.

53 *Afro-American*, 29 Jul, 1911.

54 "Immigration," Library of Congress website, loc.gov.

55 Wolff, *4th Of July*, p. 104.

56 Lynn Abbott and Doug Seroff, *Ragged But Right*, (Jackson, MS: University of MS, 2007), p. 3.

57 David A. Jasen and Trebor Jay Tichenor, *Rags And Ragtime: A Musical History*, (New York: Dover Publications, Inc.,1978), p. 12.

58 Jasen and Tichenor, *Rags And Ragtime*, p. 4.

59 Geoffrey C. Ward and Ken Burns, *Jazz: A History of America's Music,* (New York: Alfred A. Knopp, 2000), p. 11.

60 "Asbury Park," *Monmouth Inquirer,* 29 Nov, 1883, p. 2

61 Authors' conversations with Jonathon Richardson's granddaughter Rhonda Vanderveer Ladaye, Feb, 2019.

62 "Getting About At The Shore," The Story Of The Cherokee Indians, https://0201.nccdn.net/1_2/000/000/18f/cc0/Getting-About-at-the-Shore.pdf

63 "Colored Pythians To Dance," *The Journal,* [Asbury Park], 16 May, 1902, p. 8.

64 "Our Proud History," Njpythians.com

65 "Then & Now: 'Colored' Knights of Pythias, 701-703 North Senate," https://HistoricIndianapolis.com

66 "Our Proud History," Njpythians.com

67 "West Side Social Events," *Asbury Park Press*, 21 Apr, 1908, p. 2.

68 "Social Club Gives Reception," *Asbury Park Press*, 21 Feb, 1903, p. 1.

69 "Reception And Concert," *Asbury Park Press*, 13 Nov, 1903, p. 4.

70 "Local Happenings," *Asbury Park Press,* 11 May, 1906, p. 3.

71 "Gave Entertainment," *Asbury Park Press,* 12 May, 1906, p. 3.

72 "Will Repeat Concert," *Asbury Park Press*, 18 Feb, 1905, p. 3.

73 "Concert Well Attended," *Asbury Park Press,* 2 Mar, 1905, p. 1.

74 "West Side Social Events," *Asbury Park Press,* 21 Apr, 1908, p. 2.

75 "Orchestra Concert Tonight," *Asbury Park Press*, 28 Apr, 1908, p. 2.

76 "Jolly Grass Widows' Co," *Asbury Park Press*, 5 May, 1908, p. 4.

77 "Local Happenings," *Asbury Park Press*, 19 May, 1908, p. 2.

78 Ad for the Lyric Hall, *Asbury Park Press,* 25 Aug, 1903, p. 5.

79 *Asbury Park Press*, 4 May, 1908, p. 1.

80 "Chapel Rector Welcomed," *Asbury Park Press*, 17 Jun, 1904, p. 2.

81 "Local Happenings," *Asbury Park Press*, 30 Jan, 1905, p. 3.

82 "West Side Has All-Around Boom," *Asbury Park Press*, 22 Apr, 1908, p. 7.

83 Authors' correspondences with Rhonda Ladaye, Jan, 2019.

84 "K. Of P. Anniversary," *Asbury Park Press*, 1 Jun, 1907, p. 4

85 "K. Of P. Reception," *Asbury Park Press*, 24 Apr, 1908, p. 1.

86 "K. Of P. Anniversary," *Asbury Park Press*, 26 May, 1909, p. 1.

87 "Big day For K. Of P.", *Asbury Park Press,* 1 Jun, 1909, p. 9.

88 "K. Of P. Reception, "*Asbury Park Press*, 1 Oct, p. 1.

[89] "Tobacco Juice, Arguments Added Zest To Life Around Early City Post Office," *Asbury Park Press*, 28 Nov, 1943, p. 3.

[90] *Asbury Park Press*, 3 June, 1909, p. 2.

[91] "Burial Of Musician," *Asbury Park Press*, 11 Jan, 1910, p. 8.

[92] Ad for Richardson's Orchestra, *Asbury Park Press*, 13, Aug, 1915, p. 15.

[93] "Testimonial Given To Retiring Principal," *Asbury Park Press*, 6 Jun, 1929, p. 21.

[94] "West Side Has All-Around Boom," *Asbury Park Press*, 22 Apr, 1908, p. 7.

[95] "A Hot Chicken Supper," *Asbury Park Press*, 18 Mar, 1908, p. 1.

[96] "Band At Easter Service," *Asbury Park Press*, 18 Apr, 1908, p. 2.

[97] "West Side Social Events," *Asbury Park Press*, 21 Apr, 1908, p. 2.

[98] "Preaches To Veterans," *Asbury Park Press*, 25 May, 1908, p. 1.

[99] Ad for Howe's Great London Show," Asbury Park Press, 3 Aug, 1908, p. 9.

[100] "First Circus Of Season Is Here," *Asbury Park Press*, 26 Aug, 1909, p. 2.

[101] "West Side Has All-Around Boom," *Asbury Park Press*, 22 Apr, 1908, p. 7.

[102] "Local Happenings," *Asbury Park Press*, 16 Oct, 1908, p. 2.

[103] "Belmar's Mayor Is Given Rousing Serenade," *Asbury Park Press*, 4 Nov, 1909, p. 1.

[104] "Manasquan Enjoys Great Celebration, *Asbury Park Press*, 5 Jul, 1910, p. 1.

[105] "2 Church Bazaars Open Same Time," *Asbury Park Press*, 21 Nov, 1908, p. 1.

[106] "Concert And Supper," *Asbury Park Press*, 30 Jan, 1909, p. 2.

[107] "Queen City Honors Memory of Lincoln," *Asbury Park Press*,12 Feb, 1909, p. 1.

[108] "Squan Club Held Gay Celebration," *Asbury Park Press*, 19 Mar, 1909. P. 2.

[109] "Local Happenings," *Asbury Park Press*, 7 May, 1909, p. 2.

[110] "Events This Week," *Asbury Park Press*, 10 May, 1909, p. 9.

[111] "Honor Prof. Wheeler," *Asbury Park Press*, 14 May, 1909, p. 2.

[112] "Merry Maskers Enjoy Sunset Ice Carnival," Asbury Park Press, 14 Jan, 1910, p. 1.

[113] "Local Happenings," *Asbury Park Press*, 6 Apr, 1910, p. 2.

[114] "Band Benefit Concert" *Asbury Park Press*, 15 Apr, 1910, p. 1.

[115] "K. Of P. Band Busy," *Asbury Park Press*, 15 Apr, 1910, p. 3.

[116] "Eureka Patrol On Exhibition," *Asbury Park Press*, 28 Jul, 1910, p. 10.

[117] "Band Leader's Birthday," *Asbury Park Press*, 15 Nov, 1910, p. 3.

[118] "Rivals In Fight Over A Bandman," *Asbury Park Press*, 6 Mar, 1911, p. 1.

[119] "G. W. Henson Dead," *Asbury Park Press*, 6 Sep, 1912, p. 2.

[120] "Testimonial Given to Retiring Principal," *Asbury Park Press*, 6 Jun, 1929, p. 21.

[121] "Church Bazaars Open Same Time," *Asbury Park Press*, 21 Nov, 1908, p. 1.

[122] "Victor Orchestra," *Asbury Park Press*, 10 May, 1909, p. 9.

[123] "New Italian Band," *Asbury Park Press*, 30 Dec, 1908, p. 4.

[124] "New Italian Band," *Asbury Park Press*, 30 Dec, 1908, p. 4.

[125] "New Musical Education," *Asbury Park Press*, 15 Feb, 1906, p. 4.

[126] Tom Chesek, *Legendary Locals of Asbury Park*, (Charleston: Arcadia Publishing, 2015), p. 26

[127] Wolff, *4th Of July*, p. 83.

[128] "Casino Will Be Ready On Time," *Asbury Park Press*, 14 Jun, 1905.

[129] Lynn Abbott and Doug Seroff, *Ragged But Right*, (Jackson, University Press of MS, 2007), pp. 38 - 44.

130 "Purchase Of Square Seems Now Assured," *Asbury Park Press*, 5 Jan, 1906, p. 1.

131 "Black Patti Said To Have Caused Withdrawal of Auditorium Option," *Asbury Park Press*, 16 Jan, 1906, p. 1.

132 *Ibid.*

133 Ad for Black Patti at the Casino, *Asbury Park Press*, 27 Apr, 1910.

134 Boyd's Directory of Asbury Park, Ocean Grove…, 1916.

135 "Theatrical Jottings," *New York Age*, 26 Sep, 1912, p. 6.

136 "Resent Attack By Dr. Atchley," *Asbury Park Press*, 19 May, 1913.

137 "Theatrical Jottings," *New York Age*, 18 Jul, 1912, p. 6.

138 "Black Patti Co.," *New York Age*, 5 Jan, 1911, p. 6.

139 "New Club in Essex County," *New York Age*, 14 Mar, 1912, p. 1.

140 Ad for the Royal Theatre, *New York Age*, 26 Sep, 1912, p. 6.

141 Ad for Billy Ward at the Majestic Theatre, *Asbury Park Press*, 1 Jul, 1912, p. 10.

142 "Theatrical Jottings," *New York Age*, 26 Sep, 1912, p. 6.

143 "Royal Theatre - Asbury Park, New Jersey," *Indianapolis Freeman*, 14 Jun, 1913.

144 "Theatrical Jottings," *New York Age*, 7 Aug, 1913, p. 6.

145 "Two Meetings Tonight," *Asbury Park Press*, 22 Sep, 1913.

146 "Asbury Emerging From Great Storm," *Asbury Park Press*, 3 Mar, 1914, pp. 1-2.

147 Record of Sanitary Inspection for 1206 Springwood Avenue, 27 Jul, 1914.

148 Ad for the Metropolitan Hotel, *New York Age*, 15 Aug, 1907.

149 *Indianapolis Freeman*, 18 Sep, 1915.

150 "Theatre Jottings," *New York Age*, 6 Jul, 1916, p. 6.

151 "Royal Theatre to Open on Decoration Day," *New York Age*, 18 May, 1918, p. 6.

152 "Gets Another Theatre," *Asbury Park Press*, 19 Nov, 1919.

153 "Sherriff's [sic] Sale," *Asbury Park Press*, 15 Jun, 1923, p. 23..

154 *Insurance Maps of the New Jersey Coast, Vol. 2*, (New York, Sanborn Map Company, 1927).

155 Mark Tucker and Duke Ellington, *The Duke Ellington Reader*, (New York: Oxford University Press, 1993), pp. 10.

156 Terry Teachout, *Duke: A Life Of Duke Ellington*, (New York: Gotham Books, 2013), p. 31.

157 https://www.allmusic.com/artist/luckey-roberts-mn0000303166/biography

158 Ad for *Victor Records, Evening Star* [Washington, DC], 1 Feb, 1914, p. 70.

159 Ad for "The Junkman Rag," *Evening World* [NYC], 6 May, 1913, p. 2.

160 Terry Teachout, *Duke*, end notes.

161 Terry Teachout, *Duke*, p. 31.

162 Tucker and Ellington, *Duke Ellington Reader*, p. 12.

163 Ad for the Criterion Theatre, *Asbury Park Press*, 6 Jun, 1912, p. 10.

164 "At The Theaters," *Asbury Park Press*, 2 Jul, 1915, p. 9.

165 "Big Night at Bridge Water Inn," *Asbury Park Press*, 31 Aug, 1916, p. 1.

166 https://en.wikipedia.org/wiki/Houston_riot_of_1917

167 "Parade Tomorrow For 18 Draft Men," *Asbury Park Press*, 18 Jul, 1918, p. 1.

168 "Welcome Home For Colored Fighters," *Asbury Park Press*, 10 Jul, 1910, p. 1.

169 "Big Parade For Colored Soldiers," *Asbury Park Press*, 12 Jul, 1919, p. 1.

170 https://www.history.com/topics/world-war-i/1918-flu-pandemic

171 "Influenza Claims 50 More At Camp Dix," *Asbury Park Press*, 3 Oct, 1918, p. 1.

[172] "Welcome Home For Colored Fighters," *Asbury Park Press*, 10 Jul, 1910, p. 1.
[173] "Epidemic Shows No Indications Of Falling Off," *Asbury Park Press*, 11 Oct, 1918, p. 1.
[174] Jasen and Tichenor, *Rags And Ragtime*, p. 249.
[175] Robert Gottlieb, ed., *Reading Jazz: A Gathering of Autobiography, Reportage and Criticism From 1919 to Now*, (New York: Vintage Books, 1999), p. 51.
[176] Maurice Waller and Anthony Calabrese, *Fats Waller*, (New York: Schirmer Books, 1977), p. 41.
[177] *Asbury Park Press*, 15 Nov, 1920.
[178] "Neptune Looks Back at a Century of Progress," *Asbury Park Press,* 14 Jan, 1979, p. 152.
[179] Waller and Calabrese, *Fats Waller*, p. 41.
[180] New York State Census 1905; New York State Census, 1915; 1920 Unites States Federal Census; Gerald Williams U.S. Social Security Application and Claims Index, 1936 - 2007.
[181] "Extra," *Asbury Park Press*, 23 Jun, 1919, p. 1.
[182] "Women Demand Work At Morgan," *Asbury Park Press*, 24 Sep, 1918, p. 2.
[183] "T. A. Gillespie Company Shell Loading Plant Explosion," *Wikipedia*.
[184] "Extra" *Asbury Park Press*, 23 Jun, 1919, p. 1.
[185] Count Basie and Albert Murray, *Good Morning Blues,* (New York: Donald J. Fine, Inc, 1985), p. 34,
[186] Waller and Calabrese, *Fats Waller*, pp. 30-31.
[187] Waller and Calabrese, *Fats Waller*, pp. 37-38.
[188] "Jazz Band," *Asbury Park Press*, 21 Jun, 1921, p. 1.
[189] "Corky's," *Asbury Park Press*, 1 Aug, 1921, p. 1.
[190] Waller and Calabrese, *Fats Waller*, p. 41.
[191] "To Wed Monday," *Asbury Park Press*, 1 Oct, 1921, p. 2.
[192] "Pianist," *Asbury Park Press*, 23 Nov, 1921, p. 13.
[193] "Cabaret News," *New York Age,* 4 Oct 1924, p. 6.
[194] "Spend Vacation At The Clef Country Home," *New York Age,* 23 May, 1925, p. 2.
[195] Radio listing, *Brooklyn Times Union*, 19 Sep, 1927, p. 9.
[196] "On The Air," *Brooklyn Citizen Sun*, 1 Jul, 1928, p. 21.
[197] Brian Rust, *Jazz Records: 1897 - 1942, A - K,* (London: Storyville Publications and Co., 1969), p. 901.
[198] Robert M. W. Dixon and John Goodrich, *Blues and Gospel Records: 1902 - 1943*, Essex, UK: Storyville Publications and Co., 1982), p. 44.
[199] Ted Yates, "I've Been Around, *New York Age*, 28 May, 1938, p. 7.
[200] *Asbury Park Press*, 22 Mar, 1937, p. 6
[201] "Andy Razaf," from *Wikipedia*.
[202] 1930 Federal Census.
[203] Leonard Feather, "Two Men to Thank for Ain't Misbehavin' and Other Hits," *Winnipeg Free Press*, 8 Jul, 1978, p. 40.
[204] Waller and Calabrese, *Fats Waller,* pp. 81 - 83.
[205] William Gibson, "'Fats' Waller Got Idea for 'Ain't Misbehavin' in Gary," *Baltimore Afro-American*, 8 Feb, 1930, p. 8.

Chapter Four

Black Vaudeville and the Birth of the Blues

The end of World War I began the start of the first Great Migration, where 1.6 million African Americans moved from mostly rural areas of the South to northern industrial cities to escape racial oppression and the poverty-stricken conditions of sharecropping. The booming resort economy of Asbury Park, though seasonal, suggested an abundance of service and maintenance jobs. As African Americans poured into the Springwood Avenue area, the Italian American population, still confined to the West Side, gradually moved north toward Asbury Avenue.

In 1916, the West Side did get a champion, of sorts, when Clarence Hetrick was elected Mayor of Asbury Park. Hetrick had gained the respect of the city's African American population several years earlier as the city's sheriff. On November 9, 1910, a ten-year-old white girl, Marie Smith, vanished on her way home from school. Marie had been attending the newly-built Bradley School at Third Avenue and Pine Street, in the recently annexed area west of downtown but north of Asbury Avenue. After the annexation, the city spent money renovating this area. While technically west of downtown, this area was distinctly different from the African American and Italian, Springwood Avenue section called the "West Side." Improvements to the Springwood Avenue area would come much slower.

Mayor Clarence Hetrick
Courtesy of the Asbury Park Museum

Marie Smith would have walked west on Asbury Avenue toward her home in Whitesville, a neighborhood even farther west of the city. After an exhaustive search, the child's body was found a couple days later. She'd been raped, beaten and strangled. From the beginning, authorities, and especially the press, sought to pin the crime on a black, former prize fighter who'd spent time in prison for larceny. A handyman, Thomas Williams was known locally as "Black Diamond." Never mind that Williams had denied the crime and that there was no evidence. The front page of the local newspaper screamed, "NEGRO IS PLACED NEAR SCENE AT THE TIME OF BRUTAL MURDER" and went on to proclaim, "This is a negro crime [rape and murder of a white girl] and Black Diamond was the only negro known to have been near the scene at the time the murder was committed." With Black Diamond's arrest, a mob formed around the jail with sledgehammers, axes and crowbars, bent on lynching the suspect.[1] Clarence Hetrick, sheriff at the time, secretly whisked Black Diamond away to a jail in Freehold for his safety. Convinced of his innocence, Hetrick hired the nationally known Burns Detective Agency to investigate the case. Burns detectives proved, through the new science of fingerprints, that the real culprit was a German immigrant who had fled Germany after molesting a girl there. The German eventually confessed and was executed. And Hetrick was elected mayor thanks to support of the West Side.[2] Hetrick was Asbury Park's mayor from 1916 to 1941.

Black Vaudeville

American Vaudeville, a type of variety show featuring a series of unrelated acts presented on stage together on a common bill, was extremely popular in the United States, beginning around 1880. Vaudeville shows might contain comedians, singers, musicians, animal acts, contortionists, magic acts, fire eaters or other types of entertainment. By the beginning of the 20th Century, vaudeville shows were gradually replacing minstrel shows in theater circuits around the country. They would last into the 1920's when their popularity would be reduced due to the growing interest in motion pictures.

Racial segregation dictated that African American vaudeville develop separately. Black vaudeville - vaudeville by black performers for black audiences - began gaining momentum in the South after 1900. Performed at first on makeshift stages in saloons and public parks, by 1910 it had mushroomed into a network of theaters that touring black vaudeville troupes could rotate through. The next year, black vaudeville troupes brought their form of entertainment to northern audiences. By 1921, these vaudeville houses organized into the Theater Owners' Booking Association (TOBA). Presenting "legitimate" black musical comedies, black vaudeville "weaned mainstream audiences away from the crude character delineations of nineteen century" minstrel shows.[3]

Abbott and Seroff firmly establish in their groundbreaking book, *The Original Blues,*[4] that blues music emerged on the stages of black vaudeville. But, early black vaudeville songs owed more to ragtime than to what would later be called the blues.

"The blues did not emerge onstage fully formed. The blues remained mutable and multiform long after it was institutionalized on the black professional stage. Gifted artists put their personal stamp on the blues songs they sang and played a big part in the development of a modern blues style."[5]

Blues became publicly recognized as a distinct music entity around 1909. While male vaudeville singers lingered in the roles of blackface comedians, female "coon shouters" emerged as the first blues singing stars. This coincided with the music industry discovering a market for "race records" - recordings made of black artists for sale to African American buyers. Mamie Smith's 1920 recording of "Crazy Blues" for *Okeh* Records ushered in a proliferation of female blues recordings by the likes of Ma Rainey and Bessie Smith. Male blues singers would follow a few years later.

Unlike with country blues, which would develop soon after, black vaudeville blues singers were typically accompanied by piano, drums and sometimes a brass instrument.[6]

Lawrence Deas performing in the
Deas & Deas team at the Hippodrome in
Asbury Park, November 21, 1911.

Lawrence Deas

One black vaudeville star with ties to Asbury Park's West Side was Lawrence Deas. Deas was reportedly born in Toronto, Canada, and entered show business in 1896 as a partner of legendary ragtime pioneer, "Jack The Bear" Wilson. Jack the Bear was said to be one of the greatest ragtime pianists of his time. Wilson and Deas joined the ragtime minstrel troupe, *The South Before The War* briefly, before settling in New York City. They were remembered as the "first colored act to use a piano on the stage singing their own compositions. One of their compositions, "All I Want Is My Chicken" was one of the most popular ragtime songs of 1899. Deas and Wilson continued partnering in other black vaudeville troupes until parting ways around 1900.[7]

In 1907, Deas performed in the musical comedy *The Oyster Man* in New York City.[8] By 1909 he was doing song and dance in New York with the Octoroon Burlesque Company as "Deas and Deas." The female Leas partner was possibly his wife. He also performed as a straight man to comedian Harry Reed in that company.[9] The act "Deas, Reed and Deas" ventured on as their own vaudeville company, playing in Milwaukee[10] and Cincinnati[11] before arriving in Asbury Park in November of 1911. There they played the Hippodrome Theatre on Main Street at the head of Wesley Lake. Newspaper reviews describe them as a "trio of colored performers" doing a song and dance act with comedy.[12]

Lawrence Deas must have liked Asbury Park, for in June of 1913, he oversaw the grand opening of Royal Theatre on Springwood Avenue. Leading the orchestra at the grand opening was Mrs. Dolly Deas of Boston.[13] Dolly may have been the woman in Deas

63

and Deas. [Reference to a "Deas & Deas" theater on Springwood Avenue in May of 1913[14] may be an early name for the Royal Theatre.]

For awhile in the 1910's, the Royal Theatre was the crown jewel of Springwood Avenue's entertainment scene. Lawrence Deas stayed in Asbury Park through 1917, when he produced "The Goofer Trust," a vaudeville act that, featuring Deas & Parker, played the [white] Savoy Theatre in November of that year.[15]

In 1921, Lawrence Deas joined Noble Sissle and Eubie Blake in the ground-breaking Broadway production of *Shuffle Along*. There he choreographed all the dances and also played the part of Detective Jack Penrose.[16] He also choreographed the less successful musical, "Change Your Luck" in 1930.[17]

Baby Mack, Star of Black Vaudeville and Blues Pioneer

Asbury Park's biggest West Side contribution to black vaudeville was Baby Mack [sometimes spelled "Mac"]. Wilhelmina "Baby" Mack, was born in Asbury Park, August 3, 1897,[18] to a white woman and her black lover. Not wanting to face her friends and family and not caring about the welfare of the child, Wilhelmina's mother gave her up to an impoverished black woman, a widow named Mrs. Anna Mack, and moved to New York City.

Living in a small wooden shack at 37 Avenue A on Asbury Park's West Side, Wilhelmina learned what poverty meant. "I always went to school without breakfast and never came home for lunch because I had left nothing there," said Wilhelmina. "[I] came home hoping [for food] in the afternoons."[19]

While her foster mother worked as a maid in nearby Ocean Grove, Wilhelmina took small jobs washing and cleaning to help out until she was fourteen years old. The young girl completed seventh grade in the segregated public school for black children but dropped out to look for work. She was overheard singing by Lawrence Deas. Deas helped her put together a song act and had her change her name to "Baby" Mack. Baby Mack soon became extremely popular on Springwood Avenue, where she sang and danced, earning $18 a week.

Lawrence Deas, with the aid of Samuel Tolson, manager of a motion picture house on Springwood Avenue, recommended Baby Mack to S. H. Dudley. Star singer, comedian and producer, S. H. Dudley, is most often associated with one of the most important black vaudeville shows, *The Smart Set*. Music historians Abbott and Seroff have stated that "*The Smart Set* was a singular vehicle for the constructive change on the American stage."[20] Dudley was playing in Philadelphia for much of 1914, so Baby Mack's first out of town gig was in Philadelphia.

In January, 1914, The *Asbury Park Press* carried a front page article that Mrs. Anna Mack had asked the police to locate her 16 year-old daughter, Wilhelmina, who'd gone to Philadelphia to seek employment at a theater. The daughter had written back that she had secured theatrical employment but failed to come home that weekend like she'd promised.[21] The next day, the newspaper reported that Baby Mack was safe. An illness had prevented her from visiting her mother.[22]

S. H. Dudley gave Baby Mack a contract to perform on the TOBA circuit for $25 weekly. Baby Mack looked younger than her age and used that to her advantage. At times she was harassed by well meaning child service organizations but was allowed to continue performing since she was sending $10 of her $25 back home weekly to her foster mother.[23]

Baby Mack's foster mother was in dire need of money. Ten months after Baby left to tour, her home at 37 Avenue A was completely destroyed by fire. Mrs. Anna Mack lost what little possessions she had.[24]

In May 1914, Baby Mack was performing in a show at the Crown Garden Theatre in Indianapolis, Indiana. A reviewer wrote, "Yes, Baby Mack is some baby all right. She sings three delightful numbers, 'Wait Until Your Daddy Comes,' 'When I Lost You' and 'What It Takes To Make You Love Me, You've Got It'. Her numbers stand for variety. Her second number is especially pathetic, touching. She sits down until the close, when she rises, going off the stage, singing in a heartbreaking manner the last lines. Baby Mack's closing number shows vivacity, shows that she is a performer already, and also that she is going to be among the top notchers. Her eyes, smile, steps, are all indicative of her ability as a performer. The little lady has the stage essentials. She is pretty. She is versatile and knows how to look well. She will make a good number on any bill."[25]

Sheet music ad in the
Indianapolis Freeman, 3 July 1915

Also on the Crown Garden Theatre show was Butler "String Beans" May.[26] While composer W. C. Handy has been crowned the "Father of the Blues," it was String Beans who was the stage performer most responsible for popularizing early blues. Handy's songs were published, giving him a sense of immortality. At the peak of String

Beans' popularity, the recording industry had not caught up to vaudeville blues. Were it not for Abbott and Seroff's painstaking research of the existing black press, String Beans would have all but been forgotten. String Beans mixed comedy and song, spreading the blues throughout the country, as a pianist and singer. "String Beans was the greatest attraction of the pre-1920 African American vaudeville and the first blues star."[27]

A reviewer for the *Indianapolis Freeman* later wrote, "Baby Mack ... a pleasing creature, very impressionistic ... came near going into hysterics over 'String Beans' work, insisting on seeing him every night after her own turn, which was first... They got together as a team before the week was over."[28]

The team of String Beans and Baby Mack opened at the Lincoln Theatre in Cincinnati. From there they moved on to the Monogram Theatre (Chicago) in June 1914 and then to the 81 Theatre in Atlanta. Then it was on to the grand opening of the Champion Theatre in Birmingham, where they drew capacity crowds.[29]

Baby Mack's teaming up with String Beans lasted only a few months, but it was enough to kick start her career in black vaudeville. By late August 1914, Butler "String Beans" May was again performing solo.[30] The next three years would solidify his fame as the greatest blues piano player of his time in the world. Unfortunately, String Beans time in this world was short. In November 1917, he died of a broken neck after a hazing accident while being initiated into a Masonic lodge. String Beans was only in his mid-twenties.

By 1916, Baby Mack had teamed with Tommy Parker, soon to be her first husband. Parker & Mack (Tommy & Baby) became very popular as a black vaudeville song, dance and comedy team. They began touring with Alexander Tolliver's Smart Set of 1916, said to be one of the most brilliant collection of entertainers in the history of the African American stage. The traveling show was viewed in a four-pole tent containing a forty-foot stage in the center. The show featured legendary blues singers Ma Rainey and (at times) Clara Smith, one-legged dancer Peg Leg Lightfoot and scores of others. The show went on the road from New Orleans to Birmingham, Bessemer, Atlanta, Raleigh, Petersburg, Norfolk, Newport News, Richmond, Winston-Salem, Savannah and numerous other cities.[31] Though Ma Rainey and Clara Smith would not make their first records until 1923, they were honing their skills as the first generation of blues singers.

In February, 1920, Mamie Smith recorded for *Okeh Records*. This was the first recording by a black blues singer. Smith's second record later that year, "Crazy Blues," sold more than a million copies, opening the floodgates for record companies to record female black blues vocalists. Prior to that, record companies believed there was no real market for blues.[32]

As a result of "Crazy Blues," Mamie Smith formed her own company and began touring. Parker and Mack joined Mamie Smith on tour in Dallas in April, 1921, where "Tommy

Parker and Baby Mack went over big."[33] From there The Mamie Smith Review moved to the Standard Theatre in Philadelphia.[34] By the time they reached Douglass Theatre in Baltimore the next year, newspaper reviews proclaimed, "Parker and Mack, Tommy and Baby, are still keeping busy and are as popular around here as ever despite the fact that they have not been in town for some months."[35] In Baltimore, "Parker and Mack opened with their sailor act, the feature of which was the closing dance and caught a good hand."[36]

Moving to the Hippodrome in Richmond, VA, the couple drew this comment from a reviewer. "Parker and Mack, who always register highly, elicited much laughter and applause from their audience and were a big hit. Miss Mack still holds her charm, juvenile mannerisms and baby voice. She injected all these into her number and easily drew an encore. Tommy's dancing is still his best bet... Both danced Tom Delaney's 'New York Glide' for their closing."[37]

In 1923, Baby Mack separated from her husband, Tommy Parker. They would eventually divorce. Baby Mack's new partner and rumored love interest was Sam Robinson. Robinson was formerly of the vaudeville team, Burton and Robinson. Robinson and Mack were seen playing the Grand Central Theatre in Cleveland, along with the Bob Russell All Star Company in March of 1923.[38]

Though most of Baby Mack's appearances during this time were with Sam Robinson, she also found time to appear as a soloist. In September, Baby Mack played the Star Theatre in Baltimore where she was described as "one of the cleverest little soubrettes in the business with her charming style of rendering her song and some nifty hoofing."[39]

Baby Mack, clipping from Sara Martin's scrapbook ourtesy of Pen Bogert and Doug Seroff

One description of the Robinson & Mack act is as follows: "Baby Mack and Sam Robinson started the bill, moving fast... Baby Mack put her song over in good style and Robinson with his 'Moonshine' song, a parody on 'That Dog,' was a scream. The team closed with a novelty dance and a 'blues' number."[40]

At Baltimore's Regent Theatre in October, a reviewer noted, "Mack and Robinson, the former once of the team Parker and Robinson, offered a song, dance and talking skit which was intelligently gotten together and which they put over in the same manner.

Baby Mack has progressed far since last seen here and is now a genuine comedienne, a bit in which she carried a police whistle to keep Robinson from striking her was nicely done. Robinson is a fine comic, dances well and and has a good singing voice. He put over the best 'hootch' song ever heard here and proved a riot. Robinson worked under cork [in black face]."[41]

Working at Chicago's Monogram Theatre with Butterbeans and Suzie and Jackie "Moms" Mabley in December 1923, Robinson & Mack "... open with a snappy domestic argument, which goes big. Baby Mack sings 'If You Want To Keep Your Daddy Home,' to good effect, while Robinson uses his own song, 'Moonshine Liquor,' and takes the house. They close with 'Desperate Blues,' and it was with difficulty they were allowed to leave the stage."[42]

The manager of the Booker Washington Theatre in St. Louis commented, "A word of praise for an act worthwhile," referring to Sam Robinson and Baby Mack, "'The Bootlegger and the Girl,' who played my house last week. They have a real 'honest to goodness' act. They have brought a new and timely idea and they really handle it in a splendid manner... They have new songs and new and original gags in keeping with the 'down to the minute' comedy, singing and dancing sketch."[43]

In 1924, Robinson and Mack performed at Gibson's Standard Theatre in Philadelphia[44] and the Hippodrome in Richmond,[45] to name a few.

The year 1925 started with Robinson and Mack with the Bob Russell Company playing the Grand Theatre (Chicago?). Baby Mack sang "Honolulu Isle" assisted by the chorus, to heavy applause.[46] At the same time, newspapers reported that Baby Mack was now divorced from Tommy Parker. They surmised that Sam Robinson would soon be husband number two.[47]

In May 1925, Robinson and Mack joined blues star Sarah Martin's company at the Temple in Cleveland.[48] Martin, who had begun recording a few years earlier, was one of the most recorded blues singers of her era. Robinson and Mack would be with Sara Martin for much of 1925.

On August 16, 1925, Baby Mack's ex-husband, Tommy Parker died. He had been ill for some time and had entered the hospital for treatment. His obituary stated that he and Baby Mack had played "every house on the colored time. His [Parker's] peer as a dancer and song delineator would be difficult to find. The team of Parker and Mack, being small of stature, were always considered the best juvenile impersonators in the country. ... His death has removed another who did much to elevate vaudeville."[49]

Baby Mack went to Washington to make the funeral arrangements.[50] Back on the road by September, Robinson and Mack played the Koppin Theatre in Detroit with Sara Martin and black vaudeville legend, S. H. Dudley. A newspaper review said that "Robinson and Mack... have been seen over here on several occasions and they still make them like it, judging by the applause given them on all their numbers. Robinson is funny with his wit. Miss Mack with her wonderful personality puts over her songs numbers to good effect. The act was well received and went over big."[51]

Robinson and Mack again joined S. H. Dudley at the Washington Theatre in Indianapolis in October 1925. Press reports relayed, "Robinson and Mack, male and female, were good. Remember Mack? Baby Mack, an old Washington favorite. These two team well. There was no slipshod work in their act, which was clean, clever and laughable. Thanks for the new songs."[52]

In November, Robinson and Mack continued with Sara Martin's unit in Baltimore. Reviews stated "Robinson and Mack were next with their always pleasing collection of entertainment material. Notwithstanding the evident knowledge that 'Baby' has grown up, she is as appealing in characterizations as ever."[53]

Of all the times in Baby Mack's career, the end of 1925 and beginning of 1926 was probably one of the most exciting. After watching all the female blues singers around her make records, Baby Mack finally got a chance to record.

On November 13, 1925, Robinson and Mack made their first recordings for *OKeh Records* in New York. *OKeh Records* was the company that was most responsible for releasing blues recordings at that time. Sam and Baby recorded two duets, "Don't Lose Your Head And Put Your Hands On Me" and "I Beg To Be Excused." Both were written by Sam Robinson and accompanied on piano by music veteran Clarence Williams who was *OKeh*'s Director of Race (African American) Recordings in New York City. The songs were both taken from the team's comedy act and more suited to a live audience than on record. They were released as *OKeh 8259*.[54]

With sales of "race records" doing well, *OKeh* then opened another recording studio in Chicago, the center of jazz in the 1920's, where jazz pioneer and composer, Richard M. Jones, was hired as "race" recordings director. Jones put out a call for African American musicians and singers to come in and record. Jones sought to assemble an ensemble of former New Orleans musicians. The result was one of the most

Baby Mack's 1926 blues recording of "You've Got To Get Home On Time." Accompaniment by Louis Armstrong.

respected groups in jazz history - Louis Armstrong's Hot Five. The Hot Five recorded for *OKeh* for the first time on November 12, 1925.[55]

Baby and Sam started 1926 in Ohio with Jack Reid's Black & White Review[56] but were quickly sent to Chicago to record again. This time their songs were produced by Richard M. Jones. Jones played piano and called Louis Armstrong back in to accompany him on the sides.

The recording session on February 23, 1926, featured Baby Mack singing two blues numbers solo, backed by Louis Armstrong on trumpet, with Richard M. Jones on piano. While the industry was moving toward the more modern integrated system of electrical microphones, amplifiers and electromechanical recorders, *OKeh* made these recordings with their own "TrueTone" electric process. The process was not very good, sound wise, and was soon abandoned by *OKeh* in favor of the new industry standard by Westing-house. On "You've Got To Get Home On Time" (written by Sam Armstrong), Baby Mack takes full command of the record, vocally. Her voice is powerful and her diction is excellent. Armstrong's and Jones' accompaniment is subdued but appropriate. On the reverse side of *OKeh 8313*, Armstrong and Jones dominate the first third of the record with an outstanding jazz instrumental introduction. From there, Baby Mack takes over, belting out the blues vocal, "What Kind Of Man Is That."

Two days later (February 25, 1926) Robinson and Mack recorded two more sides, "It's All The Same To Me" and ""Make Room For Someone Else" (*OKeh 8298*). Both have only Richard M. Jones accompanying on piano and comedy skits taken from the pair's live show. The same day, Sam Robinson also recorded a couple of sides solo.[57]

Robinson and Mack would have one more recording session together. Performing with Dave Marion's show at the Columbia Theatre in New York in the Fall of 1926,[58] they recorded two songs for *Vocalion Records* on November 27. "I'm Sure Gonna Put You In Jail" and a remake of "Make Room For Somebody Else" remain unreleased to this day.[59]

Ad for Baby Mack and Sam Robinson playing Pittsburgh's Elmore Theatre
with Drake & Walker. *Pittsburgh Courier*, 28 May, 1927.

Even as they recorded together, Baby Mack and Sam Robinson were beginning to go their separate ways.

By October 1926, Baby Mack had joined the Drake and Walker Company as a solo act to play the Royal Theatre in Baltimore. "Baby Mack, another beauty, displays some real toe dancing, assisted by the chorus she puts 'Animal Crackers' in a novel manner. Sure enough they threw animal crackers out to the audience."[60]

When they reached Washington DC in November, the Drake and Walker Company, with Baby Mack, was drawing record crowds.[61]

May of 1927 saw Baby with the Drake and Walker Company playing the Grand Theatre in Chicago[62] and then the Elmore Theatre in Pittsburgh. Baby Mack and Sam Robinson were both on those shows, but performing separately.[63] When the Drake and Walker troupe performed in Baltimore's Royal Theatre in August, one reviewer noted, "Ethyl Walker, 'Baby' Mack, Estelle Edwards, and Jackie [Moms] Mabley take the spotlight by turns, each starring in her own specialties. Miss Mack has 'it' with her light comedy, singing and dancing."[64]

That Fall, Baby Mack traveled to the West Coast with the Doc Straine & Sam Russell Company.[65] In November they were working the Lincoln Theatre in Los Angeles, presenting a comedy called "The Wilds Of Arizona". The band appearing with the Straine & Russell Company was the Dixieland Blueblowers,[66] led by Curtis Mosby. While performing with the Straine & Russell Company, Baby Mack met saxophonist Charles "Leslie" Hite of the Curtis Mosby Band and the two were married in a quiet wedding ceremony before a judge in the Los Angeles County Courthouse in April, 1928.[67]

Later in 1928, Les Hite left Curtis Mosby's band and started his own orchestra. They began working at Frank Sebastian's Cotton Club in Culver City, just outside of Los Angeles. Baby Mack was one of the star attractions.[68]

Sebastian's Cotton Club was Culver City's premier jazz venue. It was opened in 1926 and was one of the area's first to feature bands with exclusively black musicians. The club opened late and stayed open until breakfast.[69] It was right across the street from the MGM movie studios so many film stars frequented it. [The Cotton Club audience was primarily, if not exclusively, white.] Among the many things Les Hite's band was known for is giving a start to the career of Lionel Hampton. Hite and Hampton had grown up in the same neighborhood in Chicago. Hite and Hampton had even played in the same teenage band and when Hite went to Los Angeles, he invited Hampton to come out and join him.

"We were a bunch of young cats," recalled Hampton of the Les Hite Band. "And we could swing, man... When Frank Sebastian hired us for his Cotton Club, man, we all felt we'd made the big time. We went in under the name Leon Herriford's New Cotton

Leon Herriford's Orchestra (soon to become Les Hite and the New Sebastian's Cotton Club Orchestra. Photo taken at Sebastion's Cotton Club in Culver City. Is that Baby Mack standing to the left of center?

Club Orchestra, because Sebastian wanted Herriford to front us, but very soon we were Les Hite and His New Sebastian Cotton Club Orchestra."[70]

Les Hite's Orchestra backed all the famous black acts that came through the Cotton Club, from the Mills Brothers to Louis Armstrong.[71] They also performed as a unit between other acts, giving Baby Mack plenty of stage time. In fact, a 1931, newspaper reported that, "A Negro radio hour sponsored by the *California Eagle* started last Monday night. Baby Mack, widely known blues singer, was on the first program."[72]

Les Hite and Baby Mack played Sebastian's Cotton Club for the next four years, with the exception of one six-month period when they were displaced by McKinney's Cotton Pickers.[73]

But singing on stage was just a part of Baby Macks' career as an entertainer. Another aspect was motion pictures. As far back as 1928, newspapers mentioned that Baby Mack (Mrs. Leslie Hite) would be in the Foxtone movie, "The Kentucky Handicap" with Lincoln Perry, Perry, better known as Stepin Fetchit, was the first black film superstar.[74]

We could find no record of "The Kentucky Handicap" ever being released. Stepin Fetchit's big film of that year was "In Old Kentucky," an MGM film where he starred with Carolynne Snowden, an established black actress, singer and dancer. Stepin Fetchit's next film was "The Ghost Talks," which was done for Fox Studios. Carolynne

Ad for "The Ghost Talks" in
Photoplay magazine, 1929.
Baby Mack is pictured on the left.

Snowden was so confident of her stardom, that she reportedly showed up at the Fox Studio casting office for an interview with her maid and chauffeur. She was turned down and the role was given to Baby Mack.[75]

In the 1929 farce comedy, "The Ghost Talks," Baby Mack and Stepin Fetchit play a honeymooning couple in a haunted house.[76] Feature length movies with sound ("talkies") were in their early stages then, having just been introduced to the public in late 1927. While Stepin Fetchit would later be demonized for his negative stereotypical portrayal of African Americans, it's important to remember that those were the only roles open to black actors and actresses in major films. Dignified roles for blacks in mainstream motion pictures would have to wait another thirty years, and Stepin Fetchit helped open doors for those that came after him.

Baby Mack would also have parts in at least two more talking motion pictures. She played the part of Syvil in "Close Harmony" (1929), a film that starred bandleader Charles "Buddy" Rogers and featured an uncredited chorus girl extra, Jean Harlow. Baby Mack's last credited role was as Julia in "Crazy That Way" (1930).[77] However, one newspaper article stated she appeared with Buck and Bubbles in several talkie comedies.[78]

Baby Mack's Famous Dog

As early as 1927, Baby Mack could not resist showing off her prized bulldog pup. She had publicity photos taken with him and taken the dog with her as she traveled the country on tour. Baby Mack's fans knew one of her slogans was "Love me, love my dog!" Unfortunately newspapers reported in 1931, "Baby Mack, clever night club and motion picture actress... is reportedly seriously ill on the Coast, suffering from an infection that set in after her dog bit her."[79] Baby Mack did recover from the illness and as a dog lover was reported to own many dogs in her kennels. But this dog was her favorite. It was not surprising then that newspapers carried the story of the death of Baby Mack's dog in January, 1934.[80]

"Love Me, Love My Dod"

Baby Mack and her dog. We assume the title is a typo. Baby Mack's slogan was "Love Me, Love My Dog".

Out On Her Own Again

Baby Mack sent a letter to the *Pittsburgh Courier* in February of 1933 reporting that she and her husband were taking a much needed rest in the country at Elsnor, California, after closing a four-year engagement at the Cotton Club in Culver City.[81] When Les Hite's Band returned to Sebastian's Cotton Club in June, Baby Mack was not with them, preferring to work at a different club.[82] While she and Les remained happily married, Baby Mack chose to strike out again on her own, career-wise. As Les Hite continued at the Cotton Club, Baby joined Leon Herriford who'd left to form his own seven piece band at the Backstage Club in Hollywood.[83]

Baby Mack was sorely missed by not only the Cotton Club audiences, but also a whole fan base on radio. The Cotton Club shows were broadcast live on radio and fans "used to sit up nights to hear her on the Cotton Club program."[84]

In November 1933, Baby Mack left Los Angeles for the first time in six years to accept a spot as an entertainer at the Radio Cafe in Portland, Oregon.[85] There she began working with C. L. Burke's band. The Radio Cafe (Club) was a "whites only" club with black entertainers.[86]

Baby Mack in Portland, Oregon

Some time in 1933, white residents of Portland, Oregon, developed a taste for black entertainment. The idea of bringing black entertainment to Portland was conceived by Herman Whaley, a former dining car waiter, who first tried it out in Portland's Cotton Club. The show was a huge success as throngs of patrons abandoned the white clubs to fill the Cotton Club. Soon other clubs followed suit, hiring black entertainers for exorbitant pay. Newspapers proclaimed, "The lumberjacks of the great Northwest have doffed their Makinaws, their leather boots, laid down their two-edged axes and donned soup and fish to visit the night clubs. Harlem hotcha introduced during the past year, with brown-skinned maidens shaking their shimmy and a band of sepia musicians blasting hot tunes in the true Ellington jungle rhythm is responsible for the arousing of interest on the Oregon capital's dawn patrol."[87] Crowds deserted the white night clubs for the Cotton Club and others like the Radio Club, who'd brought in Baby Mack from Los Angels. The Radio Club was the most exclusive of all of these clubs.

Baby Mack's stay in Portland lasted fewer than three months. In spite of the gossip that she had broken many hearts there,[88] she was back in Los Angeles by the first week in February, 1934. By Baby Mack's account, the musicians union in Portland ousted all the black musicians from the Radio Club. It seemed there was no union for black musicians in Portland and musicians of color were not allowed in the white musicians union.[89]

In March, Baby Mack was back performing in Southern California. She entertained with the "Change Your Luck" company at the Burbank Theatre for a month[90] and then moved to the heart of Hollywood at the popular night spot, Caesar's. Baby was now referred to as the "The Coast's Sweetheart."[91]

Apparently soured by her experiences in Portland, Baby turned down a chance to go on tour with her husband, Les Hite, and his band. She told the press in November 1934 that she preferred "keeping house rather than traveling all over the country."[92]

Sticking close to home, Baby Mack was performing with Leon Herriford's Orchestra at Bud Taylor's Cafe, on Vermont and Washington Streets in Los Angeles, in May and June of 1935.[93] Newspapers described her as "the charming Baby Mack who warbles catchy tunes 'Lullaby [of] Broadway' and 'What's The Reason.'"[94]

In January 1936, Leon Herriford's band moved to the Club Skyline Cafe, 746 South Figueroa in Los Angeles. Baby Mack captivated the audiences with "Dinner For One, Please James." The shows were broadcast over radio stations KFVD and KFCA resulting in hundreds and hundreds of fan letters.[95] They played there through at least April.[96]

The last newspaper reference we could find of Baby Mack as an entertainer was when she was playing the Swanee Inn on North La Brea Street in August 1937. The Swanee Inn was a white club.[97] It would be the same club that hosted the first incarnation of the Nat (King) Cole Trio that same year.

In 1948, Mr. And Mrs, Les Hite did attend an award ceremony for Louis Jordan in Los Angeles.[98]

Baby Mack's husband, Les Hite, continued leading his orchestra for several years. The band's popularity and proximity to Hollywood studios allowed them to appear in numerous movies.

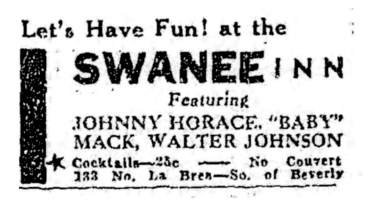

Besides Lionel Hampton, members of his band at times included Dizzy Gillespie, Marshall Royal and T-Bone Walker. Les Hite died of a heart attack in 1962 at the age of 58.[99]

At some point, Baby Mack apparently remarried. Wilhelmina "Baby Mack" Hite Myatt died in Los Angeles on January 6, 1987.[100] In 2017, the Asbury Angels Foundation honored Baby Mack with a plaque on the Asbury Park Boardwalk of Fame.

Other West Side Blues Pioneers

Baby Mack was not the only pioneer blues vocalist from Asbury Park's West Side. Reese DuPree was a key figure in Springwood Avenues' music scene when he made what very well may be the first blues vocal recording by an African American male singer with guitar accompaniment in 1923. But that story will appear in Chapter Eight.

Notes to Chapter 4

[1] See coverage in the *Asbury Park Press*, 14 Nov, 1910, pp. 1, 5, and surrounding dates.

[2] Daniel Wolff, *4th of July, Asbury Park*, (New York: Bloomsbury Publications, 2005), pp. 93 - 96.

[3] Lynn Abbott and Doug Seroff, *Ragged But Right: Black Traveling Shows, "Coon Songs," and the Dark Pathway to Blues and Jazz*, (Jackson, MS: University of MS, 2007), p. 81.

[4] Lynn Abbott and Doug Seroff, *The Original Blues: The Emergence of the Blues in African American Vaudeville 1899 - 1926*, (Jackson, MS: University of MS, 2017).

[5] Abbott and Seroff, *The Original Blues*, p. 4.

[6] Abbott and Seroff, *The Original Blues*, p. 5.

[7] Lynn Abbott and Doug Seroff, *Out Of Sight: The Rise of African American Popular Music, 1889 - 1895*, (Jackson, MS: University of MS, 2002), p. 455.

[8] https://www.ibdb.com/broadway-cast-staff/lawrence-deas-37700

[9] "Octoroon Burlesque Company," *New York Age*, 20 May, 1909, p. 6.

[10] "Theatrical Jottings," *New York Age*, 28 Apr, 1910, p. 6.

[11] *Cincinnati Enquirer*, 22 May, 1910, p. 46.

[12] "Theaters Offer Good Vaudeville," *Asbury Park Press*, 21 Nov, 1911, p. 7.

[13] "Royal Theatre - Asbury Park, New Jersey," *Indianapolis Freeman*, 14 Jun, 1913.

[14] "Resent Attack by Dr. Atchley," *Asbury Park Press*, 19 May, 1913, p. 1.

[15] Ad for Deas & Parker at the Savoy Theatre, *Asbury Park Press*, 28 Nov, 1917, p. 7.

[16] Robert Kimball and William Bolcom, *Reminiscing with Noble Sissle and Eubie Blake,* (New York: Viking Press, 1973).

[17] https://www.ibdb.com/broadway-cast-staff/lawrence-deas-37700

[18] Eric S. LeBlanc and Bob Eagle, *Blues: A Regional Experience*, (Santa Barbara, Praega, 2013), p. 517.

[19] "Lack of Regular Meals Drove Singer To Stage," *The Afro-American*, 13 Aug, 1927.

[20] Abbott and Seroff, *Ragged But Right*, p. 81.

[21] "Fears For Daughter Who Went To Philadelphia," *Asbury Park Press,* 28 Jan, 1914, p. 1.

[22] "Baby Mack Safe," *Asbury Park Press*, 29 Jan, 1914, p. 1

[23] "Lack of Regular Meals Drove Singer to Stage," *The Afro-American*, 13 Aug, 1927.

[24] "Early Blaze Does Damage of $2,500," *Asbury Park Press,* 11 Nov, 1914. p. 1.

[25] *Indianapolis Freeman*, 16 May, 1914.

[26] Abbott and Seroff, *The Original Blues*, p. 85.

[27] Abbott and Seroff, *The Original Blues*, p. 67.

[28] "Stage Notes," *Indianapolis Freeman*, 30 Jan, 1915.

[29] Abbott and Seroff, *The Original Blues*, p. 86 - 88.

[30] Abbott and Seroff, *The Original Blues*, p. 88.

[31] Abbott and Seroff, *Ragged But Right*, pp. 140 - 156.

[32] Barry Mazor, *Ralph Peer and the Making of Popular Roots Music*, (Chicago: Chicago Review Press, 2015), p. 37.

[33] *Chicago Defender*, 2 Apr, 1921. All *Chicago Defender* references courtesy of Doug Seroff.

[34] *Chicago Defender*, 13 Aug, 1921.

[35] *Chicago Defender*, 27 May, 1922.

[36] *Chicago Defender*, 3 Jun, 1922.

[37] *Chicago Defender*, 24 Jun, 1922.

[38] *Chicago Defender*, 10 Mar, 1923.

[39] "Vaudeville and Pictures," *Afro-American*, 28 Sep, 1923, p. A4.

[40] *Chicago Defender*, 12 May, 1923.

[41] "Regent," *Afro-American*, 5 Oct, 1923.

[42] *Chicago Defender*, 1 Dec, 1923.

[43] *Chicago Defender*, 26 Jan, 1924.

[44] *Chicago Defender*, 28 Jun, 1924.

[45] *Chicago Defender*, 9 Aug, 1924.

[46] *Chicago Defender*, 3 Jan, 1925.

[47] *Chicago Defender*, 7 Feb, 1925.

[48] *Chicago Defender*, 23 May, 1925.

[49] "The Spotlight," *Afro-American,* 29 Aug, 1925, p. 5.

[50] *Chicago Defender*, 29 Aug, 1925.

[51] *Chicago Defender*, 5 Sep, 1925.

52 *Chicago Defender*, 3 Oct, 1925.

53 *Chicago Defender*, 14 Nov, 1925.

54 https://archive.nationaljazzarchive.co.uk/archive/journals/storyville/storyville-017/46919-storyville-017-0009?#prettyPhoto/0/

55 Laurence Bergreen, *Louis Armstrong: An Extravagant Life,* (New York: Broadway Books, 1997), p. 262.

56 *Chicago Defender*, 9 Jan, 1926.

57 Baby Mack and Robinson & Mack recordings directed by Richard M. Jones can be found on the CD, "Richard M. Jones and the Blues Singers," *Document DOCD-5390.*

58 *Chicago Defender*, 25 Nov, 1926.

59 Robert M. W. Dixon and John Godrich, *Blues & Gospel Records 1902 - 1943,* (Chigwell, Essex, UK, Storyville Publications, 1982), p. 628.

60 "Royal," *Afro-American*, 30 Oct, 1926, p. 10.

61 Charles Smythe, "Georgia Minstrels," *Afro-American*, 6 Nov, 1926, p. 6.

62 *Chicago Defender*, 7 May, 1927.

63 *Pittsburgh Courier*, 28 May, 1927, p. 13.

64 "Royal: Drake & Walker," *(National) Afro-American*, 13 Aug, 1927, p. 19.

65 *Chicago Defender*, 26 Nov, 1927.

66 "Baby Mack in California," *Afro-America,"* 12 Nov, 1927, p. 8.

67 *Chicago Defender*, 21 Apr, 1928.

68 "Stage and Screen Gossip," *Afro-American*, 22 Dec, 1928, p. 8.

69 Devon McReynolds, "Vintage Photos From Culver City's Lively Prohibition Era Jazz Scene,http://laist.com/2016/01/27/culver_city_jazz_scene.php#photo-7, 27 Jan, 2016.

70 Lionel Hampton with James Haskins, *Hamp: An Autobiography,* (New York: Warner Books, 1989), p. 34.

71 Harry Levette, "Movie Gossip," *Afro-American,* 23 Aug, 1930, p. A9.

72 "Actors Busy in West as Easterners Loaf," *Afro-American*, 27 Jul, 1931.

73 "Taking Movies Singer's Hobby," *Afro-American*, 4 Feb, 1933, P. 10.

74 *Chicago Defender*, 29 Sep, 1928.

75 "Morning Glories in Hollywood," *Afro-American*, 6 Apr, 1936, p. 8.

76 "Story of Southwest Leads Regent Bill," *Afro-American*, 29 Jul, 1929, p. 9.

77 "Baby Mack," http://www.imdb.com/name/nm0532936/

78 "Dog Bit the Hand That Fed Him," *Afro-American*, 10 Oct, 1931, p. 9.

79 *Ibid.*

80 "Baby Mack's Dog is Dead," *Afro-American*, 27 Jan, 1934, p. 20.

81 Floyd G. Snelson, "Newsy Newettes," *Pittsburgh Courier*, 11 Feb, 1933, p. 16.

82 "Band Back in Club," *Afro-American*, 10 Jun, 1933, p. 9.

83 Ray Buford, "In Hollywood," *Afro-American*, 15 Jul, 1933, p. 11.

84 Harry Levette, "In Hollywood," *Afro-American*, 5 Aug, 1933, p. 18.

85 "For Oregon," *Afro-American*, 11 Nov, 1933, p. 19.

86 *Afro-American,* 25 Nov, 1933, p. 18.

87 Ralph Matthews, "Black And Tan Craze Sweeps Portland; Lumberjacks Fall Hard For Harlem Hotcha," *Afro-American*, 24 Mar, 1934, p. 5.

88 "Train Thoughts," *Afro-American*, 3 Mar, 1934.

[89] Ray Bufford, "On The Coast," *Afro-American*, 10 Feb, 1934, p. 7.

[90] "Baby Mack At Club," *Afro-American,* 14 Apr, 1934, p. 21.

[91] "Baby Mack Back at New Hollywood Club," *Afro-American*, 10 Mar, 1934, p. 7.

[92] *Afro-American*, 3 Nov, 1934,

[93] Fay M. Jackson, "Hollywood," *Afro-American*, 15 Jun, 1935, p. 8.

[94] Bernice Patton, "The Sepia Sound of Hollywood," *Pittsburgh Courier*, 25 May, 1935, p. 22.

[95] *Pittsburgh Courier*, 25 Jan, 1936, p. 16.

[96] Ad for the Club Skyline Cafe, *Los Angeles Times*, 9 Apr, 1936, p. 36.

[97] "Sepia Stars in L.A. Night Clubs," *Pittsburgh Courier*, 21 Aug, 1937, p. 4.

[98] Lawrence F. LaMar, "Jordan Honored By Press Club," *Afro-American*, 20 Mar, 1948, p. 6.

[99] "Les Hite," Wikipedia.

[100] Eric S. LeBlanc and Bob Eagle, *Blues: A Regional Experience*, (Santa Barbara, Praega, 2013), p. 517.

Chapter Five

Basie, Greer and the Lamb

William "Count" Basie, World Telegram Photo by James J. Kriegsmann
Public Domain. Courtesy of the Paul Ressler Archives

William James Basie (the name "Count" would come later) was born in Red Bank, New Jersey, on August 21, 1904. Red Bank is a small town on the banks of the Navesink River about ten miles north of Asbury Park. Bill Basie's mother, Lilly Ann (Childs) Basie was a laundress[1] and his father, Harvey Lee Basie, was the coachman and caretaker for influential political leader and district attorney, Henry Simmons White. Contrary to what is implied in Count Basie's autobiography, young Bill Basie never met "Judge" White, who died of typhoid fever in 1901, three years before Basie was born.[2]

William Basie's father, Harvey Basie, next to a piano in what appears to be a
dilapidated structure. There's probably an interesting story that goes with this
photo but unfortunately it's been lost with the passage of time.
Previously unpublished photo, courtesy of Dorn-Severini Classic Images.

However, Bill Basie's father continued to work for Judge White's widow, Annie and
daughter, Margaretta, for the next sixteen years. The White family owned one of Red
Bank's big estates at the end of Prospect Avenue on the Navesink River. The Basie
family lived about three blocks inland, at 183 Stout Street which in 1910 was renamed
Mechanic Street.[3],[4] [The 229 Mechanic Street address incorrectly cited as Basie's
birthplace by many jazz music sources was, instead, where the Basie family moved to
in the early 1920's.[5]]

It's been reported that William Basie's father could play the mellophone and his mother
was a pianist.[6] "As long as I can remember," Count Basie wrote in his autobiography,
"We always had a piano. And I had taken piano lessons because my mother made me
take them. She paid twenty-five cents a lesson. ... I took a few lessons from a German
lady, Miss Vandevere and I could play things like 'The Midnight Fire Alarm' [a march
and two-step written by Harry J. Lincoln in 1900] and selections from 'Rigoletto.'"[7]

At a young age, William Basie displayed a unique talent for playing by ear. "I could pick out just about any song I heard," recalled Basie. "I liked ragtime. It was the big thing in those days and all I had to do was hear somebody else playing something and I could start right in and repeat it. That wasn't anything for me. And of course, in those days you also picked up things from piano rolls."[8]

William Basie also practiced piano at the estate of his father's employer, the White family. "Lady Margaretta, as I used to call their daughter, ... was always very nice to me. I guess she used to be in her early twenties. ... When I started taking piano lessons she used to have me come into the house and go over the keyboard exercises for her. I can still remember that room and the piano with the neat stack of sheet music."[9]

William Basie's father, Harvey Basie, was president of the board of trustees and later a deacon of the Pilgrim Baptist Church in Red Bank. He was instrumental in getting the church incorporated and acquiring property for the church building to be erected.[10] William Basie's mother, Lilly Ann, sang in the church choir.[11] Harvey Basie was also vice chancellor and co-organizer of Red Bank's chapter of the Colored Knights of Pythias lodge.[12] [*See Chapter 3 for more on the Knights of Pythias*] As such, Harvey helped supervise lodge musical activities. One such event was a benefit concert the Knights of Pythias gave for the Pilgrim Baptist Church in August of 1918. Chaired by Harvey Basie, it featured vocal and instrumental music.[13] Young William Basie would perform at events at the Knights of Pythias Hall.

The earliest newspaper mention of Bill Basie as a musician is from May, 1914. The then ten-year-old Basie took part in the entertainment at a benefit for "the colored young men's association." The proceeds were applied to a fund providing uniforms for the African American boy scout troop. The event was held at the Odd Fellows Hall on Beech Street in Red Bank and raised $18. William Basie and Charles Holmes played piano. William Rock, president of the association was active in the Knights of Pythias.[14,15] Rock was also editor of the local black newspaper, *The Echo Press.*[16]

Bill Basie's interest in show business undoubtedly got a boost when he began helping out at Red Bank's Palace Theatre.

The Palace Theatre began as the Lyric Theatre, built in 1912 at 17 E. Front Street, about a six-block walk from William Basie's home. Through its existence, it functioned as a vaudeville house and moving picture theater. The Lyric was managed by M. E. McNulty, who also managed Red Bank's Empire Theatre. McNulty remodeled the Lyric and reopened it as the Palace Theatre in April of 1920,[17] when Bill Basie was 15 years old.

"As far back as I can remember, my favorite place in Red Bank was the Palace moving-picture theater," wrote Count Basie. "I used to go down there and do chores for the manager every chance I got. I would sweep out the auditorium and the lobby, polish the brass rails and fixtures, put up the extra seats and clean up the dressing room under the stage so that they would be ready for the vaudeville shows that used to play there on weekends. I also used to meet the entertainers when they arrived at the station and show them the way to the hotel."[18]

In the days before motion pictures had sound, silent films were accompanied by a pianist or organist who'd provide musical background for whatever was happening on the screen.

The Palace's pianist used to come in from New York to play, every day. "One day something happened and he didn't get there, and Mr. McNulty, who was the manager, couldn't find anyone to fill in," recalled Count Basie. "So I said I could do it. And I could. ... I'd been taking piano lessons for a while by that time and I knew how that kind of music went, because I had been hearing it over and over all the time. I was the type of guy who could hear something once and work it out on my own. All you had to do was watch the screen and play something that was happening in the story. Sometimes you got the cue from the captions. I had spent enough time down there watching the regular piano player to know what that was all about."[19]

M. E. McNulty at first laughed off the offer to fill in, but young Basie sat down at the piano and played for the matinee. When that was over, McNulty asked him to come back and play for the evening show.

Later known as a great pianist as well as band leader, Bill Basie's first choice in musical instruments was not the piano. He really wanted to be a drummer.

"I was attracted to trap drums very early," said Basie. "There was a drummer known as Chick something who played for quite a few of the dances that my mother used to take me along to. So I got to know him and he taught me a few little things. Before long he used to let me sit in on drums during intermission. By that time I was so wrapped up in drums that my father bought me a little trap set. ... I actually started to play drums along with a piano player whose name I've forgotten, and we picked up a little change from a few little jobs around town," recalled Basie in his autobiography. "In those days a lot of organizations giving a little dance used to just hire a piano player and a drummer. So in a little while, I was beginning to play for a few dances with almost any piano player who could play dance music."[20]

But Bill Basie's career as a drummer only lasted until he heard Sonny Greer play.

Sonny Greer

William Alexander "Sonny" Greer, Jr's date of birth has long been questioned. His birth certificate lists his date and place of of birth as December 13, 1902. in Long Branch, NJ. Sonny, himself, gave several different birth years ranging from from 1895 to 1904 and the birth certificate had a delayed filing date of 1933.[21]

Sonny Greer ca. 1946 as a member of Duke Ellington's Orchestra.
Photo in Public Domain. Gottlieb, William P. Portrait of Sonny Greer,
Aquarium, New York, N.Y., ca. Nov. United States, 1946. ||||, Monographic.
Photograph. https://www.loc.gov/item/gottlieb.03521/.

"My mother was a modiste," said Sonny. "She copied original gowns for wealthy white people. My father... was a master electrician with the Pennsylvania Railroad." Greer was the second oldest of four children but no one else in his family was musically inclined. As a youngster he sold fish after school, delivered groceries and had a paper route. But Sonny's real interest was playing pool. "My first love was playing pool, ten cents a game. I practiced pool like other kids practice violin or piano. I'd practice two hours a day. We had [B. F.] Keith's [Theatre] vaudeville in Long Branch and when J. Rosamond Johnson brought his company through, he had a drummer named "Peggy" Holland - Eugene Holland."

J. Rosamond Johnson along with his brother James Weldon Johnson would compose "Lift Every Voice And Sing," now considered the African American National Anthem.

"[Holland] could sing and dance and play," related Greer. "He fascinated me. The company was in town for two weeks, and every time he came to the poolroom I'd beat him. I told him I admired his playing and he said, 'Kid, teach me how to play pool like you play and I'll do the same for you'. I bought him a box of cigars just to put an edge on it and he gave me six or seven lessons." It so happened that after that Holland's band had a week off so Sonny invited him to stay at the Greer home and give him more drum lessons.[22]

Sonny Greer attended Chattel High School in Long Branch where they had a twenty-five piece band. After demonstrating his drumming skills, Sonny was added to the band. "We also put together a small band and it had six white boys, two white girl singers and me, the Indian," said Sonny. Sonny also sang with the band. The band was doing songs like "Avalon." The group played at basketball games and local dances. Greer quit high school a year before graduation to concentrate on music.[23]

"It was Sonny Greer, who later on went on to become one of the greatest and most famous drummers in the world with the Duke Ellington Orchestra, who got the notion of [me] being a drummer out of my head for once and for all," recalled Count Basie. "I would be playing some little job around town, and every time Greer would happen to come in from Long Branch, which was only a few miles away, and you let him sit in on drums, that was it for me. A few times like that and I didn't want to play another lick. I had sense to know I'd never be able to do what he did... I could see that playing drums was not going to be my gig."[24] Thus, William Basie stuck to piano.

Basie recalled that Greer was already playing as a professional with Chester Arthur's Band which used to play the Red Bank annual fireman's ball. Indeed, the American Federation of Musicians does list a Chester Arthur's Band of Red Bank, NJ, in 1918 - 1920. It's on the union's "Unfair List," possibly for hiring non-union musicians.[25]

On Halloween night, 1920, Sonny Greer and Howard Butterfield played the Long Branch Hotel, 661 Broadway in Long Branch NJ, one of many local gigs for Greer. The Long Branch Hotel had dancing and dining every night, but having Sonny Greer play there was considered a special night.[26]

Besides Basie, another musician that Sonny Greer had an influence on was future drummer, Cozy Cole. Cole was a youngster living in Leonardo, NJ, very near Long Branch. Born in 1909, Cole was only 7 or 8 when Greer was playing locally. Cole used to carry Greer's drums to and from gigs for him [*See Chapter 10*].

"I used to carry [Sonny Greer's] drums from his gigs, used to take them to my

1916 Ad for Chester A. Arthur's Orchestra. Sonny Greer was said to play with them.

house and then the next day I would get a bus and take them to his home," recalled Cozy Cole. Cole recalled Greer playing public dances at fire halls, libraries and other halls around Red Bank, Asbury Park, Sea Bright, Long Branch and Keansburg. "I would read about where he was playing and I'd go and see Sonny."[27]

While it's likely William Basie entered different piano contests, one on January 10, 1921, stands out. "One time there was a piano contest down in Asbury Park," wrote Basie, "And my mother went down with me, and when we got there, Greer was there, and he came over to me and said, 'Hey, I'll play with you.' And I won first place. And I think he was the reason."[28] Indeed, there was a long list of competitors and each was afforded only three minutes of playing. For first prize, Basie took home $2.50 in gold.[29]

After that, Bill Basie and Sonny Greer did a number of area gigs together. Basie's connections with Red Bank's Palace Theatre got them a three-night gig on that theater's vaudeville stage. "They used to have those amateur talent contests known as Opportunity Night and my big pal, Raymond McGuire, won the vocal prize," recalled Basie. "So I asked Mr. McNulty about letting me get a group together for a weekend there with Raymond and he went for it. So I got Greer and Duffan on C-melody sax and Bill Robinson on violin. That was really my introduction to show business and it was wonderful."[30]

The Palace Theatre gig occurred on Thursday, Friday and Saturday, January 20, 21 and 22, 1921. The headliner was Red Bank native son, Frank Bush, who was a world traveled monologist. Basie's group, dubbed the "4 Jazz Hounds" included Basie, Robinson, Duffan and Greer. Advertisements mentioned they were "all local boys," saying "These Boys are Masters of Syncopation." Ads made no mention of vocalist McGuire.[31]

Basie, Greer, Robinson and Duffan performing as the 4 Jazz Hounds at Red Bank's Palace Theatre, 1921.

I got to go out on a few jobs with Bill Robinson," wrote Basie. "He used me on piano at the beginning of the season, and then when the summer hit full swing, they brought in Freddy Tunstall because the music they were playing was a little too heavy for me."[32]

On July 1, 1921, Basie's small combo, calling themselves "The Basie Orchestra," played a dance held in the Navesink Library. Admission was 50 cents.[33]

Sonny Greer Moves On

Meanwhile, [circa late 1921] Sonny Greer would join Fats Waller in a gig at Asbury Park's Grand Plaza Hotel. "I played in the Plaza Hotel on the boardwalk in Asbury Park," recalled Greer. "Fats Waller was on piano and Shrimp Jones on violin. A string ensemble called the Conaway Brothers worked there too and I became friendly with them."[34]

CONAWAY BROTHERS
Novelty Society
Orchestre de Danse

SUPERIOR COLORED MUSICIANS

THE ONLY SOCIETY ARTISTS FEATURING REAL JAZZ AND GENUINE HAWAIIAN MUSIC, as well as entertaining during intermission and supper periods.

Have filled engagements for seven successive seasons on the Jersey Coast and are now playing third summer at ROSS-FENTON FARM.

Music furnished for all occasions. Private Parties a Specialty.

CLARENCE F. CONAWAY, Manager.

Asbury Park, N. J.   New York City
138 Ridge Ave.   35 West 131st St.
Phone 336-W.   Phone Harlem 4515

The Conway Brothers were based on Ridge Avenue in Asbury Park before relocating to

The Conaway Brothers had been well known along the Jersey Shore since 1910. Referred to as "superior colored musicians" they entertained mainly in white hotels and higher class white clubs like the Ross-Fenton Farm, playing "real jazz and genuine Hawaiian music." Manager, and presumed member, Clarence F. Conaway, maintained offices at 138 Ridge Avenue in Asbury Park's West Side as well as in Harlem.[35]

"They were from Washington DC," said Sonny Greer, "And they invited me down for three days, and I stayed several years."[36]

In Washington DC, Sonny Greer met and began playing with Duke Ellington's group. Greer was responsible for bringing Ellington to New York City. He stayed with Ellington's band for thirty years, cementing his legacy as one of the greatest drummers ever.

With Sonny Greer moving on as a professional musician, Bill Basie continued playing around the shore area of central New Jersey. It was now 1922.

"One day I decided I was going to put on my own dance," wrote Basie. "So I printed up my own signs and had Pop get a night at the [Knights of Pythias] Hall. Mama made some sandwiches and Pop was the ticket seller. Then I went and got Bill Robinson, Duffan and Cricket played the drums. It was a good thing that Pop got the [Knights of Pythias] Hall free of charge, because when I paid the musicians, I don't think there was very much money left."[37]

Basie was back at the Knights of Pythias Hall on March 31, 1922, to entertain at a cabaret to raise money for an African American girls basketball club called the Jolly Battlers. Besides Bill Basie, friend Raymond McGuire was there along with Arthur Lane and Samuel Johnson.[38]

Basie and Lane would perform together in May at the aforementioned Opportunity Night at the Palace Theatre.[39] All the contestants were local performers and were judged by audience applause. We don't know who won the $10 prize.[40]

Basie's band became mobile when his friend Elmer Williams got a job as a chauffeur and access to an automobile. Elmer Alexander Williams was born in the Pine Brook section of Shrewsbury,

Count Basie Sheet Music
From the Classic Urban Harmony Archives

New Jersey in January 1903.[41] He sent away for a saxophone and began teaching himself to play so he could join Bill Basie's band. This gave them transportation to and from gigs. Elmer Williams' first gigs with Basie's band were a couple of Saturday nighters in Keansburg. Basie's band used to average $3 - $4 per night per musician. Sometimes they would get whatever they collected by passing around a hat. Basie's main interest was finding gigs for his band. He started skipping school to hang out in the local pool hall where he could network with other musicians. He eventually dropped out of school completely to pursue a career as a musician.

"We used to play a place on Springwood Avenue when the Harlem Renaissance basketball team used to come to Asbury Park," wrote Basie. "That was always a big event, and after the game there was always a dance."[42]

Whenever Bill Basie needed a place to spend the night in Asbury Park's West Side, he'd head for Corky William's house. [*Corky Williams life is covered in detail in Chapter 3.*["He had a room where you were welcomed to flop until the next morning," wrote Basie. "But if two or more [musicians] showed up, you would have to sleep crossways on the bed. [Corky] was just a very nice guy and you were always welcomed to flop in that extra room."[43]

Donald "The Lamb" Lambert

At a house party near Asbury Park, Bill Basie first heard Donald Lambert play. Donald Lambert was born in Princeton NJ, in 1904. His mother, Alma Lambert, was a music teacher and tried to teach him to read music but the five-year-old resisted so she just let him pick out notes on the piano by ear.[44] Donald never did learn to read music but that didn't stop him from becoming a great piano player. He started buying and imitating records by stride piano pioneer James P. Johnson and at 16 quit school to travel as a musician.[45] Donald was one of the greatest, though least known, of the stride pianists. Said to be left-handed, his left hand seemed almost frantic at times. Lambert was a formidable opponent in area cutting contests (piano competitions) and a young Bill Basie once backed out of a cutting contest with him by pretending to be too drunk to play.

Donald "The Lamb" Lambert
Publicity photo.

"A bunch of my friends from Red Bank took me up there to play against him one night," recalled Basie. "I was supposed to go in there and cut him, cut him a new suit and duster. But as soon as I heard that cat playing, I knew I was in trouble. So I slipped back into the kitchen and got myself two or three big dips out of that pot they were serving the juice in. And by the time Lambert was winding up and they came looking for me to take my turn, I was into my act. ... They said, 'Old Bill Basie can't play, man. Look at him. He's drunk. He can't play.'"[46]

Donald Lambert may not have been as gentle as his nickname, "The Lamb," indicated. Word had it, he was known to carry a hatchet with him.

"That is how my first meeting with Donald Lambert turned out," remembered Basie. "I had a very narrow escape. I don't think any of my good buddies were any the wiser, but I wasn't about to let them get me all tangled up with the Lamb, because he had that hatchet even then. I didn't have to listen to but so many bars to realize that I didn't have any business messing with him."[47]

Donald "The Lamb" Lambert was one of the greatest stride pianists ever, but his legacy is hurt by the fact that he made few recordings. He preferred to play local bars in relative obscurity. Also known as "The Jersey Rocket," Lambert did appear at the 1960 Newport Jazz Festival along side of Eubie Blake and Willie "The Lion" Smith and is said to have outplayed both of them. Lambert died in 1962 and is buried in his home town of Princeton, NJ.[48]

William "Count" Basie's story continues in Chapter 6.

Notes to Chapter 5

[1] Count Basie as told to Albert Murray, *Good Morning Blues: The Autobiography of Count Basie*, (New York: Primus, 1985), p. 25 - 26.

[2] "Henry S. White Dead," *The Daily Register [Red Bank NJ]*, 2 Oct, 1901, p. 9.

[3] "Notice," *The Daily Register [Red Bank NJ]*, 27 May, 1914, p. 11.

[4] "Ordinance No. 77," *The Daily Register [Red Bank NJ]*, 13 Apr, 1910, p. 3

[5] "Home Laundry," *The Daily Register [Red Bank NJ]*, 25 Jun, 1924, p. 13.

[6] https://www.biography.com/people/count-basie-9201255

[7] Basie and Murray, *Good Morning Blues*, p. 33.

[8] *Ibid.*, p. 33.

[9] *Ibid.,,* p. 26.

[10] "A Church Incorporated,"*The Daily Register [Red Bank NJ]*, 28 Jan, 1903, p. 1.

[11] Authors' conversations with Gilda Rogers of the T. Thomas Fortune Foundation.

[12] "Another Lodge At Red Bank," *The Daily Register [Red Bank NJ]*, 3 Jun, 1903, p. 1.

[13] "Concert For Colored Baptists," *The Daily Register [Red Bank, NJ]*, 14 Aug, 1918, p. 9.

[14] "Give Benefit For R. B. Colored Boy Scouts," *Asbury Park Press*, 21 May, 1914, p. 4.

[15] "Money For Boy Scouts," *The Daily Register [Red Bank NJ]*, 20 May, 1914, p. 9.

[16] Authors' conversations with Gilda Rogers of the T. Thomas Fortune Foundation.

[17] "Palace Theatre," http://cinematreasures.org/theaters/13246

[18] Basie and Murray, *Good Morning Blues*, p. 31.

[19] *Ibid.*, p. 32.

[20] *Ibid.*, p. 33.

[21] Letter confirming Sonny Greer's birth certificate from the Deputy Registrar, Vital Statistics, Long Branch City Hall, 29 Mar, 1982. Courtesy of the Institute of Jazz Studies, Rutgers University. Greer's birth certificate is located in Book 1, Page 100.

[22] Interview with Sonny Greer by Stanley Crouch, Rutgers University Community Repository, 1979, https://rucore.libraries.rutgers.edu/rutgers-lib/52263/

[23] Whitney Balliett, *American Musicians II: Seventy-One Portraits In Jazz,*

(Jackson, MS, University Press of MS, 2005), p. 55 - 56.

[24]Basie and Murray, pp. 33 - 34.

[25] For instance, see *The Official Proceedings, Twenty-Fourth Annual Convention of American Federation of Musicians*, (Dayton, OH: May 12 - 17, 1919), p. 13.

[26] "Wilber C. Gardner," *The Daily Record [Long Branch, NJ]*, 1 Nov, 1920, p. 1.

[27] Transcript of an interview with Cozy Cole by Bill Kirchner, 16 Apr, 1980. From the Institute of Jazz Studies' Jazz Oral History Project.

[28] Basie and Murray, p. 34.

[29] "Won $2.50 in Piano Playing," *The Daily Register [Red Bank NJ]*, 12 Jan, 1921, p. 11.

[30] Basie and Murray, p. 34.

[31] Palace Theatre ad, *The Daily Register [Red Bank NJ]*, 19 Jan, 1921, p. 16.

[32] Basie and Murray, p. 34.

[33] "Dance," *The Daily Register [Red Bank NJ]*, 22 Jun, 1921, p. 11.

[34] Balliett, p. 56

[35] Ad for the Conaway Brothers, *Asbury Park Press*, 21 Jul, 1917, p. 7.

[36] Balliett, p. 56

[37] Basie and Murray, p. 34 - 35.

[38] "Jolly Battlers Made $100," *The Daily Register [Red Bank NJ]*, 5 Apr, 1922, p. 1.

[39] Ad for Basie & Lane at the Palace Theatre, *The Daily Register [Red Bank NJ]*, 24 May, 1922, p. 28.

[40] "Opportunity Night, *The Daily Register [Red Bank NJ]*, 24 May, 1922, p. 1.

[41] 1905 New Jersey State Census.

[42] Basie and Murray, p. 35.

[43] Basie and Murray, pp. 38 - 39.

[44] "Recalling The Lamb: Orange's 'Stride' Genius," *Essex Journal*, 15 May, 1986.

[45] "Orange Jazzman Shuns Spotlight," *Newark Sunday News*, 17 Jul, 1960.

[46] Basie and Murray, p. 37.

[47] *Ibid.*, p. 37.

[48] "Donald Lambert," Wikipedia.org

Chapter Six

Prohibition and Bill Basie's Summers in Asbury Park

On January 17, 1920, Prohibition went into effect. Prohibition was the nationwide constitutional ban on the production, importation, transportation and sale of alcoholic beverages. It would remain in place until December 1933.

New Jersey was one of the last states to ratify the Eighteenth Amendment and with good reason. Much of New Jersey's economy depended on the tourist business in the shore towns like Asbury Park, Long Branch and Atlantic City. And businesses along the shore resorts needed to make sure the tourists had a good time, which included access to alcohol.

Illegal speakeasies immediately sprang up everywhere and liquor was not hard to find in New Jersey. The ban on liquor in New Jersey was at different times enforced by the Federal Government and/or local authorities. But corruption was widespread and it was easy to pay off local officials to keep your establishment from being raided.

Prohibition Era sign displayed at the Morris Museum (Morristown, NJ) exhibit, "Prohibition: From Flappers to Bootleggers"

Even before Prohibition, Asbury Park had problems with alcohol and corruption. In 1917, three years before national prohibition took effect, Ocean Grove took Asbury Park to task. An 1896 New Jersey law stated that intoxicating liquor could not be sold within one mile of a religious camp. Ocean Grove was the Methodist religious campground that bordered Asbury Park. The Anti-Saloon League which was fighting for Prohibition, hired a detective to investigate. He found that intoxication, prostitution, voter fraud, gambling and corruption were rampant in Asbury Park, protected by the mayor, police chief and other town leaders.[1] It's hard to imagine things were any better three years later.

Prohibition led to the rapid rise of organized crime's involvement in the manufacture, distribution and sale of alcohol. In Asbury Park, few raids happened at the big hotels. Many raids seem to have been in Little Italy, the Italian immigrant section of the West Side just behind the railroad tracks. Anti-immigrant hysteria was high in the United States with the influx of millions of immigrants prior to World War I. This was not helped by a number of high profile crimes committed by the Italian Mafia which was heavily involved in the bootlegging of alcohol.

For the most part, West Side African American nightclubs that illegally sold alcohol flew under the radar for the time being. That was, until they started to attract large numbers of white tourists with cutting edge musical entertainment.

In 1922, Bill Basie and his friend Elmer Williams left home and set off for Asbury Park to make their name as musicians. Unfortunately they chose to go in the fall when most of the summer tourists had left and gigs were scarce. Arriving by train from Red Bank, they decided not to wear out their welcome at Corky Williams' house. They ended up sleeping on benches at Joe Brown's poolroom on Springwood Avenue. Joe Brown's was where all the West Side musicians hung out and it was where they found out about potential gigs.

"Joe Brown... was a very friendly guy and he was nice enough to let us spend a few nights there," wrote Basie. "So wherever else we went during the day, we would make it back around to the poolroom by closing time, and after everybody else cleared out, Elmer Williams would take one of those benches and I would grab myself another one and that was our hotel room. Then we would cut out early the next morning and come back when everybody else would begin dropping in."[2]

With limited work as musicians and very little money in their pockets, Basie and Williams had to resort to stealing loaves of bread from the early morning deliveries of baked goods, left outside of local restaurants. While the two never got caught, they did have one close call at Water's Restaurant, 922 Springwood Avenue, when they were surprised by a restaurant employee.

"All I could do was just look at him and smile," wrote Basie, "And I guess he must have thought I was working there too, so he just went on doing what he was doing. But for a split second there I really thought he had caught me in the act."[3]

After about a week, Basie and Williams got discouraged and returned to Red Bank for the rest of the fall and winter, vowing to come back to Asbury Park the next summer.

When Bill Basie and Elmer Williams did return to Asbury Park in the summer of 1923, they met drummer Harry Richardson. Richardson hired them both into his band,

Harry Richardson's Kings of Syncopation. Also in the band was Jimmy Hill, violinist. Harry Richardson had already been hired for a return engagement as the house band at the area's Hong Kong Inn. He allowed Basie and Williams to sleep at his home while performing with his band.

An ad placed in the local newspaper in October, 1922, showed Harry Richardson living in a home at 1118 Adams Street, a block off of Springwood Avenue in Asbury Park's West Side. In the ad Harry was looking for gigs for his "Harry Richardson Orchestra" to perform at "white or colored" functions. He described his then band as dance specialists with music specially arranged by Paul Whiteman.[4]

Harry Richardson's Kings Of Syncopation. Left to right: Jimmy Hill (violin), Bill Basie (piano), Elmer Williams (tenor sax), Harry Richardson (drums). From the Basie Collection. In public domain.

Actually, the first mention of Harry Richardson's band in the area seems to be in May of 1922 when he played a benefit for disabled soldiers at the Long Branch (NJ) casino. The dance was sponsored by the Long Branch Post of the National Veterans' League and drew a couple hundred people from Long Branch, Asbury Park, Red Bank and Keyport. Harry's band was called a "New York Novelty jazz band which played Broadway's latest hits."[5]

Richardson's band then worked at the Hong Kong Inn for the first time later that summer. Many restaurants in the shore area were only open on a seasonal basis. The Hong Kong Inn had opened May 27, 1922, with entertainment by Jesse Stork and his Lords of Melody.[6] But by July 29, 1922, the Hong Kong Inn was advertising the house band "Harry Richardson's Sunny Syncopators."[7]

Basie described the Hong Kong Inn as a roadhouse on the outskirts of Asbury Park. "It was not just another joint," wrote Basie. "It was really a pretty classy place."[8]

The Hong Kong Inn had an interesting history. The building itself was built in 1885 on a beautiful spot on the southern shore of the Shark River, at the head of Shark River Bay. The area was considered part of Belmar, just south of Asbury Park. Around 1905, the venue was purchased by a Mrs. French, who turned it into the popular French's Restaurant.[9] (It's said that the restaurant during the early days was a favorite meeting place for the Monmouth County Ku Klux Klan[10] but we could not confirm that.) From there it became the River Crest before being acquired by a man of Chinese descent named Joseph Wong-Akie in 1922.[11] Akie operated the Hong Kong Inn, along with his two brothers Charles and Tommy Akie, as a Chinese American restaurant. Visitors were instructed to take the scenic drive west on River Road from Belmar "for an

Hong Kong Inn.
River road, west from Belmar. Best American and Chinese dishes. Dancing. The Harry Richardson Country Club Orchestra. Big Shore Dinner.

August 2, 1924 ad for Harry Richardson at the Hong Kong Inn

enjoyable repast at moderate expense." It was advertised as "Unmistakably clean, morally and otherwise. Good music. Excellent floor for dancing."[12]

Basie went on to describe some customers at the Hong Kong Inn having too much to drink. Remember, this was during Prohibition and the Hong Kong Inn even had a sign posted saying that no intoxicating liquors were sold there and another sign forbidding any of his waiters or other employees handling liquor in any form.[13]

These signs and advertisements of the Inn's moral character did not fool the Feds who investigated the Hong Kong Inn six months before Basie came to play there. During a trial, detectives testified that on August 5, 8 and 13, 1922, they bought drinks of

Post card of the Hong Kong Inn, ca. 1910, when it was French's Restaurant intoxicating liquors at the Hong Kong Inn and that Thomas Akie had told a waiter it was all right to serve them. They said on another occasion, Thomas Akie had taken them to a side room and treated them to a drink of whiskey from a teapot. The local sheriff was then called to testify the results of a search he made of the premises on September 10. He said he found no liquor at the Hong Kong Inn, and the Akies' attorney had the charges dismissed. Later the sheriff told a reporter that while he found no liquor on the premises, he had found hundreds of empty [bottles]![14] [For the record, the Hong Kong Inn would be raided again in 1924 and this time a small quantity of liquor would be found.][15]

Bill Basie played with Harry Richardson's band at the Hong Kong Inn until mid-summer. Then a better piano player, Johnny Montague, came down to Asbury Park from New York, and Basie was replaced. Not wanting to go back to Red Bank, Basie asked Mr. Akie if he could stay on and park cars. He soon found himself making more money parking cars than he had been as a musician there.

"I was meeting the cars as they pulled in," wrote Basie. "And I would let them out near the entrance, brush them down with a whisk broom and then park the car, dust it off, and when they came back out, I would either get the car or escort them to it, and the tips were great. And sometimes the fringe benefits were even better. When somebody came back out and couldn't quite make it to his car on his own because he had too much to drink, I would support him all the way and then lay him in there. Sometimes one customer like that was worth the whole night. I will not say how the money got out of his pocket and into mine but somehow it always did. And he was feeling too good to miss it or need it. ... When he woke up he still had his wallet and watch and jewelry. I didn't bother anything like that. But whatever amount of cash he still had in his pocket when he came back out by himself feeling too good to make it to his car was what my tip was for helping him."[16]

In spite of the money, Bill Basie couldn't stay away from his piano for too long. By the end of the summer he was looking for gigs with other West Side bands. One band that Bill Basie was said to gig with was the Dickerson Band, run by James E. Dickerson and his wife, Christina Richardson Dickerson.[17]

James A. Dickerson was born in Virginia in 1891[18] and moved to West Park as a child. He purchased his first trombone from C. G. Conn Ltd. when he turned 16 in 1907.[19] At the time, Conn was the largest band instrument manufacturer in the world. James was confirmed in St. Augustine's Church on April 22, 1908.[20] Actually, James E. Dickerson and Christina F. Richardson had met while attending the Asbury Park Grammar School for Colored Children on Springwood Avenue some years before. Both shared an early interest in music.[21]

By 1913, James Dickerson's trombone could be heard performing locally with a trio that also contained Estelle Hazel on piano and George H. Haynes on violin.[22] The following year Dickerson was organizing dances for the Arion Social Club at Morrow's Hall, though the music was supplied by Franklin's Orchestra.[23]

In 1916, the Negro Business League held a meeting at Bethel A. M. E. Church which featured speeches by different dignitaries, including Asbury Park's Mayor Hetrick. James Dickerson played trombone selections between the speeches.[24] Dickerson's trombone playing was also featured in a war-related Red Cross fund raiser in 1918.[25]

As the 1920's began, the Elks Club on Atkins Avenue just off Springwood Avenue was becoming one of the leading venues for music, especially the young genre called jazz. James Dickerson was treasurer of the Elks Club and helped bring entertainment there.[26] At the time, Dickerson was living at 1611 Springwood Avenue.[27]

James E. Dickerson and Christina F. Richardson were married at St. Augustine's Epis-

"The Trombone I purchased from C.G.Conn, of Elkhart, Indiana, is certainly a 'pet.' It is perfect in every respect."

James E. Dickerson, Asbury Park, — N.J.

Conn advertising card donated to the Asbury Park Historical Society by the Dickersons' granddaughters.

Christina Richardson
Courtesy of her grandnephew,
Bill Carter

copal Church on Sylvan Avenue, Asbury Park in the early 1920's.[28] [Their family reported a wedding date of 1925, but newspapers refer to them performing as Mr. & Mrs. J. E. Dickerson in 1923.[29] [30]]

Christina Richardson was the first cousin of Jonathan T. Richardson, leader of Richardson's Orchestra and the Colored Knights of Pythias Brass Band [see Chapter 3]. Both were descendants of Sand Hill Indians. [Jonathan's father, Isaac W. Richardson and Christina's father, Joseph Richardson, were brothers.][31]

Christina was born in 1891 in the Sand Hill area of Neptune, later called Richardson Heights. It was an area directly west of West Park that her extended family of Sand Hill Indians had received from James Bradley in return for building many of the hotels and houses in Asbury Park. She was to become a life-long member of her family's St. Augustine Church on Sylvan Avenue in West Park.[32]

On March 4, 1923, a musicale was held at St. Stephen's A. M. E. Church by the People's Lyceum Choir and orchestra of that church. Listed among the performers was a trio consisting of Mr. James E. Dickerson (trombone), Mrs. James E. Dickerson (piano) and Alfred H. Haynes (violin). They performed "O Dry Those Tears."[33] Also listed among those performing, was a Fred Duffan.[34] James Dickerson and Alfred Haynes would also perform separately at a St. Augustine Church musical services from February[35] to April,[36] 1924, and probably longer.

James and Christina Dickerson
on their wedding.
Photo courtesy of Bill Carter.

All the while, Christina Dickerson gave piano lessons from the Dickerson home at 5 Bloomfield Avenue, Maywood section of Neptune, NJ.[37]

Around this time, the Dickersons formed a small band to play around Asbury Park. They both brought their musical knowledge and respective instruments to their band, "The J. E. Dickerson Band." A rare photo post card, reprinted here shows members James E. Dick-

The Elks Club on Atkins Avenue became a hot spot for jazz. Here, James Dickerson is treasurer.

Photo of the J. E. Dickerson Band taken on Third Avenue in Long Branch, NJ.
Donated to the Asbury Park Historical Society by the
Dickersons' granddaughters, Anita D. Clark and Phyllis J. Jackson.

erson (trombone), Christina Dickerson (piano), Ed Duffan (sax), Fillmore Scudder
(drums) and a Mr. Butler (cornet).

Ed Duffan is most likely E. B. Duffan who in the 1930's would direct the choir of Bethel
A. M. E. Zion Church.[38] In the early thirties, E. B. Duffan and this choir would have
their own weekly twenty-minute radio program over local station WCAP.[39] It was one
of the first, if not the first Asbury Park radio program hosted by African Americans.
Ed Duffan's brother, Fred Kendall Duffan [mentioned earlier], was also a part time
musician when not working as a hotel waiter.[40] It's also possible that one of the Duffan
brothers was the Duffan who played piano in Bill Basie's first band at Red Bank's Palace
Theatre, but we can't confirm that.

Drummer, Fillmore Scudder, also has an interesting story. Fillmore (also shown as
Philmore) M. Scudder was born in New Jersey in the mid-1890's. [Records alternately
list 1893, 1894 and 1896.] In 1915 he was living with his parents at 137 Atkins Avenue
on the West Side. Fillmore served in the Army during WWI. After returning home,
he lived briefly in Trenton where he worked in an orchestra. He'd eventually move to
Princeton.[41] It would seem likely that he was related to Katherine Scudder Patterson,

wife of West Side dance hall manager and journalist, Frank Patterson [*see Chapter 3*], but we could not confirm that.

The Dickerson - Duffan Orchestra played the Coterie Club Exhibit at the Elks Hall (Atkins Avenue & Adams Street) in June of 1924.[42] By the time the orchestra played a dance in Point Pleasant's high school gymnasium in November 1924, it was referred to as the Duffan Colored Orchestra of Asbury Park.[43]

James Dickerson died at his home at 5 Bloomfield Avenue, Neptune, on October 7, 1952, at the age of 61.[44] Christina Richardson Dickerson died May 21, 1979 at the age of 87.[45] She continued giving piano lessons at her home until shortly before she passed away. The Dickersons told their grandchildren they had fond memories of Bill Basie gigging with their band.

James and Christina Dickerson
Photo courtesy of Bill Carter

More Bill Basie

As for young Bill Basie, as gigs became scarce in late 1923, he and Elmer Williams

Willie Gant

moved into Elmer's Uncle Ralph's house in Asbury Park for the rest of the summer. Another of the great stride pianists, Willie Gant, would come into Asbury Park to play. When he did he would stay at the home right next door to where Basie was staying.

William D. Gant was born in New York City in 1900.[46] As a youngster, he worked in the Brill Building for the Brill Brothers. Living in the Hell's Kitchen area, he began playing piano at the age of 12. A year later he met James P. Johnson and persuaded the stride master to take him on as a pupil. Gant and Fats Waller learned Harlem Stride from Johnson. By 1917, Gant was playing professionally and soon became known as one of the top pianists around. He was particularly fond of the piano "cutting contests" that he usually won.[47]

"I used to go around to all the places [Willie Gant] used to work just to hear him and I got to know him pretty well," wrote Basie. "Then sometime after I got to know Gant, Don Lambert also came down to Asbury Park to work in a place down there, and I remembered him, and we also got to be friendly." Basie invited Lambert over the house to play some piano and then called Gant to come over. Gant put on his bathrobe and hopped the fence to see who this fellow was who "thinks he can play piano." Gant and Lambert each tried to outdo one another on piano. When they were done, Gant said of Lambert, "Well, he's alright."

"I guess you can say I learned something about playing the piano from Don Lambert," Basie recalled. "And I learned to stay out of the way of the Lamb and that hatchet."

By the end of the summer of 1923, Bill Basie and Elmer Williams headed to New York City to try to make their mark in the entertainment business. But they would return to Asbury Park for a number of gigs over the next couple of years before "Count" Basie headed to Kansas City.

We need not recount the rest of Count Basie's story, for as one of America's greatest pianists, bandleaders and composers, his music career is well covered elsewhere. But Basie never forgot his roots and would on occasion return to play Asbury Park's West Side once he became famous.

Notes to Chapter 6

[1] "Asbury Park: Why "Prohibition Did Not Prohibit," (Newark, NJ: Anti-Saloon League of New Jersey, 1917) from *The Bootlegger Era: Prohibition in New Jersey*, Exhibit at the Monmouth County Library Headquarters, 2013.
[2] Count Basie as told to Albert Murray, *Good Morning Blues: The Autobiography of Count Basie*, (New York: Donald I. Fine, Inc, 1985), p. 40.
[3] Basie and Murray, p. 40.
[4] "Harry Richardson Orchestra," *Asbury Park Press*, 25 Oct, 1922, p. 1.
[5] "Benefit Dance Well Attended," *Asbury Park Press*, 18 May, 1922, p. 2.
[6] "Hong Kong Inn will Open Saturday May 27th," *Asbury Park Press*, 3 Jun, 1922, p. 5.

7 "Hong Kong Inn," *Asbury Park Press*, 29 Jul, 1922, p. 1.

8 Basie and Murray, pp. 40 - 41.

9 "Hong Kong Inn Leveled by Fire," *Asbury Park Press*, 3 Feb, 1930, pp. 1 - 2.

10 Richard Napoliton, *Images of America: Wall Township*, (Charleston, SC: Arcadia Publishing, 1999), pp. 12-13.

11 "Hong Kong Inn Leveled by Fire," *Asbury Park Press*, 3 Feb, 1930, pp. 1 - 2.

12 "Hong Kong Inn," *Asbury Park Press*, 2 Aug, 1924, p. 13.

13 "Inn Proprietors Held Guiltless: No Liquor Sold at Hong Kong Inn, Jury Finds," *Asbury Park Press*, 28 Nov, 1922, p. 1.

14 *Ibid.*

15 "Federal Raiders Busy," *Red Bank Register*, 30 Jul, 1924.

16 Basie and Murray, p. 42.

17 The authors' correspondences with the Dickersons' granddaughter, Anita D. Clark, Jan, 2019.

18 "She's an Indian Without a Tribe," *Asbury Park Press*, 14 Jan, 1979, p. G4.

19 Correspondences between the Asbury Park Historical Society and the Dickersons' granddaughters, Anita D. Clark, Neptune, NJ, and Phyllis J. Jackson, Woodbridge, VA.

20 "Class Confirmed At St. Augustine," *Asbury Park Press*, 23 Apr, 1908, p. 1

21 Correspondences between the Asbury Park Historical Society and the Dickerson's granddaughters, Anita D. Clark, Neptune, NJ, and Phyllis J. Jackson, Woodbridge, VA.

22 "Local Happenings," *Asbury Park Press,* 23 Jan, 1913, p. 2.

23 "Arion Club Dance," *Asbury Park Press*, 3 Jan, 1914, p. 1.

24 "Mayor Speaks To Business League," *Asbury Park Press*, 5 Apr, 1916, p. 2.

25 R. C. Auxiliary In Patriotic Rally," *Asbury Park Press*, 26 Aug, 1918, p. 2.

26 "Local Happenings," *Asbury Park Press*, 4 Feb, 1920, p. 2.

27 "Local Happenings," *Asbury Park Press*, 15 Feb, 1921, p. 2.

28 Correspondences between the Asbury Park Historical Society and the Dickerson's granddaughters, Anita D. Clark, Neptune, NJ, and Phyllis J. Jackson, Woodbridge, VA.

29 "Sunday Musicale," *Asbury Park Press*, 3 Mar, 1923, p. 1.

30 "Memorial Display," *Asbury Park Press*, 26 May, 1923, p. 17.

31 The authors' correspondences with Christina Richardson's granddaughter, Anita D. Clark and Claire T. Garland, Director of the Sand Hill Indian Historical Society, Jan, 2019.

32 "She's an Indian Without a Tribe," *Asbury Park Press*, 14 Jan, 1979, p. G4.

33 "Memorial Display," *Asbury Park Press*, 26 May, 1923, p. 17.

34 "Sunday Musicale," *Asbury Park Press*, 3 Mar, 1923, p. 1.

35 "St. Augustine's Church," *Asbury Park Press*, 23 Feb, 1924, p. 9.

36 "St. Augustine's Church," *Asbury Park Press*, 19 Apr, 1924, p. 3.

37 *Asbury Park Press*, 3 Feb, 1925, p. 2.

38 "Bethel Choir to Sing," *Asbury Park Press,* 14 Jun, 1930, p. 17.

39 Radio Listings, *Asbury Park Press*, 7 Jan, 1932, p. 7.

40 Census research by genealogist Jayme Klein.

41 *Ibid.*

42 "Coterie Club Exhibit," *Asbury Park Press*, 5 Jun, 1924, p. 14.

43 "Point Pleasant," *Asbury Park Press*, 24 Nov, 1924, p. 3.

44 "Obituaries: James Dickerson," *Asbury Park Press,* 8 Oct, 1952, p. 2.

45 "Obituaries: Mrs. James E. Dickerson, 87; Was Oldest Member of Indian Group," *Asbury Park Press*, 23 May, 1979, p. 20.

46 "Willie Gant," *Wikipedia.*

47 Mike Lipskin and Len Kunstadt, "This Is Willie Gant," *Blues Research*, No. 4 (1960).

Chapter Seven

Never A Dull Moment at the Smile-A-While Inn

One of the most popular nighttime destinations on the West Side of Asbury Park during the "Roaring Twenties" was a place called the Smile-A-While Inn. In March, 1924, *Billboard* magazine carried the news that a property in the Springwood section of Asbury Park had been purchased by Misters Mossell and Suarez for $35,000. Mossell and Suarez planned to invest an additional $15,000 to convert the property into an amusement park for people of color. Its name would be Smile-A-While Park. The idea was that African Americans, who were restricted from beachfront amusements, deserved their own park. A scenic railway and pony track were planned. The property already contained a twenty-four room hotel and the new proprietors would build an 80- by 40-foot pavilion dance floor in the basement, where an orchestra would play. *Billboard* thought the idea had every promise of success in view of the large African American population as well as tourists and hotel workers.[1] We don't know if the amusement park was ever built (probably not), but the Smile-A-While soon became one of the hottest nightclubs in town. The owners of the establishment were Dr. Aaron A. Mossell Jr. and Mr. Julius Suarez.

Dr. Mossell was Aaron Albert Mossell Jr., member of a very distinguished family. His father of the same name was the first African American to obtain a law degree from the University of Pennsylvania.[2] His uncle, Nathan Mossell, was the first African American graduate of Penn's School of Medicine and founder of Philadelphia's first black hospital, Frederick Douglass Memorial Hospital (now Mercy-Douglass Hospital).[3] An uncle on his mother's side was the famous artist, Henry Osawa Tanner. Mossell's sister, Sadie Mossell Alexander, was the first African American woman to earn a doctorate degree in Economics from Penn's prestigious Wharton School and then the first African American woman to earn a law degree at Penn.[4] She would later be appointed by President Truman to the President's Committee on Civil Rights.

Dr. Mossell was born in 1893 in his parents' home at 2908 Diamond Street in North Philadelphia. He studied and took up pharmacy in Philadelphia but in 1916 he applied for and became registered as a pharmacist in New Jersey.[5] After serving in the armed forces during World War I, Mossell moved to Asbury Park. He is mentioned there in 1924 as the president of the Second Baptist Church's Men's Brotherhood Club.[6]

By 1925, Mossell had acquired a business partner in Julius Suarez. The two co-owned the Mossell & Suarez Pharmacy at 1051 Springwood Avenue.[7] Suarez was Cuban and had lived in Asbury Park since at least 1922. He would later become an entertainment promoter, assembling the traveling black variety show, *The Ginger Snaps of 1928*.[8]

Running a pharmacy during Prohibition was a lucrative business, especially in a wide-open area like the West Side. The Volstead Act proclaimed, "No one shall manufacture, sell, purchase, transport or prescribe any liquor without first obtaining a permit from the commissioner so to do, *except that a person may, without a permit, purchase and use liquor for medicinal purposes when prescribed by a physician as herein provided.*"[9] Of course, it was up to the doctor to determine what ailments could benefit from a good stiff drink. And doctors began prescribing liquor as a cure for cancer, tuberculosis, anemia, diabetes, high blood pressure, influenza and even old age. There were some restrictions to this loophole. You had to obtain a prescription from a doctor (at a cost of about $3) and then have it filled legally by a pharmacist (at a cost of another $3). And you could only get one pint of liquor per person every ten days. Then you had to go back to the doctor and pharmacist. All of this proved quite a windfall for doctors and druggists. In Chicago, druggist Charles Walgreen saw his chain expand from 20 stores in 1920 to nearly 400 a decade later. This was, of course, the start of today's Walgreen Drugstore empire.[10]

Mossell and Suarez continued to operate both the drug store and the Smile-A-While Inn until December 1925 (by some reports, 1926), at which point they sold the drug store.[11]

The hotel that Mossell and Suarez purchased to turn into the Smile-A-While Inn was located at 1144 Atlantic Avenue. The Atlantic Avenue of the early Twentieth Century has no relation to later present-day streets of that name. It was once located two blocks south of Springwood Avenue between Atkins and Sylvan Avenues. The property surrounding the hotel was bounded on the north by Atlantic Avenue and on the south by the Wesley Lake Brook. Years later, in 1939, Atlantic Avenue and several other streets would be vacated to make room for the Asbury Park Village public housing projects along Boston Way.[12] In fact, the street Boston Way

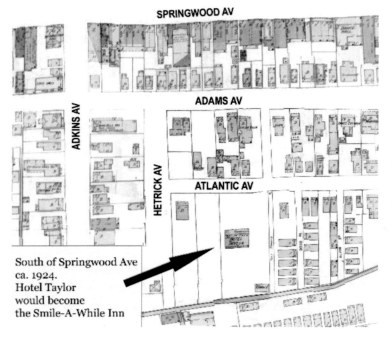

South of Springwood Ave
ca. 1924.
Hotel Taylor
would become
the Smile-A-While Inn

106

This 1925 dark newspaper photo is the only known image of the Smile-A-While Inn.
From the *Pittsburgh Courier*, 8 August, 1925

would be created overtop of the encased drainage pipe that once was Wesley Lake Brook. However by 1924, the hotel that Mossell and Suarez purchased already had quite a history.

The 1911 voter registration rolls show a Eugene Renna owning a hotel at 1144 Atlantic Avenue.[13] By 1914, the Renna Hotel also headquartered and held meetings for the Woodrow Wilson Colored Democratic Club and the Joseph Waters Colored Democratic Club (probably the same political organization).[14] The president of the Woodrow Wilson Colored Democratic Club in 1916 was an African American, Powell Banks, who in 1915 was listed as the hotel's owner.[15] That year, the Renna Hotel was renamed the Magnolia Hotel.[16]

Powell Banks was described as a "charitably disposed man" who had "given aid freely to many needy persons in the West Side."[17] Powell apparently also had a lucrative side business at the hotel, selling liquor illegally. By 1918. Powell had been arrested eight times for illegal sale of liquor and had served several months in jail for the offenses.[18] And all of this was before Prohibition! You may recall, liquor sale in Asbury Park was already illegal because it was within one mile of a religious camp - Ocean Grove. Prior to being purchased by Mossell and Suarez, the hotel was also listed as the Hotel Taylor.[19]

Major hotels along the beach like the Plaza Hotel often had black entertainers but patronage was restricted to whites. At the Smile-A-While, on the other hand, all were welcomed. As word got around of the great bands playing in the black clubs, scores of white people would make the short trek to the West Side each summer evening to hang out in clubs like the Smile-A-While.

The Smile-A-While Inn seems to have opened in time for the 1925 summer season. Of all the entertainers to play the Smile-A-While, the one most associated with the venue is famous pianist and bandleader, Claude Hopkins. Hopkins would later lead the house band at New York City ballrooms like the Savoy and Roseland where his dexterity with the ivories would earn him the nickname, "Crazy Fingers."

Trained in the stride piano tradition, Hopkins was born outside of Washington DC. In the early 1920's Hopkins met and became friends with Sonny Greer who undoubtedly told him stories about Asbury Park.

Claude Hopkins was just twenty-one in 1925, when he was offered a summer job playing at the Little Belmont Bar in Atlan-

Claude "Crazy Fingers" Hopkins

tic City, NJ. This was Hopkins' first gig outside of Washington and the chance to play in a glamorous resort city seemed exciting. He had no trouble rounding up local musicians to go with him as his band - Henry Goodwin (trumpet), Daniel Doy (trombone), Joe Hayman (sax) and Tommy Miles (drums). They boarded a train for Atlantic City with such high hopes. When they got to the club they found that club owner, Herndon Daniels, had also added tuba player Ernie Hill to the band. Unfortunately, after just a couple of months, the Belmont was raided by Prohibition agents and shut down. By then the summer season was in full swing and there were no prospects for work in Atlantic City. However, Hopkins had heard so much about the entertainment scene in Asbury Park, he wanted to give that a try. The group had no money for train fares but new member Ernie Hill owned an old Buick touring car that had seen better days. Tommy Miles, disgusted with the situation, quit and returned to Washington. He was replaced by Percy Johnson.

So the six musicians, their instruments and everything they owned, were loaded into the car and they headed north for the 80 mile drive to Asbury Park. Roads in the 1920's were not what we have today. Hopkins, who was driving, got lost several times. He took a back road riddled with potholes and the Buick hit a huge hole on the way and rolled over. No one was hurt and the band members were able to right the car and continue. By the time the group finally reached Asbury Park they were exhausted, hungry and broke with no idea of where to go.

Hopkins' band stumbled on the Smile-A-While Inn by accident, hearing the music from the outside. Group members questioned Hopkins for stopping there, since the club obviously already had a band. However Hopkins insisted they at least give it a try. Hopkins had but $3 in his pocket and used it to buy drinks for the band while they checked out the five-piece band that was playing. When the owner appeared, Claude Hopkins told him the band was from Washington and would like to play a few numbers. Dr. Mossell wanted to know how Hopkins knew the Smile-A-While was holding auditions. "A friend told me," Hopkins improvised.

Claude Hopkins' band members hurried out to the car and brought in their instruments. When the other band took a break they got up and put every ounce of talent they had into the audition. When they finished, Dr. Mossell asked them "When can you start?" Mossell walked over to the other bandleader and said something to him. Then he came back and told Hopkins his band could start the next evening.

"Who's the other bandleader?" Claude asked. "I hope he makes out all right." "Oh, he will," Mossell replied. "He's local - comes from Red Bank which isn't too far from here. His name is Bill Basie."[20]

Not having any immediate work in New York that summer, Basie had assembled a few musicians including Elmer Williams and drummer Jazz Carson and brought them back to Asbury Park. He secured a gig at the Smile-A-While Inn.

"We weren't there very long before Claude Hopkins and his band came to town," Basie wrote. "They were out of our league and we knew it. They had a real band. They'd been working together for a while and they could play a lot of their own things because Claude was also an arranger. I came to work the next night and the club manager called me into his office and said he wanted to find out how much I had drawn and how much I still had coming. But then I felt a little strange, and my feeling was right, because he said what I was afraid he was going to say. 'We have to settle up the account because Claude Hopkins is going to take over.' That was the end of my first career as a bandleader so I went back to New York."[21]

For Claude Hopkins, the Smile-A-While job was a career starter. Near the end of the summer, Mrs. Carolyn Dudley Reagan arrived from Harlem, looking to audition bands for a troupe to tour Europe.

Carolyn Reagan was a thirty-year old promoter who had secured a contract with the Theatre des Champs-Elysees to bring a black review to Paris. She enlisted the help of bandleader Will Marion Cook to secure talent for the review and settled on a young Josephine Baker who was working at the Plantation Club in Harlem. From there, Reagan and Cook began looking for a good jazz band. They auditioned forty bands without success. Then they heard about the hot band that was playing at the Smile-A-While Inn in Asbury Park.[22]

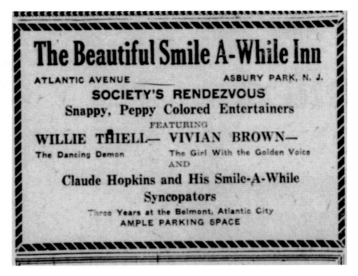

Ad for Claude Hopkins at the Smile-A-While. 1925. Note: "Three Years at the Belmont, Atlantic City" is certainly an exaggeration. It was more like three weeks!

Near the end of July, rumors started circulating around the Asbury Park Clubs that a wealthy woman from New York was auditioning bands for a tour of Europe. Claude Hopkins heard the rumors but didn't think much of them. Then one night, Claude got word that Mrs. Carolyn Reagan was in the Smile-a-Way audience to hear his band. Claude was ready with some of his band's best numbers including "O Katharina," "Prince Of Wails," which featured his own piano playing and a novelty version of "St. Louis Blues." The latter was a ten- to fifteen-minute comedy tune that left the audience in stitches and Carolyn Reagan hysterical. Claude's band was offered the European job without auditioning anyone else. Claude's gig with the Smile-A-While was due to end after Labor Day and he would start rehearsals in New York City then.[23]

In addition to Claude and his band, Mrs. Reagan also selected several chorus girls from the *Smile-A-While Creole Review*, including Evelyn Anderson. Claude Hopkins had recently gotten married and persuaded Mrs. Reagan to take along his wife Mabel as an additional chorus girl. According to Anderson, Mrs. Reagan got Mabel Hopkins, Bea Foote and Marguerite Ricks from a different cabaret in Asbury Park.[24] (Bea Foote would later surface as a blues singer with *Decca Records*.) The European tour that followed would also launch the career of Josephine Baker.

La Revue Negre was a huge success and ran for nine weeks at the Champs-Elysees Theatre with a special performances at the Moulin Rouge. After that it moved to the Theatre L'Etoile in Paris for ten weeks and then on to the Cirque Royal in Brussels, Belgium for six weeks. Then the show moved on to Berlin but closed after a couple weeks when Josephine Baker left the *Revue*.

Claude Hopkins then formed a new band with some European musicians and played in Spain and Portugal.[25] He returned to the United States in the Spring of 1926 and started a new band with Doc Clarke (trumpet), Balos Alexander "Sandy" Williams (trombone), Bernie Addison (guitar), Bob Brown (drums), Hilton Jefferson (alto sax) and Elmer Williams (tenor sax). Elmer Williams is undoubtedly the same sax player who grew up playing with Bill Basie.

Meanwhile, the Smile-A-While Inn opened the 1926 season in April with entertainment by The Cooks (Hartwell & Louise), New York sensational dancers direct from the Club Alabam.[26] In July, the entertainment consisted of "snappy and peppy songs and dances" by Toussaint Duer's *Smile-A-While Revue* and the band, Bernie Robinson's Maryland Ramblers.[27]

In mid-July, the Smile-A-While Inn announced the return of Claude Hopkins and his Band, "after their most successful European engagement." They called Claude's band, "the best band on the Coast last summer."[28] Claude Hopkins' band stayed on at the Smile-A-While through the end of the summer.

Program frpm *La Revue Negre* in Paris, 1925. Show included Josephine Baker and Claude Hopkins' Orchestra.

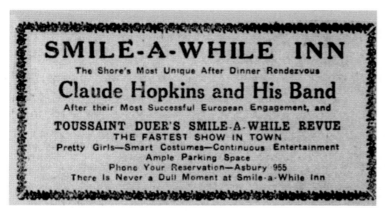

1926 ad for Claude Hopkins at the Smile-A-While following his return from Europe.

Newspapers reported that on Labor Day weekend 1926, the Smile-A-While was one of two popular West Side cabarets raided by county authorities looking for evidence of alcohol (this was still the Prohibition Era). A half dozen detectives and constables "found the Smile-A-While jammed to the doors with a seething mob of white persons when they swooped down on the place about 12:30 o'clock Saturday night."

111

The raiders were armed with search warrants and began a hunt for liquor. They found only a few bottles of liquor under the tables, most likely stashed there by some patrons. The raiders refused to allow anyone to leave until those connected with the place had been rounded up. In spite of the meager evidence, they insisted on charging Mossell and Suarez with illegal sale of alcohol and running a disorderly house. The two owners and eighteen of their employees (musicians, entertainers and waitresses), all black, were arrested. Among those arrested were members of Hopkin's band; Elmer Williams, Hilton Jefferson, Bernard Addison, John [Doc?] Clarke and Sandy Williams, along with Claude Hopkin's wife Hattie [sic] Hopkins. Claude Hopkins was not found and probably avoided capture. When it was announced that the place was going to be closed, the three hundred persons in the place began a mad rush for the only exit in the front. Hundreds of patrons, almost all of them white, were turned out into the street."[29]

Claude Hopkins business card.
Courtesy of the Institute for Jazz Studies,
Rutgers University

After all employees were bailed out of jail, they were arrested again on a second raid the next night. This time Claude Hopkins was among those arrested. When the raiders returned a third night, they found the Smile-A-While Inn closed.

It's important to point out that West Side clubs still had a valuable ally in Mayor Hetrick. While Hetrick, a Republican, publicly supported Prohibition, in actuality he often looked the other way. Prohibition raiders who shut down the Smile-A-While were county detectives, not Asbury Park officers! To implement the nationwide ban on alcohol, the Prohibition Bureau in Washington, DC set up local enforcement offices around the United States. Agents made anti-alcohol raids around the state, shutting down speakeasies, stills, breweries, bottling plants, and other illegal operations. Mayor Hetrick's permissiveness and reluctance to enforce West Side "morality laws" quickly drew the ire of the Anti-Saloon League and the Ku Klux Klan who shared their support of Prohibition. By 1924, the KKK boasted of sixty thousand members in New Jersey.[30] Hetrick, it is said, kept the KKK out of Asbury Park at a time when four thousand Klan members paraded through nearby Long Branch, New Jersey, while twenty-five thousand looked on.[31] Still Asbury Park remained a segregated city.

While African American clubs on the West Side may have been spared early on during Prohibition, they now became frequent targets of raids, especially when they were drawing large numbers of white patrons. Speaking to a meeting of black voters in 1930, former County Prosecutor John J. Quinn charged that East Side bosses were padding the census to gain votes for themselves and were "getting drunk with power, shaking down every [West Side] speakeasy... ."[32] Of course, politics played a role in

Quinn's accusations. Quinn was a Democrat and former county employee. Hetrick and the "East Side bosses" were Republicans. And raids on the Smile-A-While and other West Side cabarets seem to have been carried out by county agents.

Aaron Mossell and other leaders in the West Side's black community seemed to have been big supporters of Mayor Hetrick. In fact, in 1925, when Mayor Hetrick needed popular support to build a glorious Convention Hall, Aaron Mossell, Julius Suarez and local noted sand sculptor and outspoken civil rights advocate, Lorenzo Harris, chipped in to purchase a full page ad in the local newspaper entitled "The Convention Hall WILL Benefit Colored Taxpayers And Citizens of the West Side."[33] In 1931, Mossell and Harris co-edited a booklet entitled "Asbury Park and its Colored Citizens 1911 - 1931," essentially a re-election instrument for Hetrick, describing the progress black residents of the West Side had made under his administration.[34] And in the same year, Mossell paid for a large add in the *Asbury Park Press*, imploring voters to give credit to Hetrick for having "made those things happen which have glorified Asbury Park."[35]

The September 1926 raids seem to have targeted the establishments on the busiest weekend of the year, trying to crush them financially. But a November 1926 newspaper ad showed that the Smile-A-While Inn could not be defeated so easily. It announced it would be open every evening of the Fall and Winter season. Their motto was "There's never a dull moment at the Smile-A-While Inn."[36]

Meanwhile, while in New York City, Claude Hopkins made the acquaintance of S. H. Dudley, Jr., The son of the famous black vaudeville entertainer. Dudley was rehearsing a variety show and needed some original music written for the opening. Hopkins offered to help and was invited to join the show. Julius Suarez, Smile-A-While co-owner was brought in as a sponsor and promoter of the show, presumably through Hopkins.[37] Initially the show premiered on July 1, 1927 at the West End Inn, located at the corner of Brighton and Ocean Avenues in nearby Long Branch, New Jersey. It was called *Cotton Land* and starred S. H. Dudley Jr., *Victor* recording star Ozie McPherson and Mary Clemmons ("the Black Bottom Queen") along with Sid Straton and his famous Plantation Serenaders.[38]

Re-titled *The Ginger Snaps of 1928*, the show then went on the road in September of 1927. Now added to the bill were Claude Hopkins and his band, Sandy Burns, Billy Higgins, Lottie Gee and others.[39] Hopkins toured with the show on the TOBA (Theater Owner's Booking Association) circuit for a few months before it folded in Louisville, Kentucky.

Newspaper coverage of the Smile-A-While Inn was spotty from then on, but operating the cabaret must have been difficult under frequent harassment by local authorities. An October 1927 ad invited patrons to visit the Smile-A-While's Creole Grill.[40] But a December 1927 article stated the Inn was recently closed down [again] for selling intoxicating liquor. The article further stated that Julius Suarez was running an illegal West Side numbers racket.[41]

May of 1928 marked the reopening of the Smile-A-While Inn and the return of Claude Hopkin's band.[42] Julius Suarez offered a $100 reward for anyone who could prove that the Smile-A-While Band, under the leadership of Claude Hopkins, was not the best on the whole Jersey coast.[43] Now, $100 was a lot of money in 1928, but how could you "prove" such a thing?

In the Spring of 1928, the Smile-A-While Inn even contributed an engraved silver tray as a prize for the city's annual baby parade. The parade drew tens of thousands of viewers each year, though it's doubtful any African American babies were allowed to participate (except dressed an coachmen or servents). Still, so many white vacationers frequented the Smile-A-While Inn, it was good publicity. The tray now is in the possession of the Asbury Park Historical Society.

Before the end of the year, the Smile-A-While Inn closed for good at that location. Aaron Mossell returned to being a pharmacist at the Johnson and Poland Drug Store at 1045 Springwood Avenue, just a few doors down from the drug store he and Suarez had sold in 1925. This was in clear violation of the contract they had signed when they sold the store, promising not to compete for five years. Mossell was ordered to terminate his involvement with the pharmacy, an order he ignored.[44] Found in violation a second time, Aaron Mossell was sent to jail for three months.[45] By 1933, Aaron Mossell had left Asbury Park for good, moving from his West Side house on Dewitt Avenue back to his home town, Philadelphia. There he continued practicing pharmacy until his death in 1959.[46]

"Baby Parade, 1928, Asbury Park NJ, Smile-A-While Inn Prize" Courtesy of Don Stine and the Asbury Park Historical Society

On November 27, 1928, someone tried to torch the already closed up Smile-A-While Inn. The fire department was called at 1:10 in the morning to find pools of unburned kerosene in the depressions in the concrete floor around the entrance and the dance floor. The steps leading to the second floor were saturated with the same liquid. A fire had been started in a corner of the dance floor and was burning slowly when firemen arrived but had made little headway. No damage had been caused by the fire. The article went on to say that "the building was unoccupied at the time but had been famous during the past few summers when it was operated by Julius Suarez as the Smile-a-While Inn where a Creole review and a snappy jazz band were presented for both colored and white pleasure seekers of the shore." The building's current owner was listed as Eugene Renna of New Brunswick, not Suarez and Mossell.[47] Renna had been the original property owner back in 1911. Could it be that Mossell and Suarez never bought the hotel, but just rented it from Renna? Police believed that this fire and two other arsons, one at a hotel and one at a private residence, were all set by the same person.[48]

The property at 1144 Atlantic Avenue appeared in the news again in 1934 when an offer was made to rent the property to the city of Asbury Park for one dollar. Proposed uses included an isolation hospital (for treating numerous infectious diseases like small pox and tuberculosis), a playground[49] and a West Side health center.[50] A month later the city granted use of the property to The B.P.O. Reindeer to hold a carnival there at a later date.[51] The property later became part of the Boston Way housing projects.

The name "Smile-A-While" would be used twice more for night spots in the Springwood Avenue area, but any connection with the original club remains a mystery. A Smile-A-While club existed at 904 Prospect Avenue in 1936 and a Smile-A-While Tavern once stood at 110 Lincoln Place, both in the West Side. On August 25, 1938, the latter Smile-A-While was the scene of a murder suicide. Jesse Hall walked into the Smile-A-While and killed his wife, Alfreda Hall, with four shots from his .45 before killing himself.[52] Both Jesse Hall and his wife were entertainers in the tavern, owned by Bobby Brown.[53] No further mention of the Smile-A-While can be found. By 1939, the 110 Lincoln Place establishment reopened as Jackie's Cotton Club.[54]

Notes to Chapter 7

[1] "Smile -A-While Park - New Jersey," *Billboard*, 15 Mar, 1924.

[2] "Penn Biographies: Aaron Albert Mossell (1863 - 1951)", http://www.archives.upenn.edu/people/1800s/mossell_aaron_a.html.

[3] "A Principled Man," *The Pennsylvania Gazette*, Nov/Dec, 2014, pp. 50 - 55.

[4] "Sadie Alexander," http://blackhistorynow.com/sadie-alexander

[5] *Practical Druggist and Pharmaceutical Review of Reviews*, Volume 34 (Dec, 1916), p. 52.

[6] "Asbury Park, NJ," *New York Age*, 29 Mar, 1924, p. 3.

[7] "Local Druggists Win State Actions," *Asbury Park Press*, 9 Jul, 1925, p. 23.

[8] *Pittsburgh Courier*, 27 Aug, 1927, p. 15.

[9] Section 6 of the Volstead Act, http://www.historycentral.com/documents/Volstead.html

[10] "Walgreens," wikipedia.org

[11] "Druggist Must Answer in Suit," *Asbury Park Press*, 19 Jun, 1928, p. 21.

[12] "City Creates New Roadway," *Asbury Park Press*, 11 Oct, 1939, p. 1.

[13] "Qualification of Voters," *Asbury Park Press*, 21 Oct, 1911, p. 6.

[14] *Asbury Park Press*, 17 Oct, 1914; *Asbury Park Press*, 2 Nov, 1914.

[15] "Colored Democrats Meet," *Asbury Park Press*, 3 Aug, 1916, p. 2.

[16] "Lamp Causes Fire," *Asbury Park Press*, 17 Jul, 1915, p. 12.

[17] "Powell Banks Is Given Jail Term," *Asbury Park Press*, 24 Jan, 1917, p. 2.

[18] "Banks Arrested Again," *Asbury Park Press*, 28 Dec, 1918, p. 2.

[19] *Insurance Maps of the New Jersey Coast, Vol. 2*, (New York: Sanborn Map Company, 1927).

[20] Warren W. Vache, Sr., *Crazy Fingers: Claude Hopkins' Life In Jazz*, (Washington, DC: Smithsonian Institution Press, 1992), pp. 9 - 12.

[21] Count Basie and Albert Murray, *Good Morning Blues*, (New York: Primus, 1985), pp 76 -77.

[22] Jean-Claude Baker and Chris Chase, *Josephine Baker: The Hungry Heart*, (New York: Cooper Square Press, 1993), pp. 93 - 94.

[23] Vache, *Crazy Fingers*, pp. 12 - 13.

[24] Baker and Chase, *Josephine Baker*, p. 94.

[25] Vache, *Crazy Fingers*, pp. 17 - 25

[26] Ad for Smile-A-While Inn, *Asbury Park Press*, 16 Apr, 1926, p. 4.

[27] Ad for Smile-A-While Inn, *Asbury Park Press*, 8 Jul, 1926, p. 15.

[28] Ad for Smile-A-While Inn, *Asbury Park Press*, 13 Jul, 1926, p. 5.

[29] "Raiders Close Up Leading Cabarets In Negro District: Hundreds of White Patrons Are Driven Into Street As Officers Arrest All Employs of the Inns," *Asbury Park Press*, 7 Sep, 1926, p. 1.

[30] Daniel Wolff, *4th Of July, Asbury Park*, (New York: Bloomsbury Publishing, 2005), p. 97.

[31] For a history of the KKK in New Jersey, see Joseph G. Bilby and Harry Ziegler, *The Rise And Fall of the Ku Klux Klan in New Jersey,* (Charleston, History Press, 2019).

[32] "Quinn Charges 'Shakedown' Of Legitimate Merchants: Former Prosecutor Tells Negros "East Side Boss' Padded Census to Offset Vote Lost by 'Numbers King'," *Asbury Park Press*, 30 Oct, 1930, p. 3.

[33] "The Convention Hall Will Benefit Colored Taxpayers And Citizens of the West Side," *Asbury Park Press*, 2 Nov, 1925, p. 17.

[34] Lorenzo Harris Sr. and Aaron A, Mossell, ed., *Asbury Park and its Colored Citizens 1911 - 1931,* (New Jersey: Privately printed, 1931). Provided by Rutgers Library, New Brunswick, NJ.

[35] "To The Voters Of Asbury Park," *Asbury Park Press*, 30 Apr, 1931, p. 4.

[36] Ad for Smile-A-While Inn, *Asbury Park Press*, 1 Nov, 1926, p. 16.

[37] Vache, *Crazy Fingers*, p. 29.

[38] Ad for "Cotton Land", *Asbury Park Press*, 2 Jul, 1927, p. 12.

[39] Ad for Ginger Snaps of 1928, *New York Age*, 17 Sep, 1927.

[40] Ad for Smile-A-While Inn, *Asbury Park Press*, 5 Oct, 1927, p. 18.

[41] "Various Runners Still Actively Plying Numbers Game On West Side," *Asbury Park Press*, 10 Dec, 1927, p. 1.

[42] Ad for Smile-A-While Inn, *Asbury Park Press*, 2 May, 1928, p. 4.

[43] Ad for Smile-A-While Inn, *Asbury Park Press*, 22 May, 1928, p. 4.

[44] "Druggist Guilty Of Court Contempt," *Asbury Park Press*, 15, Aug, 1928, p. 2.

[45] "Mossell Jailed for thirty Days," *Asbury Park Press*, 22 Aug, 1928, pp. 1-2.

[46] "Death Notice: Aaron A. Mossell," *The Philadelphia Inquirer*, 17 Jun, 1959, p. 10.

[47] "Two Shore Blazes Believed Incendiary," *Asbury Park Press*, 27 Nov, 1928, pp. 1 - 2.

[48] "Continue Sift of Three Shore Fires," *Asbury Park Press*, 3 Dec, 1928, p. 2.

[49] "Budget Can Be Cut, Silverstein Claims," *Asbury Park Press*, 14 Feb, 1934, p. 3.

[50] "Engage Director for Health Center," *Asbury Park Press*, 23 May, 1934, p. 1.

[51] "Session Disrupted by Budget Debate," *Asbury Park Press*, 27 Jun, 1934, p. 2.

[52] "Husband Kills Wife and Self in Night Club,"*Pittsburgh Courier*, 27 Aug, 1938, p. 4.

[53] "3 Killed in Fair Haven, City Murders," *Asbury Park Press*, 21 Aug, 1938, pp. 1-2.

[54] "More Bright Spots Open: Band Gets Fame Chance" *Asbury Park Press,* 24 Jun, 1939, p. 5.

Chapter Eight

Reese DuPree and the Roseland Cabaret

That same 1926 Labor Day weekend when Prohibition raiders shut down the Smile-A-While Inn, they also shut down the Inn's nearest competitor, the Roseland Cabaret. The Roseland was a couple of blocks away at 1155 Springwood Avenue at Atkins Avenue. The newspaper accounts called the Roseland Cabaret the largest on the West Side and found it also packed with patrons (mostly white). The raiders found no liquor at the Roseland but arrested the "alleged proprietor," Henry Hart, and thirteen other employees (bartenders, waitresses and musicians), all black, on charges of running a "disorderly house." The employees were promptly bailed out by the Roseland's real owner, Reese DuPree.[1]

REESE DuPREE

Though not that well known nowadays, Reese DuPree was once one of the country's leading figures in show business; a very successful African American singer, musician, promoter and venue owner of the 1920's, 1930's and 1940's. Reese LaMarr DuPree was born July 18, 1883, on a cotton plantation in Bibb County, Georgia. Bibb County lies about eight miles south of the city of Macon.

Reese DuPree began singing spirituals in the Swift Creek Baptist Church but left the plantation when he was thirteen. He had a series of jobs before heading north to New York City around 1900.[2] DuPree is credited by many for writing the song, "Shortnin' Bread," which he was singing in public since 1905. While some historians believe the song to be based on a folk song with roots going back much earlier, DuPree was the first to copyright the song, which he later sold to Ralph Peer, the first music publisher to recognize the value in recording roots music.[3]

Taking a job as a singer at a hotel in Laurence Beach, Long Island, DuPree was then making $25 a week. Winning an amateur contest at the Miner's Theatre in New York

City, DuPree quit his job and began making the rounds of amateur contests around the city. He appeared in the movie, "Turkey In The Straw." Eventually DuPree was hired as a singer in a fashionable night club, where he was discovered by Diamond Jim Brady, Lillian Russell and Sophie Tucker. They helped him get a lucrative job as a singer which he kept for five years. From there, DuPree began doing special engagements and concerts. He ran dances that made as much as $1000 to $1,400 a night. During that time Reese claimed to have made $150,000 but spent it all on automobiles and high living. He ran dance halls and in 1917 went to Atlantic City and opened the Egg Harbor Hotel. Unfortunately, the hotel was destroyed in a fire after a short time.[4]

In 1918, Reese came to Asbury Park, renting Lafayette Hall at 1155 Springwood Avenue. For a residence, DuPree purchased the estate of James H. Harky on Corlies Avenue in nearby Neptune, consisting of twelve acres and a private lake. He lived there until that house was destroyed by fire. He eventually sold the estate to the Ann May Hospital [now the present day the Jersey Shore University Medical Center] and built a new home on 1920 Corlies Avenue, called Duchene Lodge.

Reese DuPree turned Lafayette Hall into a popular night spot. There was dancing every night of the summer seasons until 2 a.m. Live music was provided by the Reese DuPree Jazz Band. Over the Fourth of July weekend, there was special entertainment like the Jenkins' Orphans Band and Jubilee Singers.[5] In August 1921, Lafayette Hall featured a "Monster Jazz Review" featuring two bands and "Corky, the Piano Hound" [most likely Basie's friend Corky Williams].[6]

Roseland Cabaret's dance floor. From Harris & Mossell's book.
Courtesy of Rutgers Library.

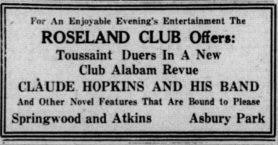

After renting Lafayette Hall for three years, he purchased it in 1921.[7] After doing some major renovations, the Hall was reopened in June 1923 as the Roseland Cabaret. Reese invited everyone to the grand opening to dance "on my new $1,800 floor under Oriental lights." The dance hall was christened by the "Belle of Asbury Park, Miss Constance Fox" and music was provided by the "Famous Jazola Boys." Mr. DuPree promised that regardless of expense, he'd have the "prettiest dance hall in the east for his race."[8]

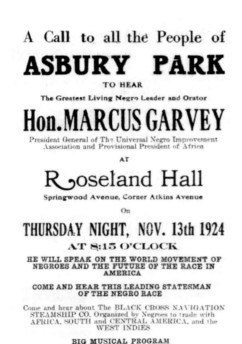

From MacKay's "The Blacks Of Monmouth County," courtesy of the Monmouth County Historical Association

Besides dances and other nightly entertainment, Roseland Hall was also used for political meetings and even civil rights rallies; something that might have made some on the East Side a little nervous. In 1924, Marcus Garvey spoke at Roseland Hall[9] and in 1928, famous black leader and editor of *The Crisis* magazine, W. E. B. DuBois addressed the Asbury Branch of the NAACP there.[10]

During the summer of 1927, while possibly the Smile-A-While Inn was shut down with another Prohibition raid, the Roseland Cabaret seems to have absorbed all of their entertainment. Through July and August, the Roseland featured Claude Hopkins and his band plus Toussaint Duers and his Review.[11]

The Roseland Cabaret was not Reese DuPree's only venture during this time. A 1923 ad lists Reese DuPree as the owner of New York City establishments; The Georgia House (241 W. 41st St.), The Henrietta House (255 W. 47th St.) and The DuPree House (241 W. 53rd St.). It's not known if these were hotels or clubs.

There's also a report of a Tuxedo Club on West Corlies Avenue, owned by Reese DuPree, being destroyed by fire in 1923. This may be a reference to the Harky Estate, if DuPree also ran a club from there.[12]

Birth of the Blues

Reese also found time to make recordings for the *OKeh* record label. In December, 1923, the *Chicago Defender* proclaimed DuPree "the first man of our race to record blues records for this company."[13] Actually, Reese DuPree may have been the first African American male blues vocalist ever to record.

Blues songs originated among African Americans in the Deep South before 1900. Ma Rainey began performing blues songs on stage as part of her act around 1902. Black composer, W. C. Handy, known for writing "St. Louis Blues" and "Memphis Blues" published his first blues song in 1912. Yet, before 1920, there were no recordings made of black artists singing blues. Even Handy's songs were only recorded by white artists such as Sophie Tucker. The reason was simple. Recording companies didn't see any commercial value to black songs sung by black artists.

Then in August 1920, *OKeh's Records* enterprising A&R man, Ralph Peer, demonstrated the commercial appeal of black artists recording black music intended for a black audience by recording Mamie Smith singing "Crazy Blues." The record sold between 800,000 and a million records, all to black record buyers. Other record companies like *Vocalion, Columbia, Paramount* and the black-owned *Black Swan* label, soon jumped on the bandwagon, recording other African American female blues vocalists. Soon there were "race" recordings out by Lucille Hegamin, Ethel Waters, Alberta Hunter, Bessie Smith and many others.[14] And though African American male blues artists were most certainly available, before 1923 all the *recorded* black blues artists were women. In November 1923, Peer recorded Sylvester Weaver on "Guitar Blues" but the song is an instrumental (guitar) solo. Although a blues song, Weaver does not sing on the record.

On December 19, 1923, the *Asbury Park Press* had a short note that "Reece [sic] DuPree of 720 Corlies Avenue, West Grove, owner of the New Roseland in West Park, and one-time Broadway singer, has recorded two popular numbers on *Okeh Records*, "Long Ago Blues" and "O Saroo Saroo." They will be released about January 1."[15] The sides (*OKeh* # 8113) featured DuPree singing with piano accompaniment. DuPree wrote "Long Ago Blues."

Reese DuPree would have two more releases on *OKeh Records* in 1924 - "Norfolk Blues" / "One More Rounder Gone" (*OKeh* # 8127) and "Mammy's Gone Coo Coo" / "Here's

Start of Fire Menacing Wide West Side Area

Press—Cole Photo
Photo shows fire which threatened a wide area in the Springwood avenue district yesterday. Originating in Roseland hall, on the right, it swept several small stores and a house before being controlled.

Firemen fight the July 1931 blaze that destroyed the Roseland Cabaret. This dark newspaper photo is the only known photo of the building's exterior.

To Your Absent Brothers" (*OKeh* # 8167). "Norfolk Blues" has Reese DuPree singing an early county blues song accompanied by a guitar. This is one of the first, if not *the first*, recorded male blues vocals with guitar by a black artist. And though there's no indication of how well DuPree's records sold, they do further indicate the innovative and diverse music styles coming out of Asbury Park's West Side.

While Reese DuPree had many interests, his main one was running the Roseland Cabaret. During its heyday, Roseland was truly the grandest music venue on Springwood Avenue. They always had big names in entertainment. For instance, in July 1930 their bill included Horace Henderson (brother of Fletcher Henderson) and his Twelve Dixie Boys plus Quintard Miller's Shuffle Along Review.[16] But the Roseland Ballroom's finest moment was when on July 7, 1930, it hosted Duke Ellington and his Cotton Club Orchestra, direct from New York City.[17] Eighteen years after he washed dishes in an Asbury Park "whites only" hotel, Ellington was back in Asbury Park's West Side.

Fires were common in the early 1900's but Reese DuPree had more than his share. In February 1931, hot ashes were inadvertently dumped into a receptacle on the west side of the building and the flames quickly spread to the northwest section of the Roseland Hall auditorium. Fortunately, firemen were able to contain the fire and save the building. There was about $5,000 in damage but it was covered by insurance.[18]

Then in July of that same year, misfortune struck again. This time it was a fire of unknown origin that completely destroyed the Roseland Hall and several neighboring buildings on Springwood Avenue. For a while it looked like the fire would wipe out a large section of the West Side, but it was finally brought under control. Fire inspectors were never able to determine the cause of the fire, since the whole building was engulfed before they got there.[19] This time the fire occurred a week after the majority of DuPree's insurance had expired. Of the loss of his $30,000 building, DuPree was only able to get back a couple thousand dollars in insurance. Just a couple years earlier, the Great Stock Market crash had relieved him of about $40,000.[20] Debts incurred in Asbury Park would lead to DuPree declaring bankruptcy some years later.

Reese DuPree was never one to give up and he re-ignited his career as a performer with the aid of a singing chicken that sang duets with him. According to newspaper reports, Reese had just finished singing the spiritual song "Deep River" one day at his home on Corlies Avenue when he heard a clucking outside. Opening the screen door that led from his music room to a side porch, he found a Plymouth Rock hen perched on the arm of one of his porch chairs. In fact, day after day, the hen returned to cluck along to Reese's singing. Moreover, the hen seemed to be trying to imitate his voice. Reese eventually brought the hen into his home and gave "Singing Jane," as he named her, voice lessons, so to speak. One day Jane was stolen along with other chickens from Reese's yard. Reese eventually found out who took them and brought charges. It fell upon Reese to prove in court that the chickens were his. To the astonishment of the Justice of the Peace and court officers, Reese started singing and the hen hopped onto his shoulder and joined in the crooning. The publicity led to a movie deal - movie houses were now featuring "talkies."[21] [We don't know that the film was ever released.]

Around 1932, Reese DuPree relocated to Philadelphia where he operated the Stand Ballroom at Broad & Bainbridge Streets for many years. Reese again was an important figure in show business, booking and /or promoting appearances by major stars like Duke Ellington and Josephine Baker.[22] He also operated the DuPree Hotel at Broad & South Streets where entertainers playing the Strand stayed. In 1946 the Strand was closed and re-leased to become an upholstery training school for returning GI's. The DuPree Hotel closed in 1950. Reese DuPree died April 30, 1963 at the age of 83.[23]

[Research for this book has recently led to greater recognition of Asbury Park's forgotten music heroes. In 2018, The Asbury Angels Foundation honored Reese DuPree with a plaque on the Asbury Park Boardwalk of Fame and Asbury Park named one of the city's alleys "Roseland Lane" in honor of his Roseland Cabaret.]

With the Smile-A-While Inn and the Roseland Cabaret in ashes, one might have expected their nearest West Side competitors, the Paradise Hall and the Old Blue Bird Cabaret to pick up much of the business and they did.

By October 1931, local newspapers proclaimed the new popular night spot for cabarets was the Paradise on Springwood Avenue.[24]

The Blue Bird Cabaret seems to have been started around 1930 by an Italian-American by the name of John Del Vecchio. It was located at 1718 Springwood Avenue (at Fisher) and it too bragged of the "Snappiest Colored Show In Town" with entertainment like "Billy Thrill's Jungle Nights - a red hot revue direct from one of Broadways' hottest night clubs, featuring Edna Taylor (the Creole Beauty), Grace Stewart, Pete Peters, Broadway Eddie and a sizzling chorus of Sepia Beauties."[25]

But in July of 1931, the Blue Bird was also raided and accused of selling alcoholic beverages.[26] Then later that year, John Del Vecchio was sued by bandleader Alfred Hill of the Hill Harmonists orchestra for $500 in back wages. According to Hill, Del Vecchio had hired his band for $160 a week. After five weeks, of the $800 that was due, only $300 was ever paid out.[27]

Hill initially won a judgment of $400[28] in civil court due to the testimony of himself and three of his band members, Charles Wells, William Brown and James Pedrick. The Hill Harmonists were a local band all residing at 26 Atkins Avenue.

What appeared to be a rare occurrence, a court siding with a black accuser against a white defendant, was short lived. Del Vecchio produced his own white witness who claimed to have overheard Hill agree to a lesser amount of money. Hill and his three band members were then served warrants by a criminal court for perjury in the previous trial.[29] The word of two white men topped the word of four black men.

However, the success of West Side cabarets was waning by 1932. Constant harassment by Prohibition raids and numerous fires, some arson and some not, combined with economic woes, brought an end to it. Influential East Side businesses, concerned that too many white tourists were traveling to Springwood Avenue for their entertainment, finally prevailed.

And the West Side demographics were shifting further. Aided by the Great Migration, the Springwood Avenue area, once a racially diverse area, had by 1930 become almost entirely African American. Other ethnic groups like the Italian Americans had moved northward toward Asbury Avenue. The 1930 census found that ninety-nine percent of Asbury Park's black population now lived in the First Ward. Unfortunately nearly a third of Asbury Park's black population were unemployed entering the Great Depression.[30]

Dunbar Manor

Growth of the area's black population didn't stop at the Asbury Park West Side city line. In 1922, the Jersey Coast Realty company announced they'd be selling 800 lots for a housing development called Dunbar Manor. Dunbar Manor was a plot of land along the (then) Springwood Avenue, just west of the West Side. The tract was being developed for "high class" homes for African Americans. The township of Neptune was at the time preparing to lay sewers and preparations were also being made to extend water mains through the various streets. [31]

Dunbar Manor was the creation of Albert Robbins, a prominent area realtor since 1901.[32] Robbins began selling lots in Dunbar Manor in 1924, advertising in African American newspapers throughout

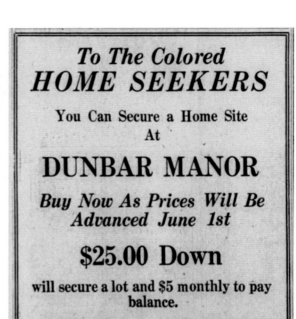

the country. Dunbar Manor, located on both sides of Springwood at Drummond, was said to be within six to ten minutes ride from "the fine brick Mt. Pisguh Baptist Church, the new $200,000 grammar school, the St. Stephens A.M.E. Zion Church, the Colored Masonic Hall and the Roseland Dance Hall. The actual seashore, where bathing can be enjoyed, is within walking distance of the property."[33] "The chance of a lifetime," ads proclaimed. "Own your own home at the 'City by the Sea'." Lots started at $150 with only $25 down and $5 a month. No wonder the "progressive colored population" flocked to Asbury Park. Newspapers had proclaimed Asbury Park the ideal city for a home with good work and good wages the year round for black citizens. "Colored" women could find work from $3 to $5 a day; men from $4 to $5 a day.[34]

But that was all changing with the stock market crash of 1929. The Great Depression was here.

Notes to Chapter 8

1 "Raiders Close Up Leading Cabarets In Negro District," *Asbury Park Press*, 7 Sep, 1926, p. 1.

2 "About A Hen That Sang Her Way Into The Movies," *Norfolk New Journal and Guide*, 2 Jan 1932, p. 8.

3 Steven Wade, *The Beautiful Music All Around Us,* (Champaign, IL: University of Illinois Press, 2012), pp. 94 - 99.

4 *Norfolk New Journal and Guide*, 2 Jan 1932, p. 8.

5 *Asbury Park Press*, 5 Jul, 1921, p. 1.

6 "Corky's," *Asbury Park Press*, 2, Aug, 1921, p. 1.

7 *Norfolk New Journal and Guide*, 2 Jan, 1932, p. 8.

8 "DuPree's Grand Opening Of New Roseland Dance Hall," *Asbury Park Press*, 18 Jun, 1923, p. 1.

9 Lenore Walker MacKay, *Blacks of Monmouth County* (1976).

10 "Local Happenings," *Asbury Park Press*, 31 May, 1928, p. 2.

11 Ad for Roseland, *Asbury Park Press*, 13 Aug, 1927, p. 5.

12 "Blaze Destroys Old Tuxedo Club," *Asbury Park Press*, 22 Mar, 1923, p. 1.

13 *Chicago Defender*, 22 Dec, 1923, p. 16.

14 Barry Mazor, *Ralph Peer and the Making of Popular Roots Music*, (Chicago: Chicago Review Press, 2015), pp. 38 - 45.

15 "Local Happenings," *Asbury Park Press*, 18 Dec, 1923, p. 2.

16 Ad for Horace Henderson at Roseland, *Asbury Park Press*, 9 Jul, 1930, p. 6.

17 "Tonight Duke Ellington," *Asbury Park Press*, 7 Jul, 1930, p. 1.

18 "Roseland Hall Is Destroyed By Fire," *Asbury Park Press,* 23 Feb, 1931, p. 1.

19 "Threatening West Side Fire Halted With $30,000 Loss: Roseland Hall and Nearby Buildings Destroyed In a Spectacular Blaze - Unable to Determine Cause. General Alarm Call a Mistake," *Asbury Park Press*, 30 Jul, 1931, pp. 1 - 2.

20 "Reese DuPree Files Bankruptcy Petition," *Afro-American*, 8 Nov, 1941, p. 16.

21 *Norfolk New Journal and Guide*, 2 Jan, 1932, p. 8.

22 "Reese DuPree Encircles His Name And Stand With Renown," *Philadelphia Tribune*, 13 Jan, 1938, p. 15.

23 "Showman Reese DuPree Succumbs at 83 in GA," *Philadelphia Tribune*, 11 May, 1963, p. 5.

24 "The West Side: Avenue Residents Seek To Advance In City's Life," *Asbury Park Press*, 7 Oct, 1931, p. 21.

25 Ad for The Old Blue Bird, *Asbury Park Press,* 22 Aug, 1930, p. 9.

26 "Pleads Not Guilty Of Fatal Stabbing," *Asbury Park Press*, 25 Jul, 1931, p. 15.

27 "Sue Blue Bird Owner," *Asbury Park Press*, 15 Aug, 1931, p. 2.

28 "Orchestra Wins Suit," *Asbury Park Press*, 21 Aug, 1931, p. 6.

29 "Threaten Perjury Action In Blue Bird Contract Tangle," *Asbury Park Press*, 10 Sep, 1931, p. 3.

30 Daniel Wolff, *4th of July, Asbury Park*, (New York: Bloomsbury, 2005) p. 134.

31 "City Suburb to be Dunbar Manor," *Asbury Park Press*, 15 Sep, 1922, p. 1.
32 "Albert Robbins Dies Suddenly," *Asbury Park Press*, 12 Nov, 1938, p. 1.
33 Ad for Dunbar Manor, *Pittsburgh Courier*, 9 Aug, 1924, p. 14.
34 *Ibid.*

Chapter Nine

West Side Music During The Great Depression

As the 1930's began, the country was in the midst of The Great Depression. Times were especially hard on the West Side, which had always been shortchanged with regard to the civic improvements given the East Side. In 1931, the West Side was still without running water, while water mains ran under most of the East Side streets. The year 1931 found almost half the streets in Asbury Park permanently paved - 14 miles out of 36. Yet, only three streets on the West Side had any paving - Springwood, Atkins and Prospect - amounting to about 3 miles.[1] The rest were gravel surfaced.

With 1930 came the completion of the huge Convention Hall, Boardwalk Theatre and Casino for entertainment along the beach. Where Asbury Avenue approached the beach, the city erected a pavilion with solariums giving the south end of the boardwalk a modern feel.[2]

The repeal of Prohibition in December 1933 was only a small reprieve from people's hardships. If you chose to drown your troubles, on a tight budget you might now do that at home.

Across the nation, the way people received entertainment was rapidly changing. Prior to 1925, phonograph records, 78-RPM shellac disks, were recorded and played back acoustically. But after 1925, records were recorded, manufactured and played back electronically with better fidelity and were cheaper to make and buy.

And in the 1930's, with unemployment high and disposable income low, fewer people could afford to go out to cabarets and live shows. Live musical entertainment was quickly being replaced with a new medium - radio. Radio was nearly "free" entertainment. You just had to purchase a radio.

The first radio broadcasts were done in the early 1900's but early radio sets lacked amplification and were not widely accepted. Besides, radio broadcast stations were few and far between. The first licensed commercial radio station did not begin daily broadcasts until 1921. What revolutionized the radio industry was the acceptance of amplifying vacuum tubes in the mid-1920's. From then on, the country was swept into the "Golden Age Of Radio" which would last into the 1950's. In 1931, two in five homes had radios. By 1938, four of five homes had one.[3] By the mid-1920's, radio broadcast stations began springing up everywhere.

Asbury Park's first radio station, WDWM, arrived in Asbury Park in the summer of 1927. It was first located on the sand hills along Bangs Avenue, about a mile west of town. But in November of that year, the station was renamed WCAP and moved to the new Charms Candy Company Building on Bangs Avenue. From there it would relocate again in late 1931 to the north side of the promenade at the newly built Convention Hall. WCAP stood for "Wonder City of Asbury Park."

Radio in the early 1930's consisted mostly of live entertainment and WCAP broadcast live dance band concerts from the Casino along with local performers. In order to feature nationally known entertainers, smaller stations affiliated themselves with one of three "networks." The National Broadcasting Network (NBC) began broadcasting in 1926 with telephone links between New York and other major cities. It soon split into the Red and Blue Networks. The competitor, the Columbia Broadcasting System, started in 1927. WCAP became affiliated with CBS in 1932.

In 1931, a young vocal quartet from Piqua, OH, the Mills Brothers, became the nation's first African American singers to become national overnight sensations, thanks to radio. The Mills Brothers broadcast live nightly on their own network program. People in Asbury Park could tune into hear the Mills Brothers over New York City's WABC.[4] Inspired by the Mills Brothers, African American vocal quartets sprang up in every urban area in the country. Other radio networks featured live quartet singing by groups like the Southernaires, who could be heard in Asbury Park on New York City's WEAF in 1933.[5] The Southernaires' close harmony spirituals were quite different than the rhythmic Mills Brothers songs but both gained enormous popularity due to radio. The Southernaires probably never sang in Asbury Park but they did make an appearance in nearby Long Branch on June 5, 1936.[6]

The Southernaires performed in Long Branch NJ in 1926. This 78 RPM album set from the Classic Urban Harmony Archives

In the 1930's, radio vocal quartets, both black and white, were popular among all races. However, African American quartets did receive a significant amount of harassment due to their race. Numerous letters sent to the Four Vagabonds vocal quartet, now found in the Classic Urban Harmony Archives, dealt with questions about the group's race.[7] Orlandus Wilson, bass singer for the popular radio spiritual group, the Golden Gate Quartet, once told of receiving so much racist hate mail, it brought tears to his eyes.[8]

The Harmony Kings of Asbury Park

Recognizing the popularity of African American vocal quartets on radio, WCAP featured its own local group. That group was Asbury Park's Harmony Kings. [*The term "quartet singing" refers to a genre of harmony, where each member sings a different part, not the number of singers.*]

The first newspaper mention of the "Four Kings of Harmony" was on November 16, 1933, when they performed at a victory celebration at Convention Hall for Edward Banker, who was just named city magistrate. Also performing were a number of white artists including the Fort Monmouth Band, Bugle and Drum Corps of the American Legion and Veterans of Foreign Wars Posts and Mrs. Paula Phoenix, vocalist.[9] Speaking that night was recently-elected Freeholder and bandleader Arthur Pryor.[10]

Arthur Pryor must surely have been impressed with the Four Kings of Harmony for he added them to a December 1933 charity event he was hosting at Convention Hall. The diversified two hour program also featured the Alice Moore School of Dancing pupils, the Fort Monmouth Military Band, organist G. Howard Scott and dancer Miss Hazel V. Geary along with other entertainment. Following the concert there was dancing to Pryor's concert orchestra.[11]

On January 3, 1934, the Four Kings of Harmony entertained at the Jeffersonian Democratic Association meeting held at the Reindeer Restaurant, 39 Sylvan Avenue on the West Side. The Association's president was listed as Harry Richardson, most likely the same Harry Richardson whose band Bill Basie had once played in. Richardson lived only a few blocks from the Reindeer Restaurant.[12] The Four Harmony Kings were surely becoming popular. By January 1934, they began their own radio show, singing live over WCAP every Thursday evening from 10:15 to 10:30 PM[13]

One can only speculate as to the Four Harmony Kings' repertoire, but there's every indication they sang a mixture of spirituals and popular songs of the day, similar to the nationally known Southernaires. In February 1934, the Four Harmony Kings sang in a church in Farmingdale, NJ. Described as "The Harmony Kings of Asbury Park, Negro quartet from station WCAP," the group sang in a special program with the theme, "Lincoln and the Negro."[14] Later that evening, the Harmony Kings gave a musical presentation at the Methodist Church, also in Farmingdale.[15]

Later in February 1934, the Four Kings of Harmony entertained at the American Legion Home on Drummond Avenue in Asbury Park.[16]

In April 1934, the Four Kings of Harmony were back entertaining at the Jeffersonian Democratic Association on Sylvan Avenue. On that night representatives for the NAACP presented the case of David Fearce who was sentenced to life in imprisonment for the murder of Asbury Park's Strand Hotel manager William Potts in 1931. They were trying to secure Fearce a new trial.[17] Police charged Fearce and friend Ernest Jackson who were together the night of the murder. Jackson, who was tried after Fearce, was acquitted when he produced an alibi. Fearce's bid for a new trial was eventually turned down.[18]

The Harmony Kings were not the only black vocal quartets in the area. In fact, they may have themselves inspired several others. An annual memorial service held in the auditorium of the city high school featured the Elks' Choir, the Traveling Four Quartet of Bates Lodge 22 in Red Bank and the "Junior Harmony Kings," among others.[19] In later years, gospel quartets would train understudies who would sing as a "junior" quartet until graduating to the senior group. This could have been the case with the Junior Harmony Kings.

A May 3, 1934 WCAP radio listing curiously credited the group's weekly radio program to the "Five Harmony Kings."[20] Either this is a typo or the Harmony Kings added a new member, possibly from the Junior Harmony Kings. At any rate, the next day, May 4, the group sang at a Lodge sponsored program in New Brunswick, NJ, as the "Four Kings of Harmony."[21]

In July, 1934, the Four Kings of Harmony performed at a summer dance on the marine deck of the Belmar Yacht Club. Also performing was Jimmy Gervey's Biltmore Orchestra.[22]

WCAP was not the only radio station to feature the Harmony Kings. March of 1935 found the group singing at the Fourth Annual Radio Birthday Party of the American Legion, broadcast on WJZ (New York City) along with Carol Deis and an army band.[23]

Though not exactly amateurs, the Four Kings of Harmony (this time listed as being from Neptune, NJ) competed at a talent contest in Lakewood, NJ, on May 16, 1935. At least two other quartets also competed.[24]

As to the personnel of the Four Kings of Harmony and the Junior Four Kings of Harmony, it seems the members were at times interchangeable. An *Afro American* newspaper column by Ike Williams describing news from Asbury Park, told of the *Junior Four Harmony Kings* as guests at St. Stephen Church on January 17, 1935. It lists the members as Douglas Johnson (second tenor), William Jones (first tenor), Armando Martinez (baritone) and Joseph Carter (bass). Ernest Downing is listed as director.[25]

An April 1935 newspaper clipping of the *Four Kings of Harmony's* appearance at a Parent Teacher Association meeting at the Bangs Avenue School listed the personnel as Joseph Carter, Williams Biggs, Amondo Martinez and Douglas Johnson.[26] With the exception of William Biggs, the others had been in the Junior Harmony Kings four months earlier. In September, 1935, the Four Kings of Harmony made a trip to New York City to audition for National Broadcasting Company. Presumably they were auditioning for a nationally broadcast radio program. The personnel then were William Jones, Ernest Downing, Douglas Johnson Jr. and Ike Williams.[27] Only Douglas Johnson remained from the personnel of four months earlier, with William Jones moving up from the Junior Harmony Kings. Ernest Downing had previously directed the Junior Harmony Kings

Vivian Eley
Courtesy of Clifford Johnson

and Ike Williams was the one who wrote the article about the Junior Harmony Kings for the *Afro American*. How the audition went is anyone's guess, but nothing further was printed in the local newspapers about the Four Kings of Harmony of Asbury Park.

Vivian Eley
Courtesy of Clifford Johnson

Vivian Eley
West Side Broadway Star

Vivian Eley was one of the West Side's first Broadway stars. A singer, dancer and all around entertainer, Vivian toured Europe with Teddy Hill's Orchestra, appearing with the *Cotton Club Review* at Paris' Moulin Rouge in 1937. She was in the musicals *Hot Mikado* on Broadway with Bill Robinson and *Born to Swing*. She sang at the Apollo Theatre and made records.

Vivian Eley was born in New Rochelle, NY, on April 26, 1902. Her father, Rev. William H. Eley, was a pastor in the African Methodist Episcopal Zion Church and after a few years was transferred to a church in Bridgeport, CT. Vivian spent her school years in Bridgeport. Around 1920, Rev. Eley brought his family to

Asbury Park where he was made pastor of St. Stephens AME Zion Church. The Eley family resided at 143 Ridge Avenue, Asbury Park.

Vivian began singing in Asbury Park, first in church and then on Springwood Avenue. Clifford Johnson, a much respected West Side jazz artist of the 1940's and beyond, is Vivian Eley's nephew. He recalled his aunt very well.

"I was born in 1925 and as far back as I can remember [Aunt Vivian] was going back and forth between Asbury Park and New York City. I don't remember when she went to New York City for the first time. She went more than once. But she performed locally in many of the establishments here and she built her reputation in Asbury Park before she ever moved to New York City. She performed in nightclubs here."

"My mother [Vivian's younger sister] was an organist and my aunt was this great vocalist. I can recall them doing a dual concert at a church on Atkins Avenue in Asbury Park when I was a young kid. [*Clifford's mother's group, the Versatile Glee Club, sang on their own WJLK/WCAP radio program from 1948 to 1950.*] After going back and forth so often, [Vivian] decided she'd relocate to New York City because she was making connections there. But she'd come back to Asbury Park quite often, dressed in her furs and she was doing quite well."[28]

By the 1930's Vivian Eley was making frequent appearances at the Apollo Theatre and other Manhattan night spots and theaters. She had a part in the 1933 movie "The Emperor Jones" with Paul Robeson. A 1937 review proclaimed, "Vivian Eley [is a] charming Harlem actress. This young lady is most versatile. She can take a regular turn on the stage of the Apollo theater, where she is seen often. When show business is slow she can draw an audience by herself with interpretative recitals."[29]

In June of 1937, Vivian set sail for France along with the *Cotton Club Review*, a show that also featured the Berry Brothers, Bill Bailey, Rollin Smith, Jessye Scott, Whyte's Hopping Maniacs (actually Herbert "Whitey" White's Lindy Hoppers), Teddy Hill's Orchestra (including a young Dizzy Gillespie) and many others.. Vivian was a star vocalist in the review that opened June 11, 1937 at Paris' Moulin Rouge and ran for six weeks.[30] After the Moulin Rouge, the

Vivian Eley singing with Teddy Hill's Orchestra at Paris' Moulin Rouge, 1937.
Courtesy of Clifford Johnson

Scenes from the *Cotton Club Review*, Moulin Rouge, 1937
Courtesy of Clifford Johnson

Cotton Club Review moved to the London Palladium where it was to open on July 26. At this point Vivian Eley abruptly left the musical and presumably returned home. Her replacement was the blues singer Alberta Hunter, who was performing in London at the time. Hunter recalled being contacted by the William Morris Agency who had sent *The Cotton Club Review* to Europe, asking her to fill in for a month in place of

Vivian who had suddenly left the review. No reason for Vivian Eley's departure was given.[31] Newspapers reported Vivian Eley back singing in New York in October 1937, making multiple engagements at the Apollo Theatre.[32]

In 1939, Vivian Eley was in the cast in the Broadway musical, *The Hot Mikado*. *The Hot Mikado* opened on March 23, 1939, at New York's Broadhurst Theater on West 44th Street.[33] It was an adaptation of the Gilbert and Sullivan classic, *The Mikado*. Produced by Michael Todd, it was performed in modern swing tempo with an all-black cast. Starring in the musical were Bob Parrish, Eddie Green and Bill "Mr. Bojangles" Robinson as the Mikado. Also in the musical was a young vocal quartet that would later evolve into the Delta Rhythm Boys. Producer Michael Todd spared no expense in putting together this show since he'd failed at two

Program from *The Hot Mikado*
From the Classic Urban Harmony Archives

previous musical attempts. *The Hot Mikado* ran for ninety-one performances at the Broadhurst. It closed there on June 10, 1939 and moved to the New York World's Fair where it continued for the rest of the summer.[34]

In 1940, Vivian Eley was reportedly singing swing music on the RKO Circuit,[35] while a 1941 newspaper informed us that "Vivian Eley, the melodious thrush, is commuting between her summer cottage at Asbury Park and her spacious apartment in the Roger Morris Park area of New York City.[36]

By 1942, Vivian Eley had become part of a vocal quartet. As reported by *Billboard* magazine, "A new sepia outfit, Four Chimes, is being formed consisting of Charley Ford, former pianist and arranger for the Deep River Boys, David Pugh, previously with the Beale Street Boys, and two femme vocalists, Vivian Eley and Christine Royce. Combo is being handled by Gale Miniature Attractions."[37] The Deep River Boys and Beale Street Boys were two of the biggest names in black quartet singing at the time.

The Four Chimes. Photos courtesy of Clifford Johnson.

We don't know how long the Four Chimes continued singing. David Pugh would later return to the Beale Street Boys.

Vivian Eley was also the first female West Side vocalist we know of to make a record. In 1944, she recorded the blues number, "See See Rider" with Bill Campbell's Blue Notes for the *Apollo* label (#351).[38] It is the earliest release known on the *Apollo* label. *Apollo Records*, was started at the Rainbow Music Shop, 102 West 125th Street, New York City, two blocks from the Apollo Theatre. It went on to produced countless great recordings in the fields of jazz, blues, gospel and rhythm & blues. Bill Campbell's Notes recorded at least three other records for *Apollo*. Apollo #352 features Vivian singing on both sides, "Baby Don't You Cry" and "Too Hip To Be Happy." We don't know if Vivian is on the other two.

In 1944, Vivian joined the cast of *Born to Swing* which ran in Philadelphia. The musical opened at the Lincoln Theatre at Broad and Locust Streets. Produced by Irvin C. Miller, it starred Tim Moore, Eddie Rector, Fay Canty, the female tap duo, Salt & Pepper and a large black cast.[39] Unfortunately, the musical did not last long and closed shortly thereafter.

Vivian Eley's second record.
From Classic Urban Harmony Archives

Left: Vivian Eley. Right: Program from *Born to Swing*. Courtesy of Clifford Johnson.

Following a long career in entertainment, Vivian Eley, the first Broadway star from the West Side, returned to the Asbury Park area to live in Neptune. She passed away in June 1985. In 2015, the Asbury Angels Foundation honored Vivian Eley with a plaque on the Asbury Park Boardwalk of Fame.

Erskine Hawkins' West Side Connection

Erskine Ramsey Hawkins was born in Birmingham, Alabama, on July 26, 1914. He was destined to become one of the world's greatest bandleaders and trumpet players. His composition, "Tuxedo Junction," would forever immortalize the center of Birmingham's black nightlife, an area similar to Asbury Park's West Side.

In 1930, at the age of 16, Hawkins moved to Montgomery, Alabama, to enroll in the State Teachers College (now Alabama State University). Majoring in music, Hawkins joined the Bama State Collegians, as a trumpet player. The college band began touring the country to raise money for the school. Led by J. B. Sims, the Bama State Collegians played not only jazz and dance tunes but also military music and symphonic pieces. Hawkins graduated in 1934 but stayed on to teach

Erskine Hawkins
Promotional photo

138

UBANGI CLUB, 131st STREET and 7th AVENUE, featuring GLADYS BENTLEY and a cast of 40.

Postcard of Erskine Hawkins and the Bama State Collegians.
From the Classic Urban Harmony Archives.

music and play with the band. The Collegians quickly developed a reputation as one of the country's best college bands, led by Erskine Hawkins' flamboyant style and ability to hit high notes. But their career didn't really take off until playing Asbury Park in 1934.[40]

"During my last year [at State Teachers college], Hawkins once recalled, "The band had a tour up as far as Asbury Park, doing one night stands. When we got to Asbury Park, some of the musicians from New York came over to get a listen to us; John Hammond and Benny Carter came over to hear. It was the talk of the town; this young boy comes from the South - and they were talking about me - hitting all those high notes. So they wanted to come and see what it was all about. And Frank Schiffman, the owner of the Apollo Theatre and the Harlem Opera House, came over to hear us. So he booked us into the Harlem Opera House. When we got there, we did such a nice job - the place was packed. We did five, six, seven shows a day."[41]

Being heard in Asbury Park was a turning point in Erskine Hawkins' career. We're not sure where Erskine Hawkins played in Asbury Park in 1934, but he was back playing the Asbury Park "Colored" Elks Club in August 1936.[42] The Elks Club was known for its crowded weekly dances as well as late night jazz jam sessions.

Notes to Chapter 9

[1] *The Story of Asbury Park*, originally printed 1931, reprinted by the Asbury Park Historical Society, 2002, pp. 8 - 13.

[2] *The Story of Asbury Park,* p. 2.

[3] "History of Radio," Wikipedia.

[4] "Radio Programs," *Asbury Park Press*, 13 Oct, 1931, p. 7.

[5] "Radio Programs," *Asbury Park Press*, 28 Mar, 1933, p. 9.

[6] "Negro Quartet Gives Concert," *Asbury Park Press*, 6, Jun, 1936, p. 11.

[7] Letters to the Four Vagabonds (1937 - 1939), held in the Classic Urban Harmony Archives. See Charlie & Pamela Horner, "The Four Vagabonds Radio Years: 1933—1939 Discovering the Lost Letters," *Echoes of the Past*, #118 (2016), pp. 12-19.

[8] The author's Interviews with Golden Gate Quartet bass singer, Orlandus Wilson, 1994.

[9] "Edward Banker Seen Choice As Next City Magistrate," *Asbury Park Press*, 16 Nov, 1933, p. 1.

[10] "Silverstein Says Banker Sought To Buy Position: Magistrate 'Deal' Denied, *Asbury Park Press*, 17 Nov, 1933, p. 2.

[11] "Prepare Program for Charity Ball, *Asbury Park Press*, 13 Dec, 1933, p. 3.

[12] "Local Happenings," *Asbury Park Press*, 3 Jan, 1934, p. 2.

[13] "Radio Programs," *Asbury Park Press*, 11 Jan, 1934, p. 10.

[14] "Sunday Church Programs," *Asbury Park Press*, 10 Feb, 1934, p. 12.

[15] "Farmingdale," *Asbury Park Press*, 14 Feb, 1934, p. 5.

[16] "Datebook," *Asbury Park Press*, 22 Feb, 1934, p. 6.

[17] "Club to Consider Case of Fearce," *Asbury Park Press*, 4 Apr, 1934, p. 15.

[18] "Fearce Conviction Upheld by State's Highest Court," *Asbury Park Press*, 5 May, 1934, p. 1.

[19] "Memorial Service," *Asbury Park Press*, 19 Apr, 1934, p. 17.

[20] "Radio Programs," *Asbury Park Press*, 3 May, 1934, p. 11.

[21] "Attended Musicale," *Asbury Park Press*, 4 May, 1934, p. 18.

[22] "To Dance on Deck," *Asbury Park Press*, 21 Jul, 1934, p. 6.

[23] "In the World of Radio," *Asbury Park Press*, 16 Mar, 1935, p. 8.

[24] "Amateurs to Compete in Lakewood Program," *Asbury Park Press*, 15 May, 1935, p. 12.

[25] *Afro American*, 26 Jan, 1935.

[26] "Names Committee," *Asbury Park Press*, 13 Apr, 1935, p. 3.

[27] *Afro American*, 28 Sep, 1935, p. 14.

[28] The authors' conversations with Clifford Johnson, Vivian Eley's nephew, 2015.

[29] "She's The Versatile Kind," *Pittsburgh Courier*, 23 Oct, 1937, p. 24.

[30] Program for *The Cotton Club Review* at the Moulin Rouge, Jun 1937. Courtesy of Clifford Johnson.

[31] Frank C. Taylor and Gerald Cook, *Alberta Hunter: A Celebration In Blues*, (New York: McGraw Hill Book Company, 1988), p. 134.

[32] "She's The Versatile Kind," *Pittsburgh Courier*, 23 Oct, 1937, p. 24.

[33] "Hot Mikado' Opens Here This Evening," *New York Times*, 23 Mar, 1939, p.26; Brooks Atkinson, "The Play," *New York Times*, 24 Mar, 1939, p. 26.

[34] *New York Herald-Tribune*, 1 Jun, 1939, p. 18.

[35] Floyd G. Snelson, "Harlem," *New York Age,* 14 Dec, 1940, p. 4.

[36] Floyd G. Snelson, "Harlem," *New York Age*, 16 Aug, 1941, p. 10.

[37] "Gale's Four Chimes," *Billboard*, 14 Nov, 1942.

[38] www.discogs.com/artist/2407883-Campbells-Blue-Notes

[39] Cheryl M. Willis, *Tappin' At The Apollo: The African American Female Tap Dance Duo, Salt and Pepper*, (Jefferson, NC: McFarland & Company Inc, 2016), p. 200.

[40] Jeff Wanser, "Erskine Hawkins," *Encyclopedia of Alabama*, www.encyclopediaofalabama.org/article/h-1365

[41] Chip Deffaa, *In The Mainstream: 18 Portraits In Jazz*, (Metuchen, NJ: Scarecrow Press, 1992), p. 138.

[42] "Erskine Hawkins Here," *Asbury Park Press*, 5 Aug, 1936.

Chapter Ten
West Side Contributions to Big Bands

The influence of Asbury Park's West Side on the careers of Count Basie, Duke Ellington, Sonny Greer, Claude Hopkins and Erskine Hawkins have been covered in previous chapters. While these musicians have worldwide recognition, they were, by far, not the only West Side contributions to the "Big Band Era."

Leroy Vanderveer

The Vanderveer family was African American in origin but intermarried with and was closely associated with the area's Sand Hill Indians. The patriarch of the family and their first musical star was Leroy Vanderveer.

Census rolls say Leroy Alfred Vanderveer was born in Newark, NJ, on May 18, 1893[1] (while his gravestone lists 1892).[2] In the late 1890's, Leroy's family moved to 1133 Springwood Avenue in West Park, where his father worked as a laborer.[3] The first newspaper mention of Leroy Vanderveer, was as a six-year-old in 1899. He appeared in Asbury Park's tenth annual "Light Infantry On Parade" event. Later to be called the "Baby Parade," the annual parade of carriages carrying cute babies dressed in costumes would draw an audience of over 50,000 spectators. Over 400

Leroy Vanderveer, ca. 1922
Photo courtesy of his granddaughter,
Rhonda Vanderveer Ladaye

babies were entered to compete for prizes. Though babies of color were generally not part of the parade, young Leroy dressed as a coachman and rode on top of a goat-pulled carriage carrying a white baby dressed as Governor Teddy Roosevelt's daughter. The baby was awarded a prize of a large beautifully dressed doll.[4] While this was likely Leroy Vanderveer's first time in front of an audience, it would not be his last.

By 1909, Leroy was playing drums in the West Side's Victor Orchestra, that also featured James Dickerson and Charles Richardson (trombones).[5] By 1912, as a member of the Alcedion Glee Club (headed by William D. Bryant), Leroy took part in a minstrel presentation of "The South Before The War" at Morrow's Hall. The show was such a success, it was given again in Educational Hall on the East Side that Thanksgiving Day. That performance was preceded by a street parade.[6]

Reproduction of the 1921 program for *Shuffle Along*. Reprinted for the 2016 Broadway musical of the same name.

In 1913, Leroy married Rose Delvalle and the two settled in New York City where Leroy found work as a nightclub musician. Leroy Vanderveer joined Deacon Johnson's "Prize Band" in 1917. He played the bandolin, a 15-stringed musical instrument popular in Ecuador. Deacon Johnson's band played the supper dance at the Hotel Astor every Saturday evening. Deacon Johnson's band also performed at the prestigious Clef Club.[7] The Clef Club was a popular entertainment venue and society for African American musicians in Harlem, achieving its largest success in the 1910's. James Reese Europe incorporated the Clef Club in 1910. It became a combination musicians' hangout, fraternity club, labor exchange, and concert hall.[8]

Sometime prior to June, 1921, Leroy Vanderveer joined Eubie Blake's orchestras; first Blake's Jazzone Orchestra (June, 1921) and then the Shuffle Along Orchestra[9] as a banjo player. [Some sources also list him as trumpet player.[10]] The orchestra supplied the music for one of the most important Broadway musicals of all time, *Shuffle Along*. The show was the first successful African American musical, premiering on Broadway at the 63rd Street Music Hall on May 23, 1921 and closing on July 15, 1922, after 484 performances. Written by Noble Sissle and Eubie Blake, *Shuffle Along* helped launch

Arthur Gibbs & His Gang, ca. 1923
Leroy Vanderveer front left with banjo. Arthur Gibbs at piano.
Publicity photo.

the careers of Josephine Baker, Adelaide Hall, Hall Johnson, Florence Mills, Paul Robeson, Gertrude Saunders, William Grant Still and Will Vodery.[11] Leroy played on the orchestra's July 15, 1921, recordings of "Baltimore Buzz" and "Bandana Days" (*Victor* 18791).[12]

"Shuffle Along" toured successfully throughout the country up until 1924, but a salary list from April 29, 1922 showed that by then, Leroy had already left the cast.[13] In fact, by October 1921, Leroy Vanderveer was already recording with Fletcher Henderson's Dance Orchestra.[14] Leroy is believed to have played on "My Oriental Rose" (*Black Swan* 2022), Henderson's first recording. Fletcher Henderson later went on to phenomenal fame as a band leader.

In 1923, Leroy Vanderveer joined the band of Arthur Gibbs and his Gang. Arthur Harrington Gibbs was born in Savannah, GA, in 1895, but attended high school in Atlantic City, NJ. He came to New York City around 1913, working as a pianist. After serving in World War I, Gibbs returned to New York City where he led a new version of the Clef Club Orchestra.[15] The Clef Club is most likely where he met Leroy Vanderveer. Besides Leroy, Gibbs' band also contained some former members of the original Clef Club Orchestra, broken up after the murder of its leader, James Reese Europe. One member of the new Clef Club Orchestra was trombonist, James Reevy, possibly another Asbury Park musician.

On April 24, 1923, Arthur Gibbs' band made their first record, "Louisville Lou" b/w "Beale Street Mama" (*Victor* 19070).[16] "Louisville Lou" was a huge hit, reaching a combined music chart position of number seven nationwide.[17]

But that was minuscule compared to the success of the band's next record. Arthur Gibbs and His Gang, with Leroy Vanderveer on banjo, recorded the first-ever version of "The Charleston" (backed with "Old Fashioned Love," (*Victor* 19165). James P. Johnson wrote the song, "The Charleston," for the Miller and Lyles Broadway musical "Runnin' Wild" in 1923. In fact, the musical took its name from the included song, "Runnin' Wild"

which Arthur Griggs had written, but not recorded, a year earlier.[18] The Arthur Gibbs orchestra recorded their version of "The Charleston" on October 10, 1923, nineteen days before the opening of the musical. The song quickly soared to the top of the music charts, reaching #1 in January, 1924.[19] The dance steps to "The Charleston" as seen in the popular Broadway musical, caused quite a stir.

The dance, the Charleston, was fast and "used the whole body in shimmying motions. It included a fast kicking step, both forward and backward, and slapping of the hands on the body, especially on the knees, while the dancers were in a knock-kneed position. This beating out of complex rhythms was something that most show-goers had never seen before, and the dance created a sensation."[20]

Soon the Charleston (the dance associated with the song) was sweeping the nation and heading to Europe. It became synonymous with the "Roaring Twenties" and the image of young white "flapper girls" with short bob haircuts and short fringed dresses dancing to the tune. Other orchestras like Paul Whiteman's would cover the song and keep the dance popular for a few years. But without question, "The Charleston" was the song that defined the 1920's decade.

By 1925, Leroy and Rose Vanderveer were living on St. Nicholas Terrace overlooking Central Park, with their three children and Rose's mother and sister.[21] Leroy Vandereer would continue playing, rejoining Eubie Blake's Orchestra in the early 1930's. He can be heard on fourteen of Blake's recordings made in New York City in 1931.[22]

In 1933, the Vanderveers moved back to 1133 Springwood Avenue on the West Side of Asbury Park. The Vanderveers' oldest son, Leroy Jr., married Eugenia Richardson, the daughter of bandleader Jonathan T. Richardson in 1934. Prior to that, Leroy and family had moved to 107 Union Avenue[23] (some sources say 109 Union Avenue) on Asbury Park's West Side.[24]

Leroy Vanderveer's son, future musician Eddie Vanderveer was born May 8, 1915, while the Vanderveers were living in the Bronx. Leroy Vanderveer died on January 14, 1942.

Eddie Vanderveer and George Fauntleroy

Two of the West Side's greatest musicians started out performing together in high school. Asbury Park High School played a key role in introducing young students to, and inspiring them to pursue interests in, music. Considering the city's size, the number of Asbury Park students who went on to make their mark in music is astounding. This was due in part to two major factors. First, in times of extreme segregation, Asbury Park High School was integrated. Second, and undoubtedly most important, Asbury Park High School has always had at its core, outstanding teachers who understood the importance of music in education.

In 1930, when George Fauntleroy joined the Asbury Park High School Band, the band was under the leadership of A. J. Hoban. Hoban's "genial personality and amiable disposition encourage[d] musicians." George Fauntleroy played tenor saxophone in the band along with trombonist Frank Bryan and fifty-one other student bandmates. Bryan would, years later, return to teach music at Asbury Park High School. The APHS Band played at all the football games, the 29th Division Parade and even a 1930 YMCA mass meeting at Convention Hall.[25]

George Fauntleroy's music activities took place in and out of school. In February, 1933, he played a solo at a special program given by the Junior NAACP at Bethel AME Church.[26] A 1933 newspaper article describing the musical contributions of African American APHS students mentions Fauntleroy as one of six "colored" members of the school band. It also mentions George's role in the success of a high school "vaudeville" presentation.[27] The vaudeville show, which featured tributes to Cab Calloway, Blanche Calloway and others, served as inspirations for a more commercial venture called *A Night In Harlem*.

A Night In Harlem was a fast and rhythmic floor show presented by Maceo White and Henry Hart at Club Harlem in Asbury Park. The cast consisted of many Asbury Park High School students (and a couple from Neptune High School). Some of the songs performed were "I've Got A Right To Sing The Blues," "Tiger Rag," "Underneath The Harlem Moon" and "Gate, You Bring Me Down." The music was presented by George Fauntleroy and His Blue Rhythm Boys.[28] When the show ran again at the high school for subscribers of *The Beacon* (high school newspaper) the orchestra was alternately called the Ted Coles Orchestra (Ted Coles, George Fauntleroy, Kike Fraisler, Tom Hogan, Ivy Wilson, Eddie Vanderveer and Gilbert Tucker).[29] Eddie Vanderveer was the son of professional musician, Leroy Vanderveer.

Floyd Ray's Harlem Dictators, ca. 1939. Floyd Ray (left);
Eddie Vanderveer (seventh from left); George Fauntleroy (fourth from right.).
Publicity photo from the Frank Driggs Collection.

The late 1930's found both George Fauntleroy (saxophone)[30] and Eddie Vanderveer (trumpet)[31] with the nationally famous Floyd Ray Orchestra in California. Biographical information on Floyd Ray is contradictory. Some reports have him being born in Parsons, Kansas, while some say Los Angeles, California or even Grand Rapids, Michigan. At some point Floyd moved to Bordentown, NJ,[32] and later to Scranton, Pennsylvania, where he studied at the Scranton Conservatory of Music.[33] Floyd Ray's orchestra began as the Harlem Dictators around 1934, in either Bordentown or Scranton.

In 1937, Floyd Ray and his Orchestra relocated to Los Angeles. From there they continued touring the western part of the country. In November 1937, the band was traveling from Milligan, Nebraska to Wichita, Kansas when their stationwagon with six members onboard was totalled in an accident with an oil truck. Floyd Ray suffered severe head injuries, a broken nose, lacerated face and severe leg injuries. He would eventually recover. George Fauntleroy received only bruises.[34]

Back in Los Angeles, Floyd Ray and his band won a series of band contests at the Palomar Ballroom. They would eventually best bands led by Glen Gray, Tommy Dorsey and Skinny Ennis. The contests drew 2,000 to 5,000 fans and were broadcast over the nationwide Mutual Broadcasting radio system.[35] Floyd Ray's Orchestra recorded eight sides for *Decca Records* in 1939. The band broke up when Ray entered the service in 1942 but he reorganized it after the war.[36]

On February 16, 1944, a dozen jazz musicians assembled at New York recording studio to record three songs in a session that would forever redirect the course of jazz music. Eddie Vanderveer was among them. The songs were being recorded for release by *Apollo Records*, a new company operating out of the Rainbow Music Shop, just down 125th Street from the Apollo Theater in Harlem. At about the same time, *Apollo*

Records was recording Asbury Park's West Side singing sensation, Vivian Eley [*see Chapter 9*] and would soon thereafter record Mahalia Jackson, The Larks, The Five Royales and many others. But that wasn't why this particular recording session was so historic.

The band on February 16 consisted of some young musicians who would later be the biggest names in jazz; trumpeters Dizzy Gillespie, Vic Coulsen and Eddie Vanderveer; saxophonists Leo Parker, Leonard Lowry, Don Byas, Ray Abrams and Budd Johnson; pianist Clyde Hart; bassist Oscar Pettiford; and drummer Max Roach. The band leader was thirty-nine-year-old saxophonist Coleman Hawkins, the oldest by far. Hawkins had made a name for himself a few years earlier with his recording of "Body And Soul." The song featured three minutes of improvising, while dancing around the original melody. The February 16 recording session took that one step further and is largely considered to be the first real session of a new type of jazz. It would soon after become known as Bebop.

Unlike previous melodic big band music that was made for dancing, Bebop was completely improvised and too fast to dance to. Bebop would become the new hip sound in jazz and Coleman Hawkins' band's "Woody 'n You," "Bu-Dee-Daht" and "Yesterdays," recorded on that day with Eddie Vanderveer on trumpet were the first in a new genre.[37]

Both George Fauntleroy and Eddie Vanderveer continued to perform throughout their lives. Fauntleroy would inspire his nephew Dorian Parreott to pursue a career in music [See Volume Two of this book]. Eddie Vanderveer died in 1979.

Courtney Williams

Trumpeter, Courtney Williams, was born in Asbury Park on March 29, 1916. He began studying violin at the age of eight but by his teens had switched to trumpet.[38] In a long career, Courtney played with Charlie Skeets's Band, Al Henderson's Orchestra, the Savoy Dictators and bands or combos led by Fats Waller and Hot Lips Page. He's also said to have played trumpet with and/or arranged for Benny Carter, Claude Hopkins and Cab Calloway among others.[39]

In 1938 when Louis Jordan was putting together the recording version of his Elks Rendezvous Band, Courtney Williams was added as trumpet player and arranger. That band would evolve into the world renowned Louis Jordan & the Tympany Five.

"I had just come off the road after a tour with Fats Waller's big band," Courtney Williams recalled. "And I heard that Louis Jordan was looking for a trumpet player. ... So I went along and talked things over with Louis, did an audition and joined as trumpeter and arranger."[40]

Courtney Williams would become a key member of Jordan's Tympany Five, performing and recording with them through 1941. During that time he also sat in on recordings by Buddy Johnson's Band and Snub Mosley's Band.[41]

Cozy Cole, drummer

William Randolph "Cozy" Cole was born on October 17, 1909 in East Orange, New Jersey. When he was still young, his family moved to Leonardo, NJ. Leonardo is a small community twenty miles north of Asbury Park. Cozy Cole came from a musical family. The oldest of five children, Cozy's brother Teddy Cole would go on to play piano with jazz great Roy Eldridge. His brother Ruben played with different groups around New Jersey and was arranger for singer Miss Rhapsody in Newark, NJ. A sister played piano in church. A third brother, Herbert Cole, dabbled a little as a drum player but was never a professional musician. The Herb Cole who sang with Bobby Thomas & the Vibranaires [*See Volume 2 of this book*] was most likely Herbert's son. The Cole family's father was a singer who'd gather the children around the family piano and direct them at singing when they were young.

Cozy Cole actually began playing drums in first grade at the age of five. Cozy's mother died while he was in grade school and his father died when he was a freshman in high school. During high school in Leonardo, Cole took manual training. There he would fashion his own drum sticks to practice with.

Cozy Cole. Photo by William P. Gottlieb. Public domain photo courtesy of https://www.loc.gov/item/gottlieb.01491/

Cole's first inspiration was Long Branch drummer, Sonny Greer [*See Chapter 5*]. "I was still in school when Sonny [Greer] was playing around [locally]," recalled Cole. "I used to see him up there throwing his sticks around and just doing everything. He looked good and he was a great showman. [Sonny] was the only black drummer working with all the white groups there in Jersey. There was a firemen's hall where they used to play, the library and different little halls around Red Bank, Asbury Park, Sea Bright, Long Branch and Keansburg. I would read about them playing and I would go and see Sonny."

"I used to carry [Sonny's] drums from his gig," said Cole. "I used to take them to my house and then the next day I would get a bus and take them to his home. Sonny used to give me fifty cents or a dollar to do that, which was great money in those days. Believe it or not, when I first went to New York around 1929 or around there, Sonny was with Duke Ellington."[42]

Cozy Cole moved to New York City in 1926 and joined the musicians union in 1928. At that time he was playing house rent parties with piano players like Willie Gant [See Chapter 6] for $5 a night. His first music job was with Wilbur Sweatman in 1928. Cozy's first records came in 1930 when he was asked by Jelly Roll Morton to play drums on a recording session with Jelly's Red Hot Peppers. Cozy spent 1931 - 33 with Blanche Calloway; 1933 -

"Topsy II" reached #3 on the Pop Charts in 1958
From the Classic Urban Harmony Archives

34 with Benny Carter; 1935 - 36 with Willie Bryant; 1936 - 38 with Stuff Smith; and 1938–42 with Cab Calloway. In 1942, he was hired by CBS Radio as part of that network radio's first mixed-race orchestra. After that, he played with Louis Armstrong's All Stars.[43] In 1958, his recording of the double sided hit "Topsy" for the *Love* label, reached number #3 and #27. Cole toured worldwide and appeared in music-related films, including "The Glenn Miller Story" and "Don't Knock the Rock."[44] Cozy Cole died in 1981.

Notes to Chapter 10

[1] Census information researched by Jayme Klein.

[2] www.findagrave.com/memorial/35073468

[3] 1910 Census.

[4] "The Light Infantry On Parade," *Asbury Park Press*, 21 Aug, 1899, p. 8.

[5] "What's Going On In Annexed Zone,*" Asbury Park Press*, 10 May, 1909, p. 9.

[6] "To Give Minstrel Show," *Asbury Park Press*, 26 Nov, 1912, p. 4.

[7] "Clef Club Planning To Buy Modern Home," *New York Age*, 8 Feb, 1917, p. 1.

[8] https://en.wikipedia.org/wiki/Clef_Club

[9] Craig Martin Gibbs, *Black Recording Artists, 1877 - 1926*, (Jefferson, NC; McFarland & Company Inc., 2013), pp. 84, 86, 87.

[10] http://www.redhotjazz.com/shufflealong.html

[11] Program handout for the 2016 Broadway musical, "Shuffle Along: The Making Of The Musical Sensation of 1921." Held by the Classic Urban Harmony Archives.

[12] http://www.redhotjazz.com/shufflealong.html

[13] John Cort's Enterprises Salary List for "Shuffle Along," 20 Apr, 1922. Courtesy of Doug Seroff.

[14] Brian Rust and Malcolm Shaw, *Jazz And Ragtime Records (1897 - 1942) Vol. 1, A-K,* (Denver, CO: Mainspring Press, 2002), p. 769.

[15]https://grammophon-platten.de/print.php?plugin:forum.41656

[16] Brian Rust, *Jazz records 1897 - 1942 A - Kar,* (London: Storyville Publications And Co., 1969), p. 607.

[17] Joel Whitburn, *Pop Memories 1890 - 1954*, (Menomonee Falls, WI: Record Research Inc., 1986), p. 173.

[18]https://grammophon-platten.de/print.php?plugin:forum.41656

[19] Joel Whitburn, *Pop Memories 1890 - 1954*, (Menomonee Falls, WI: Record Research Inc., 1986), p. 173.

[20] James Haskins, *Black Dance in America: A History Through Its People*, (New York: Thomas Y. Crowell, 1990), p. 43.

[21] Census information researched by Jayme Klein.

[22] Rust and Shaw, *Jazz And Ragtime Records (1897 - 1942) Vol. 1, A-K,* p. 157.

[23] Census information researched by Jayme Klein.

[24] "3 Cars Stolen Here," *Asbury Park Press*, 17 Dec, 1934, p. 1; Confirmed through correspondences with Leroy Vanderveer's granddaughter, Rhonda Vanderveer Ladaye, 2019.

[25] "53 Students Now Enrolled In Band At Local School," *Asbury Park Press*, 24 Nov, 1930, p. 15.

[26] "Church Services for Sunday," *Asbury Park Press*, 18 Feb, 1933, p. 4.

[27] "Colored Students Prominent at A. P.," *Asbury Park Press*, 8 May, 1933, p. 13.

[28] Dolores O. Meyers, "School Talent In Night Club Show," *Asbury Park Press*, 8 May, 1933, p. 14.

[29] Harold Singer, "Beacon Subscribers Treated To Spirited Assembly Revue," *Asbury Park Press*, 22 May, 1933, p. 13.

[30] Earl J. Morris, "Grand Town," *Pittsburgh Courier*, 13 Aug, 1938, p. 20.

[31] "Discography Of American Historical Recordings: Eddie Vanderveer," https://adp.library.ucsb.edu

[32] "But His Band Is The Result Of A Well-Made Plan," *Washington Afro American*, 4 Mar, 1939.

[33] https://www.discogs.com/artist/4077485-Floyd-Ray

[34] "Negro Orchestra In Crash Here," *Belleville (KS) Telescope*, 25 Nov, 1937, p. 1.

[35] "Floyd Ray Wins Out Over Tommy Dorsey, Glen Gray's Band," *Pittsburgh Courier*, 6 Aug, 1938, p. 20.

[36] "Discography Of American Historical Recordings: Eddie Vanderveer," https://adp.library.ucsb.edu

[37] Mark Myers, *Why Jazz Happened,* (Berkeley, CA: University of California Press, 2019), p. 10 - 14.

[38] Barbara J. Kukla, *Swing City: Newark Nightlife, 1925 - 50*, (Philadelphia: Temple University Press, 1991), p. 225.

[39] Eugene Chadbourne, "Artist Biography - Courtney Williams," www.altmusic.com

[40] John Chilton, *Let The Good Times Roll: The Story of Louis Jordan and his Music,* (London: Quartet Books, 1992), pp. 64-65.

[41] Brian Rust and Malcolm Shaw, *Jazz And Ragtime Records (1897 - 1942) Vol. 1, A-K,* (Denver, CO: Mainspring Press, 2002), pp. 878, 912, 913, 1170, 1601..

[42] Institute of jazz, Jazz Oral History Project, Interview with Cozy Cole by Bill Kirchner, Apr 1980, https://rucore.libraries.rutgers.edu/rutgers-lib/53342/

[43] Institute of Jazz, Jazz Oral History Project, Interview with Cozy Cole by Bill Kirchner, Apr 1980, https://rucore.libraries.rutgers.edu/rutgers-lib/53342/

[44] Leonard Feather, *The New Edition Of The Encyclopedia Of Jazz*, (New York: Bonanza Books, 1960), pp. 164 - 165.

Chapter Eleven

West Side Before The Second World War

By the late 1930's, times were changing in Asbury Park. The years of Prohibition were gone and so were the cabarets. Black artists were occasionally tolerated and in some rare cases even welcomed in traditionally white venues.

In August 1938, Chick Webb's all black orchestra, featuring nineteen-year-old songstress, Ella Fitzgerald, played Asbury Park's boardwalk Casino. Advertisements proclaimed Webb's band "America's greatest swing band" and the "A-Tisket A-Tasket" girl as "The First Lady of Swing."[1] The one surviving photo shows the audience near Ella to be all white. Perhaps people of color were allowed in the back?

In many ways, Springwood Avenue had not changed much over the earlier forty years. True, the ten-block thoroughfare now glittered brighter with red and yellow neon signs. But long rows of shops, churches, barbecue stands, beauty parlors, drug stores, taverns and restaurants still lined the street. Streets that intersected Springwood Avenue were still unpaved. Yet Springwood, itself, still shone brightly, the lifeline of the African American community.

Ella Fitzgerald with Chick Webb
at the Asbury Park Casino, 1938.
Courtesy of Alamy Photos.

No time was this more evident than on Thursday evenings, the big night off for those who labored as domestic workers in the beachfront hotels. Then Springwood Avenue was crowded with little gray buses and slow moving automobiles, delivering their passengers for a night of relaxation and entertainment. Restaurants would be filled to capacity. There'd often be a big dance scheduled for the Elks Club that would go on until all hours of the night. Black musicians performing in the beachfront hotels would often gather at the Elks Club for after hours jam sessions. The sounds of swing tunes could be heard coming

Artist's representation of Cuba's, some thirty years later. *Asbury Park Press,* 17 Jan, 1971.

from Springwood Avenue venues like the Club Harlem, the Capitol Tavern, the 2 Door Tavern and the Musicians Club. But by far, the crown jewel of Springwood Avenue's nightclub scene was Cuba's Spanish Tavern.[2]

Cuba's Spanish Restaurant

The *Afro American* described Cuba's in 1938 as "where the lights are copies of beer mugs, the waitresses are garbed like Spanish peasants and where Barrington Guy sings nightly and thrills rich white women and prosperous colored with his dramatic voice."[3]

Postcard of Cuba's Spanish Tavern's interior

Cuba's Spanish Restaurant began as Henry Lopez' Spanish Tavern, which opened at 1147 Springwood Avenue on February 22, 1934.[4] An application for incorporation lists Henry O. Lopez, his wife, Minnie Lopez of 1307 Bangs Avenue, and Ben R. Abromowitz (an investor) of Lake Drive Court, Asbury Park.[5] The Lopez's would soon move to 1137 Springwood, next door to the tavern.

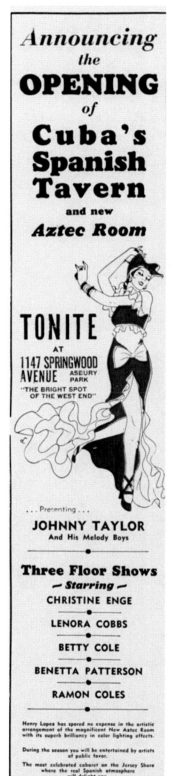

In earlier years, the 1147 Springwood Avenue property had been Silverstein's Shoe Store in the 1920's,[6] becoming the Faye Raye Dress and Specialty Shoppe in April 1933.[7]

Henry Oscar "Cuba" Lopez was born in Mayaguez, Puerto Rico, on April 11, 1895. After serving in the army during World War I, he settled down in Asbury Park around 1920.[8] In 1927, Henry married Minnie Quatrano.

Minnie was born in Asbury Park on April 15, 1904. She was the daughter of Italian immigrants, Marcellino and Mary Vetrano Quatrano. When Minnie was only four years old, her mother died, leaving Marcellino to care for the three children. He supported his family by operating a grocery at 1026 Springwood Avenue but he was also active in numerous West Side Italian community organizations and a member of Our Lady of Mount Carmel Roman Catholic Church.[9]

Before opening Cuba's Spanish Tavern in 1934, Henry Lopez dabbled in merchandise, at one point selling cigars. After operating the tavern for more than three years, Lopez undertook a major renovation on the building and in June of 1937, Cuba's Spanish Tavern celebrated a new grand opening. The various contractors who worked on the restaurant and nightclub, took out a full-page ad in the *Asbury Park Press*, congratulating Henry "Cuba" Lopez.[10]

Cuba's advertised a new "Aztec Room" built to resemble the Halls of Montezuma. Cuba's featured not only drinks characteristic of Spain and Mexico (harmonious to the surrounding decor) but also wines and liquors from around the world. Three floor shows were staged nightly. The entertainers on opening night were Johnny Taylor and his Melody Boys (band) and Christine Enge, Lenora Cobbs, Betty Cole, Benetta Patterson and Ramon Coles.[11]

By July, 1937, Cuba's was offering a cocktail hour and matinee dance every Thursday and Sunday afternoons, plus a new attraction, Reba Fields (the "hottcha girl").[12] In 1938, the house band was Garry Lee and his Jam Boys.[13] The 1939 house orchestra was now Oliver Green's and the presenter, Phil Scott (probably the club manager).[14]

Cuba's Spanish Tavern was classy. It was the kind of place you got dressed up to go to. "Cuba's had a bar in the front," recalled Clifford Johnson, who played Cuba's with Tommy McLeod's Squires of Rhythm in the early 1940's. "But then when you went past the bar to the back there was a real night club back there. They had an entrance from the bar and they also had an entrance from the outside just going into the nightclub portion. It was really like stepping into a part of New York City because they had all the curtains and spotlights, the whole nine yards. Cuba's audience then it was very racially mixed. Often times there were more whites than blacks. That would not have been that unusual on any given night, depending on who was playing. But it was very integrated."[15]

By the early 1940's, Cuba's was booking up and coming black stars like Savannah Churchill[16] and Milt Jackson.[17] Running Cuba's fell largely to Henry while Minnie ran the Midway Stationary Store next door.[18] Cuba's would exist for another thirty-two years until Henry Lopez' passing in March, 1970.[19] [*Post WWII Cuba's will be covered in Volume 2 of this book.*]

The State Ballroom

Asbury Park's West Side gained a major entertainment venue in time for the summer of 1938, with the opening of the State Ballroom at 1142 Springwood Avenue (at Atkins). Newspapers called the new ballroom a "miniature duplicate of the Apollo."[20] The management, former backers of Harlem amusement enterprises, stated their intent to bring in some of the best entertainers from the "Big City." From the beginning, they

made good on their promises, bringing in Count Basie's Orchestra in June 1938 and Duke Ellington's Orchestra in August. Tickets for the Basie concert, his first on Springwood Avenue since before he became internationally known, cost eighty cents per person. People drove in from Matawan and Keyport for the event.[21] Ellington's appearance on Sunday night, August 21, also drew well, with dancing from 10 p.m. to 2 a.m.[22]

West Side Entertainment in the Early Forties

As the 1940's began, the nightclubs on the West Side had pretty much stabilized. The Smile-A-While Tavern opposite the railroad station at 110 Lincoln Place (not to be confused with the Smile-A-While Inn) was taken over by John P. Drennan following the murder-suicide of 1938. In 1939, Drennan applied for a liquor license, intending to change the name to the Little Cotton Club.[23] By the

158

next week, when applying for a sign permit, Drennan had shortened the name to just the Cotton Club. Also applying for sign permits that month were the Turf Bar (1125 Springwood Avenue) and the Capitol Tavern (1212 Springwood Avenue).[24] Jackie's Cotton Club opened in July 1939, offering "the finest in colored entertainment." Early entertainers there included Earle & Frances (dance team), Edna Johnson (voodoo dancer), Rita Costello (songstress), Tita Henderson (torch singer) and Emily Darling. Kenny Dale was the M.C. and music was provided by Vernon O'Rara and his Swinging Sheiks.[25]

In October 1940, the Savoy Bar & Grill (1106 Springwood) Avenue celebrated its third anniversary with pianist Charles Stewart and Elouise Smith.[26]

The First 'Club Madonna' 1940 - 1941

The name, Madonna's, stirs memories of Lou Chiola's Springwood & Main Avenues nightclub and liquor store that existed from the 1950's to the early 1980's. Yet, the first incarnation of Club Madonna stretches back to 1940. It was founded by Ralph Madonna and his extended family.

Ralph Madonna was born in Italy around 1884. He met his wife in Italy and they married in Providence, Rhode Island in 1908 after migrating to the United States. They moved to the West Side of Asbury Park in 1930,[27] in the neighborhood known as Little Italy.

At the time, America was still under Prohibition and Little Italy was constantly being raided for illegal sale of liquor. By 1931, Ralph Madonna was reportedly running a speakeasy on Springwood Avenue. He was arrested on at least two occasions. The first raid occurred on the night of June 15, 1931, when a combined force of local and county authorities combined to try to clean up West Side speakeasies. They raided five speakeasies, including Ralph Madonna's at 917 Springwood Avenue. Four of the five raids took place in the Italian American section the West Side (900 and 1000 blocks of Springwood). The lone African American speakeasy was Joe Pappa's Rainbow Night Club at 1145 Springwood.[28]

Mr. & Mrs. Ralph Madonna
ca. 1958

A year later, authorities struck again, arresting some of the same proprietors. This time Ralph Madonna and the three others pleaded guilty and were fined $100 each. All paid their fines and were released except Gentry Cobb, the lone African American arrested. He was committed to county jail in default of the fine.[29]

When Prohibition ended in December 1933, Ralph Madonna continued in the liquor business, this time legally. Ralph opened a tavern and liquor store called Fifth Avenue Tavern at 812 Fifth Avenue (one block west of Main)[30] and in 1934 opened Ralph's Tavern at 817 Lake Avenue.[31] 817 Lake Avenue is just west of Main where Lake Avenue becomes Springwood Avenue. Thus 817 Lake Avenue and 817 Springwood Avenue are one and the same.

Meanwhile, in 1938, Ralph's son, Louis Madonna, began managing his father's Fifth Avenue Tavern.[32] Lou also took over Campbell's Tavern at 704 Main in 1939 and changed its name to Lou's Tavern.[33]

With another name change in 1940, Lou's Tavern became Asbury Park's first Club Madonna. At the Club Madonna, Lou Madonna hired both white and black entertainers. During the summer of 1940, they hired Sinclair and LeRoy.[34] Sinclair Rodgers and LeRoy Myers were talented black entertainers whose act consisted of tap dancing, singing, impersonations, comedy and ventriloquism. They'd made a name for themselves on the stage of the Apollo Theatre and were well on their way to becoming major stars.[35] So popular were the duo that they were held over for three straight weeks. Their success at the Club Madonna probably led Lou Madonna to consider more black entertainers.

160

From the beginning, Club Madonna suffered unfortunate setbacks. On September 24, 1940, defective wiring around the back of the orchestra stand started a fire. A portion of the club near the stage and dance floor was badly damaged.[36]

However, by October the club had been completely restored, repainted, repapered and "re-shined". The club hired an experienced chef for the winter season and offered "delicious Italian tomato pies". Club Madonna now advertised five spectacular floor shows every night. Curiously the club split the shows between "colored" and "white" shows. At 9:45 p.m. they had the first colored show, followed by the first white show at 11. The second colored show began at 12:15 a.m. and the second white show at 1:30 a.m. A late show ran at 3:15 a.m. It's not known from the advertisement whether the audiences were segregated or just the entertainers.[37]

By November 1940, Club Madonna also started showing movies every night at 8 p.m., preceding the floor shows. The club showed sound moving pictures starring Charlie Chaplin, Sophie Tucker and Bing Crosby, as well as boxing shorts, animated cartoons, travel films and a serial short. All this plus live shows with seven acts and music by Chet Johnson and All The Boys.[38]

The Club Madonna building had a second floor used for meetings by various lodges and trade organizations.

In April 1941, Club Madonna was again hit by fire. This time the damage was more extensive. An explosion blew out parts of the front of the building and caused severe damage and total loss of the first floor club.[39] This apparently marked the end of the first Club Madonna.

Ralph Madonna continued to operate Ralph's Tavern and the Fifth Avenue Tavern/Liquor Store aided in time by another son, Vincento "Vince" Madonna, and son-in-law Louis Chiola. The latter two would start a new Madonna's in the 1950's, located at the Springwood Avenue building that housed Ralph's Tavern. That will be covered in Volume Two of this book.

Notes to Chapter 11

[1] Ad for the Casino, *Asbury Park Press*, 19 Aug, 1938, p. 4.

[2] Harry B. Webber, "Rainfall Excessive, Seashore Folk Moan," *The Afro American*, 20 Aug, 1938.

[3] Webber, Ibid., *The Afro American*, 20 Aug, 1938.

[4] Ad for Spanish Tavern, *Asbury Park Press*, 21 Feb, 1934, p. 7.

[5] "New Corporation," *Asbury Park Press*, 29 Mar, 1934, p. 6.

[6] "Silverstein's 1147 Springwood," *Asbury Park Press*, 29 Jan, 1926, p. 1.

[7] Ad Faye Raye Dress and Specialty Shoppe, *Asbury Park Press*, 31 Mar, 1933, p. 1.

[8] "Henry P. Lopez, 74: Businessman in City," *Asbury Park Press*, 9 Mar, 1970, p. 11.

[9] 1930 and 1940 United States Federal Census.

[10] "Grand Opening Tonight -- Cuba's Spanish Tavern & New Aztec Room," *Asbury Park Press*, 11 Jun, 1937, p. 15.

[11] "Bright Spots," *Asbury Park Press*, 11 Jun, 1937, p. 4.

[12] Ad for Cuba's, *Asbury Park Press*, 3 Aug, 1937, p. 4.

[13] Ad for Cuba's, *Asbury Park Press*, 19 Aug, 1938, p. 4.

[14] Ad for Cuba's, *Asbury Park Press*, 25 Jul, 1939, p. 4.

[15] Authors' conversations with Clifford Johnson, 2015.

[16] Ad for Savannah Churchill at Cuba's, *Asbury Park Press*, 21 Sep, 1940.

[17] Ad for Milt Jackson at Cuba's, *Asbury Park Press*, 20 Aug, 1944, p. 4.

[18] "Minnie Lopez, 83: Ran Shop, Nightclub, *Asbury Park Press*, 13 Apr, 1988, p. 14.

[19] "Henry P. Lopez, 74: Businessman in City," *Asbury Park Press*, 9 Mar, 1970, p. 11.

[20] "State Ballroom Open For Your Pleasure In Asbury, *New York Age*, 16 Jul, 1938.

[21] M. M. Lyons, "Asbury Park," *New York Age*, 11 June, 1938, p. 11.

[22] "Ellington Here," *Asbury Park Press*, 19 Aug, 1938.

[23] "Notice," *Asbury Park Press*, 9 Jun, 1939.

[24] "Council Cracks Down on Noise on Beachfront," *Asbury Park Press*, 14 Jun, 1939, p. 1.

[25] Ad for Jackie's Cotton Club, *Asbury Park Press*, 8 Jul, 1939.

[26] Ad for the Savoy Bar & Grill, *Asbury Park Press*, 16 Oct, 1940.

[27] "Golden Jubilee," *Asbury Park Press*, 19 Feb, 1958.

[28] "Fifteen Seized In City Liquor Raids," *Asbury Park Press*, 16 Jun 1931.

[29] "Hold Six After West Side Raids," *Asbury Park Press*, 8 Aug, 1932.

[30] Ad for Fifth Avenue Tavern and Ralph's Tavern, *Asbury Park Press*, 14 Apr, 1938.

[31] "Notice," *Asbury Park Press*, 15 Jan, 1934.

[32] Ad for Fifth Avenue Liquor Shop, *Asbury Park Press*, 22 Apr, 1938.

[33] Ad for grand opening of Lou's Tavern, *Asbury Park Press*, 24 Feb, 1939.

[34] Ad for Club Madonna, *Asbury Park Press*, 9 Aug, 1940.

[35] www.leroymyers.com

[36] "Fire Damages Local Tavern," *Asbury Park Press*, 25 Sep, 1940.

[37] Club Madonna ad, *Asbury Park Press*, 10, Oct, 1940.

[38] Club Madonna ad, *Asbury Park Press*, 28 Nov, 1940.

[39] "$5,000 Fire Destroys Club Madonna Interior," *Asbury Park Press*, 14 Apr, 1941, pp. 1, 3.

Chapter Twelve

The World at War

UNITED WE STAND

THE WEATHER
Increasing cloudiness today.
Somewhat cooler tomorrow.

ASBURY PARK EVENING PRESS EXTRA
THE EVENING NEWS

FIFTY-FIFTH YEAR. NO. 288   ASBURY PARK, N. J., MONDAY, DECEMBER 8, 1941   • PRICE THREE CENTS

CONGRESS DECLARES WAR ON JAPAN
Japs Claim Sea Supremacy Won
U. S. ADMITS TWO WARSHIPS SUNK

On December 7, 1941, the war that was raging in Europe and the Pacific was suddenly thrust upon the United States. With the Japanese bombing of Pearl Harbor, all aspects of American life, including entertainment, changed. For two years, Americans had followed the destruction of London by German bombs. Now the war had been brought to them. Across the country, military recruiting offices were flooded with young men, and to a lesser extent young women, who felt it was their patriotic duty to enlist. In addition, Congress' September 1940 draft law called millions more to serve.

With the onset of war, a rationing program was set up limiting the amounts of meat, sugar, fat, butter, vegetables, fruit, coffee, gasoline, tires, clothing, shoes and fuel oil that people could purchase. Each family was issued a War Ration Book with a certain amount of ration stamps. Any excess money went into War Bonds. Communities held drives to collect scrap metal, tin cans and rubber to recycle into armaments. Sirens screamed air raid drills. Women found employment as electricians, welders and riveters in defense plants, replacing the men away at war. But as terrible as the war was, the war years also brought advances in both gender and racial equality. Evidence of progress in racial equality, however slow, was apparent in popular music.

During the war, the most popular form of music in America was swing band music. What had once been confined to black neighborhoods, like Asbury Park's West Side, had quickly caught the ear of white America. Large bands led by musicians with ties to Asbury Park, like Duke Ellington, Count Basie, Claude Hopkins and Erskine Hawkins

led the way. But white musicians began adopting this style of black jazz music during the 1930's and big band swing was now the rage in all of the United States.

Still entertainers, especially black jazz bands, had particularly hard times during the war. There were a number of reasons for this. First of all, many bands had their personnel depleted as members went off to war. Bands then raided other bands for the best musicians left. Bands played restaurants, concert halls and dance halls. But many of these venues had to limit their hours due to government enforced midnight to dawn wartime curfews. Food was rationed, so restaurants could only feed so many patrons. A twenty percent "amusement tax" was enacted to raise money for the military, meaning customers had to pay 20 cents tax on the dollar in any night club that included dancing. This hurt attendance. And with gasoline and tires rationed, entertainers had to stay close to home, no matter how few gigs were available.

Music reflected the times. Shortly after the draft law was passed, Red Bank, New Jersey native Count Basie and his band, now one of the best in the nation, revived and recorded the song "Draftin' Blues" (*Conqueror 9632*). Singer James "Jimmy" Rushing handled the vocals. "Draftin' Blues" was an old World War I song composed by black songwriter Maceo Pinkard in 1917.[1] The song warned women not to stand in the way of their men answering Uncle Sam's call.

In December, 1940, the same song was recorded by Skeets Tolbert and His Gentlemen of Swing, under the title, "Those Draftin' Blues" (*Decca 8516*). Yack Taylor sang the vocals. Other personnel on this recording are Skeets Tolbert (clarinet, alto sax), Carl Smith (trumpet), Otis Hicks (tenor sax), Red Richards (piano), John Drummond (bass), and Hubert Pettaway (drums).[2] Following the record's release in early 1941, Skeets Tolbert's band played Cuba's Spanish Restaurant on Springwood Avenue throughout the entire summer of 1941.[3] Also on the bill that summer were Smiles & Smiles ("those international favorites"), singer Jean Eldridge, conga dancer Verneda

La Selle, Lillian Fitzgerald ("Philadelphia Bombshell"), Sally Gooding (Ethel Waters' understudy), comedian Spo Dee-O Dee and emcee Ross "Chink" Collins. Joining the cast for a short time in August was singer dancer Helen Stewart. Helen would later become a part of the vocal ensemble, the Caldwells.[4] Other jazz greats Freddy Green, Kenny Clarke, Lem Johnson and a young Buddy Johnson all played with Tolbert's band, though we don't know which musicians were with him at Cuba's. Tolbert's band attracted a number of famous patrons to Cuba's including Bill "Bo Jangles" Robinson.[5]

Skeets Tolbert Band, Skeets second from left.
Courtesy of www.vocalgroupharmony.com

On Springwood Avenue, as everywhere else, everything had a patriotic, war time theme. Popular songs of the war era by black artists included "G.I. Wish" (Four Vagabonds), "Comin' In On A Wing And A Prayer" (Four Vagabonds), G. I. Jive (Louis Jordan), "Praise The Lord And Pass The Ammunition" (Southern Sons), "Stalin Wasn't Stallin'" (Golden Gate Quartet), "Till Then" (Mills Brothers) and hundreds more.

The war posed significant problems for musicians who wanted to record. The era's 78 RPM records were made of shellac, a resin created by bugs in certain parts of Asia. With the war, it became in short supply. In April, 1942, the War Production Board's rationing decree cut domestic shellac consumption by 70 percent. Shellac had military applications. All electrical wire was wrapped in cloth and waterproofed with shellac. Record companies stretched their existing shellac supplies through shellac recycling. "Shellac drives" were held where consumers turned in old records to be recycled into new 78s. But the existing supplies could only be stretched so far and production of phonograph records was severely curtailed.

In addition, on August 1, 1942, the American Federation of Musicians, led by union president James Petrillo, started a strike against American record companies due to disagreements over royalty payments. Union musicians could not make commercial recordings for any record company. Union musicians could still perform live on radio programs and live concerts, but not in a recording session. The strike would last into 1944. Musicians were allowed to record special V-Discs - recordings made for distribution to the armed forces fighting World War II. But these were not available to the general public. [*Actually, early shellac V-Disks broke in shipping overseas, so subsequent V-Discs were made of vinyl. This led to all records being made of vinyl after the War.*]

The Petrillo Strike had significant impact on recorded music, musicians, radio and even popular music itself. Some record companies began recording vocal groups "a cappella," without instrumentation. Thus, the popularity of vocalists, especially groups like the Four Vagabonds, Delta Rhythm Boys, Ink Spots and Mills Brothers, already gaining ground before the war, increased dramatically. [The Ink Spots had played Convention Hall on June,22, 1942.][6] Radio stations, having less recorded music to play, increased their number of live music programs. And finally, small independent record labels settled with the union earlier than the major companies, allowing them to get a foot in the industry. The sad effect of the Petrillo Strike is that for much of the war years, there are no recordings of many important artists during that time.

Tommy McLeod & the Squires Of Rhythm

As far as local musicians, much of Asbury Park's talent seems to have been coming out of Asbury Park High School. Asbury Park's elementary school, the Bangs Avenue School, was segregated. White students went to the northern half of the school, Bangs Avenue School North, and had white teachers. Black students went to the southern half of the school, Bangs Avenue South and had black teachers. The two sides were separated by an auditorium in the middle. Asbury Park High School, however, was integrated. Black and white students learned together, taught by an all-white teaching staff. And at Asbury Park High School, participation in music activities was not only taught but encouraged.

In the fall of 1940, an Asbury Park High School swing band was formed, called the Blue Bishops. Under the supervision of music department head Frank Bryan, the band began practicing every Monday and Thursday afternoon in the school auditorium. As a theme song, the band began using "Bye Bye Blues." Members of the band included Irving Bachman, Norman Miller, Daniel Lowenstein, Jerry Kamber (saxophones); Bob Bartlett, Herbert Blaicher, Jerry Berman (trumpets); Tommy McLeod, Walter Johnson (trombones); Paul Elisha (drums); Luke Christian (piano); Daniel Casriel (bass); Eugene Axelrod (accordion); Frank Clark (guitar); and Bernard Karasic (violin).[7]

Drawing from experience in the Blue Bishops, trombonist Tommy McLeod then organized a new jazz band in the fall of 1941 called the Squires of Rhythm. The Squires of Rhythm were a black band comprised of Asbury Park High School students and former students, though they were not directly associated with the school. The Squires of Rhythm made their first appearance at the Bangs Avenue School gymnasium. Composed of eleven young musicians, the Squires of Rhythm included leader and trombonist Tommy McLeod; a reed section of Harry Porter, Albert Tyler, Clifford Johnson and William Johnson; a brass section of Eddie Watt (also arranger), Ernie Jones, Vernon Jones, Virgil Hayes; drummer Robert Davis; and pianist Marion Grey.[8]

After a short time, Marion Gray was replaced on piano by Dolores Holland. Other members of the Squires of Rhythm in the early 1940's included Maxwell Bryant (vibraphone), his brother Ben Bryant (saxophone) and Arthur Blake.

As time went by, some members of the Squires of Rhythm would go on to become mainstays in the Asbury Park jazz scene. One was saxophonist Clifford Johnson.

Clifford Johnson was born at 143 Ridge Avenue, in Asbury Park on Christmas Day, 1925. At that time Ridge Avenue was part African American and part Italian American. Clifford's aunt was singer, actress and Broadway star Vivian Eley [*See Chapter 9*]. His mother was a music teacher.

Clifford Johnson. Photo by Joseph A. Carter Sr.
Courtesy of Madonna Carter Jackson

"In those days there was a piano in just about every home," recalled Clifford. "Music was the one outlet we [African Americans] had as a people. The music was a black thing. And most of our homes had pianos."9

"My mother was a music teacher. She taught piano and voice," said Clifford. "Students would come to our home and she'd teach them in our living room. I'd be in the kitchen and she'd be shouting to me 'fix this and fix that,' telling me how to cook things while she was giving lessons. But I'd be paying more attention to the music than what she was telling me about the food."

Almost everywhere I went, there was music," recalled Clifford. "Everybody had a piano in their house and I was around music all the time. My mother, being a musician, was the organist at Second Baptist Church on Atkins Avenue. I grew up in St. Stephen AME Zion Church where my grandfather was a pastor when I was very little. My mother left Second Baptist Church and came over to play at St. Stephens where she took over the Junior Choir. My brother and I sang in that choir."

"My mother had me playing the piano and she was stricter with me than with the other students. When I hit a wrong note she would pop my fingers with a pointer, a little baton. I thought,'Oh Lord! I can't learn this way!' I figured I needed to play something that she couldn't teach me. So she finally agreed to let me play the saxophone, because I really wasn't very good at piano anyway."[10]

"I always wanted to play the saxophone because when I visited my aunt Vivian [Eley] in New York City, she would take me to the Harlem Opera House (before the Apollo Theatre). They would have big bands there and I would be fascinated by the instruments and the saxophone solos. I just liked the sound and the lacquer and glitter of the horns. I was just attracted to it. So I started playing. Well, first I started on the flute. Then I went to saxophone. I must have been 12 years old. My mother sent me to an Italian professor here in Asbury Park, a music teacher named Professor Maraglia. He was on Bangs Avenue on the east side of the tracks. Professor Maraglia started me out reading the notes and learning the various key functions. I really wanted to start playing jazz as soon as I could. I always liked swing and jazz. He was kind of slow bringing me along. I am blessed, I guess, with good ear. I could hear certain things and that's all I needed to do. I could hear the piano or the organ, whatever the case may be playing their chords, and it was very easy for me to kind of figure out what I needed to do on the saxophone once I learned the scale. I stayed with Professor Maraglia for about two years. I stopped going because I started playing gigs when I was about 14.[11]

"Then I started to learn how to improvise by watching older musicians and hanging out with older guys. I started playing professionally with Tommy McLeod and the Squires of Rhythm when I was about 15 years old in 1941. I didn't graduate high school until 1943."[12]

In addition to playing the saxophone, young Clifford Johnson also sang in a vocal quartet called the Four Brothers Quartet. The group was aptly named as it was comprised of two sets of brothers; Clifford and his older brother William Johnson and the Harmon brothers, William and Edward. The quartet sang mostly spirituals and performed locally at community programs, churches and at Asbury Park High School where the Johnson Brothers were still students. The Harmon Brothers, being a few years older had already graduated from Asbury Park High School. The quartet was often accompanied on piano by Clifford's mother.[13] Clifford and William Johnson also sang in the Monmouth Elks Choir.[14]

Four Brothers Quartet, 1940.
Top, left to right: Clifford Johnson, William Harmon, Edward Harmon,
Bottom: William Johnson

"My mother got me involved with a lot of music activities," Clifford recalled.

Another member of Tommy McLeod and the Squires of Rhythm that went on to greater acclaim as a musician was Dolores "Queen Dee" Holland. Dee Holland was born September 18, 1923,[15] in Neptune, New Jersey, the tenth of eleven children. Also born into a musical family, her father played piano and her mother was a vocalist. They also had a piano in their home and would entertain themselves with music every Sunday. Dee also lived with her godmother whose husband was a classical pianist. As a two-year-old, she listened to him play and would then sit at the piano stool and play back classical compositions perfectly. As she grew older, Dee's mother would have her perform at school, church and community functions. Dee could listen to a song once and then play it back from memory! She did not begin taking formal piano lessons until the age of seven.

Dee Holland. Photo courtesy of "Asbury Park: Where Music Lives"

Dee continued as a child pianist, performing in shows and accompanying other vocalists and musicians, primarily in church. As word got around, she began playing popular secular venues. She was hired to play some of the white hotels along the Jersey shore, including the Berkeley Carteret and the Metropolitan in Asbury Park, and the Harbor Island Spa in Long Branch. At age nine, Dee Holland played piano and danced with a trio featuring herself, Jacque Raab on violin and dancer Vivian Holman. Dee and other black performers could entertain at the beachfront hotels in the 1930's, but the audiences were "white only."

Still a teenager, Dee Holland joined Tommy McLeod and the Squires of Rhythm around 1942. She would play with the band until sometime in 1943 when she relocated to Washington DC to work for the Federal Government. Dee Holland would return to Asbury Park in the late forties to continue her music career.[16]

Tommy McLeod and the Squires of Rhythm had just begun their professional career when the war began. "Tommy McLeod and the Squires of Rhythm had to play the night of the Pearl Harbor attack," recalled Clifford Johnson. "I had to play that very night. I think it was at Jack's Cotton Club on Railroad Avenue. It wasn't very much fun playing that night. President Roosevelt had come on the radio and talked about the bombing of Pearl Harbor. But we had to play."[17]

Throughout 1942, Tommy McLeod and the Squires of Rhythm got plenty of gigs. Most of the band members were still in high school and not yet of age to enter the service. In February, the band played a Valentine Dance in the gymnasium of the Long Branch High School.[18]

On Friday afternoon, April 24, the Squires of Rhythm and the Blue Bishops swing band both performed in the Asbury Park High School auditorium for a benefit dance to aid the sale of war stamps. Both bands donated their services and the dance drew 350 swing music fans.[19]

Both Tommy McLeod and the Squires of Rhythm and the Blue Bishops combined again to entertain at another benefit on May

Only known photo of the original Tommy McLeod & Squires of Rhythm. Courtesy of Clifford Johnson.

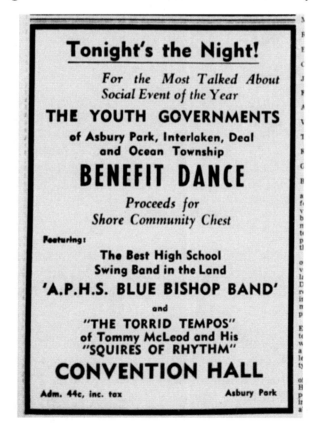

Tonight's the Night!

For the Most Talked About Social Event of the Year

THE YOUTH GOVERNMENTS

of Asbury Park, Interlaken, Deal and Ocean Township

BENEFIT DANCE

Proceeds for Shore Community Chest

Featuring:

The Best High School Swing Band in the Land

'A.P.H.S. BLUE BISHOP BAND'

and

"THE TORRID TEMPOS" of Tommy McLeod and His "SQUIRES OF RHYTHM"

CONVENTION HALL

Adm. 44c, inc. tax   Asbury Park

23. This time the event took place at Asbury Park's huge Convention Hall. It was held to raise money for the Shore Community Chest. Again, both bands donated their services.[20]

Clifford Johnson recalls Tommy McLeod & the Squires of Rhythm playing Jack's Cotton Club on Railroad Avenue but the gig he most vividly remembers is playing Cuba's Spanish Restaurant.

"We played in the back of Cuba's," said Clifford. "Many of our parents came out because most of the guys in the band were in their late teens. My mother came and other parents came. It was quite awesome to play for other people in a show with our parents sitting in the audience. I felt so privileged on that particular night. That was back when the cabs and limousines would pull up in front of Cuba's and the elite would come out with their furs and all the trappings, go into the back of Cuba's, and let their hair down."[21]

In May of 1943, Tommy McLeod and his Squires of Rhythm took part in a cabaret show called, "The Talk Of The Town," at the State Ballroom on Springwood Avenue. Also on the program were singer Alys Toombs and dancer, Naomi.[22]

After graduating high school in 1943, Clifford Johnson entered the service where he continued performing during the war. Clifford Johnson, Dee Holland and Max Bryant would return to Asbury Park after the war to continue their music careers.

ERROLL GARNER   520 Fifth Avenue
                                 New York 36, New York

Erroll Garner

In May of 1942, the Savoy Bar & Grill on Springwood Avenue advertised "one of the world's greatest piano players, Erroll Gardner."[23] Erroll Gardner was actually Erroll Garner who'd later rise to fame as a pianist, bandleader and composer ("Misty").

Erroll Louis Garner was born in Pittsburgh, PA in 1923. He began playing piano at the age of three. As a youngster, he would sit down at a piano and play anything he heard. Erroll never learned to read music - he played everything by ear. He was fond of saying, "No one can hear you read!" By the age of seven, Erroll was appearing on local radio and by eleven he was playing on Allegheny river-boats.[24]

As a nineteen-year-old, Garner arrived in Asbury Park in time for the summer of 1942. While playing at the Savoy Bar & Grill, he was discovered by local organist, Charles Stewart, who took him to Paul's Club (later Paul's Edgewater Gardens) in nearby Wanamassa.

Beginning in 1942, Garner played at Paul's Club for several summers. He was advertised as Earl Flynn Garner and was paid $75 a week. Paul's was a whites-only restaurant, but Garner

The Fried-Niesen Music Center owned by
William Friedman and Barney Niesen.
Clockwise from top left: first record store,
ca. 1938; clerk behind counter; patrons buying
records; expanded store, ca. 1941; 1941 ad
with photos of Friedman & Niesen.

172

became a favorite of the patrons there.

"People used to come in and stand at the bar and sing to his music," recalled Mrs. Jewel Walters who managed the restaurant back then. "It was a wonderful time."[25]

Some of the songs that Erroll Garner played at Paul's Edgewater Gardens he learned from William Friedman and Barney Niesen. Friedman and Niesen, who had attended Syracuse University

Paul's Club, later known as Paul's Edgewater Gardens
Photo from a postcard. Courtesy of Don Stine

together, opened the Fried-Niesen Music Center at 515 Cookman Avenue in Asbury Park in October 1938. Friedman had been a professional musician with Ted Weems' and other big bands while Niesen was a noted songwriter.[26] Friedman would later also go on to write songs like "If You're So Smart How Come You Ain't Rich" for Louis Jordan (1951) and "As You Are" for Dean Martin.[27] The music center sold records, sheet music, radios and musical instruments, and also gave music lessons and made personal recordings. By 1942 they had expanded to 501 - 505 Cookman (at Grand) and had become the largest record store and music center on the Jersey Coast. Unlike some stores in Asbury Park at the time, Friedman and Niesen welcomed customers of all races. Young Erroll Garner would drop by to purchase records and it soon became a regular stop for him. Friedman would play either saxophone or bass and Niesen would play the trumpet to perform new tunes for Garner.

"He'd come down to learn the music by ear and, God bless him, he would," said Friedman in a 1977 interview. "He was so fabulous and an absolute gentleman."

PAUL O'BRIEN

Presents

FOR THE COMING SEASON

CHARLES STEWART
At the Console of the Organ

BOB BRITTINGHAM
Singing and Playing Your Favorite Melodies

ERROL FLYNN GARNER
Wizard of the Piano Keyboard

LOGANTOWN ROAD, WANAMASSA, N. J.
JUST OFF HIGHWAY 35

For Reservations Telephone Asbury Park 9159

From the small studio in the back of the music store, Erroll Garner would return to Paul's Edgewater Gardens and play songs that he'd learned. [*Later, when William Friedman became national sales manager for Savoy Records in 1949, he helped Garner record four songs for Savoy, including "Penthouse Serenade."*][28]

173

Erroll's brother, Linton Garner, who played in Billy Eckstine's band, once told an interesting tale about Erroll. Sometime around January 1946, Erroll got word to his brother that he gotten in over his head gambling and was playing a small Mob-owned club in Asbury Park to pay off his gambling debt. In essence, he was playing piano there every night, a virtual prisoner of the Mob. Linton rented a car and drove Eckstine band members Fats Navarro and Chippie Outcalt down to Asbury Park to rescue Erroll. In a pre-planned move, Erroll stepped out of the club to have a cigarette and was whisked away by his brother and friends after flattening the club owner's tires to prevent being chased. The story can't be verified, of course, but Erroll

Garner was known to relocate to California at about that time. Three months later, he was busted in California for possession of pot. Erroll claimed he was framed and his friends wondered if this was payback.[29] Erroll Garner went on to become one of the world's great jazz pianists and composer of the well known song "Misty."

The West Side Draws Major Black Talent

The war years did see some major black entertainers visiting Asbury Park. On August 31, 1945, the State Ballroom (1140 Springwood Avenue, then called Chick's State Ballroom) featured famous comedian and actor Stepin Fetchit, along with boogie-woogie piano player, Sammy Price and the Frank Humphries Orchestra.[30] The State Ballroom had, by then, begun mixing a variety of entertainment with music. A 1943 State Ballroom bill advertised exotic dancers and a "patriotic" act of "Miss Thing and her War Bond Strip Tease" along with Johnny Green's Orchestra.[31]

On May 31, 1942, Cab Calloway's Orchestra played Convention Hall,[32] followed by Earl Hines and his Orchestra on August 4, 1942.

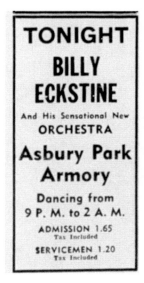

Postcard of the Asbury Park Armory. ca. 1930's.
From the Classic Urban Harmony Archives

Hines' featured vocalists included Madeline Green and Billy Eckstein. [*Eckstein and Eckstine were used interchangeably in early ads.*] Admission was only $1.10 per person and servicemen were admitted at half price.[33]

Billy Eckstine would return to Asbury Park two years later in August 1944, this time as a major star, fronting his own band.[34] In the band was young jazz trumpeter, Dizzy Gillespie. This time, Eckstine's band played the Asbury Park Armory.

The Asbury Park Armory at Lake and Bond Streets still stands today and has quite a history. Now a VFW post, the former Asbury Park National Guard Armory dates back to 1915 and housed troops heading for World Wars I and II. During the 1940's, it also played other roles. When not in use for military purposes, the large hall inside provided space for regular professional wrestling matches. It was also a venue for huge dances, featuring some of the country's leading African American music entertainers. There was no stage in the Armory then, only a large wooden dance floor with an overlook-

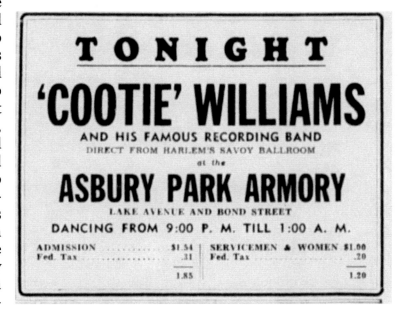

175

ing second floor balcony.[35] Located a couple of blocks from the West Side, the Armory was accessible to both blacks and whites. Cootie Williams' band played there in 1944, a couple of weeks before Billy Eckstine.[36] After the war, dances held there would become even more popular. *Billboard* magazine reported popular bandleader Jimmie Lunceford packing in 1,844 fans there on August 29, 1946,[37] though having visited the Armory, we suspect that was an exaggeration. Lunceford would die suddenly eleven months later at an autograph session in Oregon. He was 46. While the cause of death was listed as a heart attack, rumors circulated that he had been poisoned by a restaurant owner who was unhappy at having to serve a "Negro" in his establishment. It's said that other members of Lunceford's band who ate at this restaurant were also sick within hours of the meal.[38]

West Side Gospel Music
During the War

In times when those along the Jersey shore worried not only for the safety of their loved ones overseas but from attacks by German U-Boats, the Church became even more a source of emotional strength. Gospel music, be it church choirs or gospel vocal quartets, thrived in the war years.

The Harmony Singers of Asbury Park began singing in May, 1941. This gospel quintet was founded by Arthur Morris, who in his twenty-eight year career, would become one of the most important figures in West Side music.

Arthur Morris
Courtesy of Caleb Morris

Arthur Morris was born in 1916 in Williston, Florida. Arthur's father was a minister there and Arthur developed his singing skills in church. During the Depression, Florida was hit especially hard and Arthur Morris left the state as a migrant worker, picking fruit in the North. In 1934, he was picking apples in the orchards of Colts Neck when he decided to give up the harsh existence of a migrant worker and remain in nearby Asbury Park. There he joined St. Stephen AME Zion Church. When the war broke out, Arthur took a job at the Earle Navy Munitions Depot, painting ships. Arthur worked at Earle until an accident left him with a broken leg. He took the small settlement he got from the accident and invested in a friend's dry cleaning venture, a business he would eventually own. But, in 1941 he started the Harmony Singers.[39]

The first newspaper mention of the Harmony Singers was in January 1942 when the group entertained at the opening of Asbury Park's first U.S.O. club at Grand and Sewell Avenues. The event was attended by more than 550 people. The center provided servicemen a sanctuary where they could relax momentarily from the rigors of military life.[40]

In March of 1942, the Harmony Singers teamed up with the Monmouth Elks Choir to present "Belshazzar's Feast," a dramatic cantata in the auditorium of the Bangs Avenue School. This time Arthur Morris is listed as the Harmony Singers' manager and Granville Jones as assistant manager. The rest of the group is not named, but listed in the cast, along with Morris and Jones, is Ike Williams, formerly of the 1930's group, the Four Kings of Harmony. One might speculate that the Harmony Singers might have been an outgrowth of the Harmony Kings, but we can't prove that. [*Also in the cast were Clifford and William Johnson and Edward and William Harmon of the Four Brothers Quartet, and fellow Squires Of Rhythm member, Marion Gray.*][41]

By April, 1942, the Harmony Singers had their own radio program on WCAP-AM, a fifteen minute show on which they sang live every Sunday afternoon.[42]

On May 7, 1942, the Harmony Singers celebrated their one-year anniversary. The anniversary program was held at the Bangs Avenue school auditorium. As is customary with gospel group anniversaries, other groups came to sing and help them celebrate. On this occasion the Harmony Singers were joined by the Willing Workers' Quartet of Newark and the Sunshine Four of Florida, among others.[43]

May 26 saw the Harmony Singers again combine with the Elks Choir and the West Side Community Drum and Bugle Corp to raise money for the West Side Division of the Asbury Park Community Chest. Film star Canada Lee was a guest speaker.[44]

It's likely the Harmony Singers radio program brought them many opportunities to sing locally. We know only of those reported in the local paper. The end of 1942 saw the Harmony Singers giving a program of spirituals at St. Paul's Methodist Church in Ocean Grove.[45]

The year 1943 started out well for the Harmony Singers, or at least as well as could be under wartime conditions. Their radio program was now airing on WCAP every Sunday night at 9:30 p.m.[46] The group sang a set of songs at Bangs Avenue South School's Founders Day celebrations. The school for black children was now 46 years old, having been founded in 1893.[47]

The Harmony Singers and Elks Choir also sang at a program at St. Stephen AME Zion Church marking the observance of National Negro Health Week in Asbury Park.[48]

As a temporary relief from the stress of the war, Asbury Park's West Side scheduled a big four day festival for Mardi Gras, 1943. It began on Tuesday April 27 with a big parade that included units from the Kiwanis Boy's Club and the police reserve of the

Asbury Park Defense Corps, the West Side Community Center's Drum and Bugle Corps, the Blue and White Marching Club, and Boy and Girl Scouts. Many of the paraders were in costumes and there were decorated bicycles and floats. Wednesday's celebration included a paper fashion show and various games, side shows and amusements. On Thursday evening there was to be a big turkey dinner at the Community Center followed by a musical performance by the Harmony Singers.[49]

The Harmony Singers had just finished their Thursday evening performance when tragedy struck. The group's bass singer, Samuel Alston, suffered a heart attack in the basement of the Community Center where the festival exhibits were on display. Alston collapsed on the floor and was immediately rushed to Fitkin Hospital in nearby Neptune. Unfortunately, he died on route to the hospital. Samuel Alston was only fifty-five.[50]

Deciding the group should keep singing, the Harmony Singers were back performing at a P.T.A. meeting and student fashion show less than a month later, on May 20, 1943. There, they sang five songs.[51] The Harmony Singers also performed at a U.S.O. talent show in October.[52]

The year 1944 was an even busier year for the Harmony Singers. The group was still doing their live radio program each Sunday evening (now at 10 p.m.) on WCAP.[53] In January the Asbury Park Air Raid wardens of Zone 4 presented a musical show at the Asbury Park High School auditorium. Called "This Ain't The Army," the variety program featured at least fifteen acts, including the Harmony Singers.[54]

When the Republican Club of which Arthur Morris was a member held a Sunday afternoon event at the Bangs Avenue School in March, the Harmony Singers were there to sing, along with the Sky Light Singers of New York City.[55] The Sky Light Singers were just coming into their own as a major gospel group and would record their first record for the *Regis* label later that year. Arthur Morris, however, was beginning to demonstrate his ability to connect with and book gospel talent from around the country. The Second Annual Easter Sunrise service in 1944 brought the Harmony Singers in contact with Rev. James S. Pemberton. Pemberton, the pastor of the Ballard Methodist Church, conducted the service

Asbury Park High School stadium, scene of the annual Easter Sunrise services attended by thousands. The Harmony Singers sang at these. From a postcard.

in the Asbury Park High School stadium and drew close to a thousand people. A musical program, of which the Harmony Singers were a part, accompanied the Rev. James S. Pemberton's sermon.[56]

Rev. James S. Pemberton was pastor of the Ballard United Methodist Church. Ballard Methodist was founded in 1891. For many years the church stood at Asbury Avenue and Pine Street, at the northern edge of the West Side. Pemberton was born in New Jersey but graduated from the Moody Bible Institute in Chicago in 1928

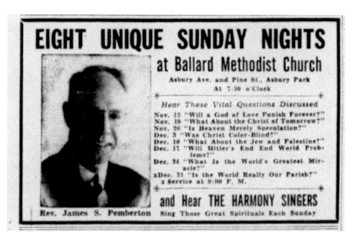

EIGHT UNIQUE SUNDAY NIGHTS
at Ballard Methodist Church
Asbury Ave. and Pine St., Asbury Park
At 7:30 o'Clock

Hear These Vital Questions Discussed

Nov. 12 "Will a God of Love Punish Forever?"
Nov. 19 "What About the Christ of Tomorrow?"
Nov. 26 "Is Heaven Merely Speculation?"
Dec. 3 "Was Christ Color-Blind?"
Dec. 10 "What About the Jew and Palestine?"
Dec. 17 "Will Hitler's End End World Problems?"
Dec. 24 "What Is the World's Greatest Miracle?"
Dec. 31 "Is the World Really Our Parish?"
    Service at 9:00 P. M.

and Hear THE HARMONY SINGERS
Rev. James S. Pemberton   Sing Those Great Spirituals Each Sunday

The Harmony Singers often sang at
Rev.. James Pemberton's services
at Ballard Methodist Church.

before returning to New Jersey.[57] He served as pastor at a number of Methodist churches in the state before becoming pastor at Ballard. Rev. Pemberton was a skilled orator and "fire and brimstone" preacher of some note. The church was packed to capacity for his sermons and he would baptize children by the dozens.[58] His 1943 sermon "Hell Holes And Fox Holes" drew attention to alleged vice in Monmouth County, gaining himself enough notoriety to run (unsuccessfully) for the state assembly on the independent Prohibition Party.[59]

Though the Ballard Methodist Church was a white church, Pemberton often incorporated black singers into his services. Starting November 12, 1944, Rev. Pemberton began a series of sermons running eight weeks. At each of the eight services the Harmony Singers sang spirituals.[60] [Unfortunately, the mostly wooden Ballard church building was completely destroyed by fire a couple of weeks after the last of this series of Rev. Pemberton's sermons.[61]

Of course, the Harmony Singers made plenty of other appearances in 1944. On April 9, they sang two spirituals at a flag unveiling to honor members of the Second Baptist Church who were in the Service. [62] Also in April, they entertained a group of black sailors from the Earle Navy Munitions Depot, along with the Smith Brothers Quartet and other entertainers.[63] In June, the Harmony Singers sang at an outdoor War Bonds rally at Springwood and Union Avenues. Additional entertainment was supplied by the "youthful Robinson Brothers Quartet," presumably a local black vocal group.[64] Another black vocal quartet, the Diamond Four Quartet joined the Harmony Singers at the 30th Anniversary service of St. Stephen AME Zion Church on October 15, 1944.[65]

Entertaining at the Asbury Park Salvation Army Citadel in September, the Harmony Singers were identified as Arthur Morris, Lawrence Flynn, S. Fauntleroy and William

Mitchell.[66] Solomon Fauntleroy was the brother of previously mentioned musician, George Fauntleroy.

By the Spring of 1945, the end of the long war was within sight, yet no one knew how much longer it would drag on and how many more lives would be lost. People started talking about "V-Day" or Victory Day. There would have to be two V-Days - VE Day for victory in Europe and VJ Day for victory in Japan. As the war in Europe began winding down, the American armed forces were still segregated. Some integration of non-combat forces was begun in early 1944,

The Willing Workers, ca. 1940's.
Annie Mae Morris, Virginia Nelson,
Leona Logan Pratts, Gladys Thornton, Rose Green.
Photo courtesy of Willie Morris.

The Willing Workers. Annie Mae Morris,
Virginia Nelson, Leona Logan Pratts,
Gladys Thornton. Courtesy of Willie Morris.

but full integration of the armed forces would have to wait until 1948.

As choirs were made up of male and female singers, so were the area quartet-style gospel groups. One prominent women's group of the time was the Willing Workers group. The Willing Workers were made up of Annie Mae Morris, Virginia Nelson, Leona Logan Pratts, Gladys Thornton and Rose Green. Gladys Thornton also played piano for the group. All the members were from nearby Long Branch except Annie Mae Morris, who was from Asbury Park. But the group would often rehearse at the Morris' home at 131 Ridge Avenue. The Willing Workers sang at many of the area churches and in fact also sang up and down the Eastern Seaboard.[67]

As talent often runs in families, Annie Mae Morris' two sons (Willie and Feoley) and three daughters (Francis, Betty and

Barbara) also grew up singing. [*Willie, Betty and Barbara Morris, especially, would play important roles in the West Side's gospel and r&b music scene in the 1950's. See Volume Two of this book.*]

In Asbury Park, "Brotherhood Week" was observed in 1945. February 18 through 25 was designated as the time for special observances of brotherhood. Local pastors and religious leaders of all denominations spoke at the U.S.O. club. Music was furnished by the "Harmony Boys," said to be a choir under the direction of Arthur Morris.[68] Whether Morris expanded the quartet or this was a misprint, is unknown. One clue is the mention of the Harmony Singers performing in Spring Lake as an octet.[69] At the Belmar Methodist Church, the Harmony Singers again sang as a "double male quartet."[70]

In April, the Third Annual Easter Sunrise service was held at the Asbury High School stadium. This time it was attended by 3000. Rev. James S. Pemberton again gave the sermon, entitled "Easter, God's V-Day." Captain John Waldron of the Salvation Army gave the prayer for a "V-Day at home with more unison on the home front and a disregard for race and religious prejudice." And the Harmony Singers sang several selections.[71]

WHY SHOULD WALTER NOT BE MAYOR of ASBURY PARK? WHY?

Come To

Asbury Park High School TONIGHT at 8.15

To Get the Answer

Meet the United Citizens League Candidates and Hear Them Speak

**GEORGE A. SMOCK, 2nd
JOSEPH R. ELY
THOMAS J. SMITH
EUGENE CAP'BIANCO
ROLAND J. HINES**

Every Interested Citizen of Asbury Park Should Attend This Meeting

Songs by the Harmony Singers

Paid for by United Citizens League

Political rally for mayor George Smock. Songs by the Harmony Singers.

As Asbury Park began gearing up for the local mayoralty elections, the Harmony Singers sang at rallies for re-election of the current mayor, George Smock.[72]

On May 8, 1945, VE Day finally arrived with the surrender of Germany. Yet the war in the Pacific looked like it would drag on. The Harmony Singers again teamed with the Pride of Asbury Elks Choir to honor an Asbury Park black soldier, Pvt. Thomas Johnson, who was killed in the war.[73]

Then on August 6 and 9, 1945, the United States dropped nuclear weapons on the Japanese cities of Hiroshima and Nagasaki, killing 129,000 people. On August 15, Japan surrendered. VJ Day was here. The war was over.

[To be continued in *Springwood Avenue Harmony*, Volume Two.]

Notes to Chapter 12

1 Guido Van Rijn, *Roosevelt's Blues: African American Blues and Gospel Songs on FDR*, (Jackson. MS, University Press of Mississippi, 1997), p. 6.

2 www.vocalgroupharmony.com

3 Ad for Skeets Talbot at Cuba's, *Asbury Park Press*, 11 Jun, 1941.

4 Marv Goldberg, "The Caldwells," www.uncamarvy.com/Caldwells/caldwells.html

5 "Bob Chester at Sea Girt," *Asbury Park Press*, 9 Aug, 1941, p. 5.

6 https://Inkspots.ca

7 Dorothy Flint, "Swing Orchestra For Asbury Park," *Asbury Park Press*, 25 Nov, 1940.

8 Shirley Jones, "Swing Occupies Asbury Attention," *Asbury Park Press*, 9 Dec, 1941.

9 Authors conversations with Clifford Johnson, 2015.

10 Asbury Park African American Heritage Project Interview Transcript, Interview with Clifford Johnson by Jennifer Souder, Charles Trott and Melissa Keeling, 8 Jan, 2018.

11 Ibid.

12 Authors' conversations with Clifford Johnson, 2015.

13 "Quartet To Sing Sunday," *Asbury Park Press*, 13 Sep, 1940.

14 "Elks Choir Gives Dramatic Cantata," *Asbury Park Press*, 7 Mar, 1942.

15 Asbury Park African American Heritage Project Interview Transcript, Interview with Dolores Holland by Jennifer Souder, Yvonne Clayton and Melissa Keeling, 12 Dec, 2017.

16 "Queen Dee," from the Jersey Shore Jazz Blues Foundation's website, www.JSJBF.org/jandbnc

17 Authors' conversations with Clifford Johnson, 2015.

18 "Valentine Dance Given by Class," *Asbury Park Press*, 9 Feb, 1942.

19 "Megaphone Has Its 2nd Dance," *Asbury Park Press*, 28 Apr, 1942.

20 "Youth Leaders to Have Dance for Community Chest," *Asbury Park Press*, 9 May, 1942.

21 Authors' conversations with Clifford Johnson, 2015.

22 League Gives Show," *Asbury Park Press*, 30 May, 1943.

23 Ad for Savoy Bar and Grill, *Asbury Park Press*, 19 May, 1942, p. 2.

24 "Erroll Garner," Wikipedia.

25 Leigh Cook, "Garner Furthered Career at Shore," *Asbury Park Press*, 5 Jan, 1977, p. 16.

26 "To Open Record Store," *Asbury Park Press*, 30 Sep, 1938, p. 3.

27 Correspondence with Douglas Friedman, 2016.

28 "Garner Furthered Career at Shore," *Asbury Park Press*, 5 Jan, 1977, p. 16.

29 Leif Bo Peterson & Theo Rahak, *The Music And Life Of Theodore "Fats" Navarro: Infatuation*, (Studies in Jazz, Book 59), (Lanham, MD: Scarecrow Press, 2009), pp. 73 - 74.

30 Ad for Stepin Fetchit at the State Ballroom, *Asbury Park Press*, 30 Aug, 1945.

31 Ad for the State Ballroom, *Asbury Park Press*, 28 Oct, 1943.

32 *Billboard*, 13 Jun, 1942, p. 18.

33 Ad for Earl Hines at Convention Hall, *Asbury Park Press*, 3 Aug, 1942.

34 Ad for Billy Eckstine at the Asbury Park Armory, *Asbury Park Press*, 30 Aug, 1944.

35 Charlie Horner, "Asbury Park Armory Important in Early Years of Rhythm & Blues," www.aphistoricalsociety.org/AP-armory.html

36 Ad for Cootie Williams at the Asbury Park Armory, *Asbury Park Press*, 9 Aug, 1944.

37 "Music - As Writer," *Billboard*, 7 Sep, 1946, p. 18.

38 "Jimmie Lunceford," *Wikipedia*.

39 The authors' interview with Caleb Morris, Arthur Morris' son, 7 Jul, 2012.

40 "550 Present at Opening Of City U.S.O. Center," *Asbury Park Press*, 5 Jan, 1942, pp. 1, 3.

41 "Elks Choir Gives Dramatic Cantata," *Asbury Park Press*, 7 Mar, 1942.

42 Radio listings, *Asbury Park Press*, 11 Apr, 1942.

43 "Singers Event Tomorrow," *Asbury Park Press*, 6 May, 1942.

44 "West Side Group Seeks Chest Funds," *Asbury Park Press*, 26 May, 1942.

45 "Datebook," *Asbury Park Press*, 9 Dec, 1942.

46 Radio listings, *Asbury Park Press*, 18 Apr, 1943.

47 "Bangs South P.T.A. Honors Founders," *Asbury Park Press*, 13, Feb, 1943.

48 "Dr. R. C. Brown Health Speaker," *Asbury Park Press*, 3 Apr, 1943.

49 "Festival Opens At West Side," *Asbury Park Press*, 27 Apr, 1943, p. 2.

50 "Singer Collapses, Dies After Concert," *Asbury Park Press*, 30 Apr, 1943.

51 "Pupils Stage Style Show," *Asbury Park Press*, 21 May, 1943.

52 "Hostesses Hear Talk on Beauty," *Asbury Park Press*, 7 Oct, 1943.

53 "Radio Programs for 24 Hours," *Asbury Park Press*, 12 Mar, 1944.

54 "Air Raid Wardens Give Musical Show in City," *Asbury Park Press*, 8 Jan, 1944.

55 "Datebook," *Asbury Park Press*, 17 Mar, 1944.

56 "Sunrise Rites To Greet Easter," *Asbury Park Press*, 7 Apr, 1944.

57 "Rev. James Saunder Pemberton," www.dvrbs.com

58 "36 Children Are Baptized," *Asbury Park Press*, 15 Jun, 1948, p. 11.

59 "Official Vote In The County," *Red Bank Register*, 11 Nov, 1943, p. 2.

60 "Pemberton Plans Series of Sermons," *Asbury Park Press*, 31 Oct, 1944.

61 "$75,000 Blaze destroys Ballard Methodist Church," *Asbury Park Press*, 9, Feb, 1945, p. 1.

62 "Asbury Class Activity," *Asbury Park Press*, 11 Apr, 1944.

63 "Earle Depot Unit Entertained Here," *Asbury Park Press*, 28 Apr, 1944.

64 "Crowds View War Equipment At City Display," *Asbury Park Press*, 29 Jun, 1944, pp. 1-2.

65 "City Church Plans Service," *Asbury Park Press*, 19 Oct, 1944

66 "Chaplain to Speak At Salvation Army," *Asbury Park Press*, 22 Sep, 1944.

67 The authors' conversations with Willie Morris, 8 Jan, 2017.

68 "Brotherhood Week Marked," *Asbury Park Press*, 18 Feb, 1945.

[69] "Como Methodist Church to Mark 75th Anniversary This Week," *Asbury Park Press*, 6 May, 1945.

[70] "Belmar to Hear Harmony Singers," *Asbury Park Press*, 29 Jun, 1945.

[71] "3,000 Attend Stadium Rites," *Asbury Park Press*, 2 Apr, 1945.

[72] "Frankel," *Asbury Park Press*, 21 Apr, 1945.

[73] "Tribute Is Paid to Pvt. Johnson," *Asbury Park Press*, 1 Jun, 1945.

SELECT BIBLIOGRAPHY

BOOKS

Abbott, Lynn, and Doug Seroff, *Out Of Sight: The Rise of African American Popular Music, 1889 - 1895*. Jackson, MS: University of MS, 2002.

Abbott, Lynn, and Doug Seroff, *Ragged But Right: Black Traveling Shows, "Coon Songs," and the Dark Pathway to Blues and Jazz*. Jackson, MS: University of MS, 2007.

Abbott, Lynn, and Doug Seroff, *The Original Blues: The Emergence of the Blues in African American Vaudeville 1899 - 1926*. Jackson, MS: University of MS, 2017.

Ayres, Shirley, *Asbury Park (Postcard History Series)*. Charleston, SC: Arcadia Publishing, 2005.

Baker, Jean-Claude, and Chris Chase, *Josephine Baker: The Hungry Heart*. New York: Cooper Square Press, 1993.

Balliett, Whitney, *American Musicians II: Seventy-One Portraits In Jazz,*. Jackson, MS: University Press of MS, 2005.

Basie, Count, as told to Albert Murray, *Good Morning Blues: The Autobiography of Count Basie*. New York: Primus, 1985.

Bergreen, Laurence, *Louis Armstrong: An Extravagant Life*. New York: Broadway Books, 1997.

Bilby, Joseph G, and Harry Ziegler, *The Rise And Fall of the Ku Klux Klan in New Jersey*. Charleston: History Press, 2019.

Chesek, Tom, *Legendary Locals of Asbury Park*. Charleston: Arcadia Publishing, 2015.

Chilton, John, *Who's Who Of Jazz: Storyville to Swing Street*, 4th Ed. New York: Da Capo Press, 1985.

Deffaa, Chip, *In The Mainstream: 18 Portraits In Jazz*. Metuchen, NJ: Scarecrow Press, 1992.

Dixon, Robert M. W., and John Godrich, *Blues & Gospel Records 1902 - 1943*. Chigwell, Essex, UK, Storyville Publications, 1982.

Ellis, Franklin, *History of Monmouth County, New Jersey*. Philadelphia: R. T. Peck & Co, 1885.

Feather, Leonard, *New Edition of the Encyclopedia of Jazz*. New York: Bonanza Books, 1960.

Friedman, Douglas E., *Four Boys and a Guitar: The Story and Music of the Mills Brothers*, West Long Branch, NJ: Harmony Songs Publications, 2016.

Garland, Claire Thomas, *Isaac Revey Richardson, Cherokee Indian Ike*. Self-published, ca. 2009.

Gibbs, Craig Martin, *Black Recording Artists, 1877 - 1926*. Jefferson NC: McFarland & Company, 2013.

Goldberg, David E., *The Retreats of Reconstruction*. New York: Fordham University Press, 2017.

Gottlieb, Robert, ed., *Reading Jazz: A Gathering of Autobiography, Reportage and Criticism From 1919 to Now*. New York: Vintage Books, 1999.

Haskins, James, *Black Dance in America: A History Through Its People*. New York: Thomas Y. Crowell, 1990.

Harris, Lorenzo Sr., and Aaron A, Mossell, ed., *Asbury Park and its Colored Citizens 1911 - 1931*. New Jersey: Privately printed, 1931.

Hodges, Graham Russel Gao. *Black New Jersey: 1664 to the Present Day*. New Brunswick: Rutgers University Press, 2019.

Jasen, David A., and Trebor Jay Tichenor, *Rags and Ragtime: A Musical History*. New York: Dover Publications, Inc., 1978.

Jackson, Madonna Carter, *Asbury Park: A West Side Story*. Denver: Ourskirts Press, 2007.

Jackson, Madonna Carter, *Asbury Park: A West Side Story – Second Edition*. Denver: Ourskirts Press, 2011.

Kimball, Robert, and William Bolcom, *Reminiscing with Noble Sissle and Eubie Blake*. New York: Viking Press, 1973.

Kukla, Barbara J., *Swing City: Newark Nightlife, 1925 – 30*. Philadelphia: Temple University Press, 1991).

LeBlanc, Eric S., and Bob Eagle, *Blues: A Regional Experience*. Santa Barbara, Praega, 2013.

Lewis, Evelyn Stryker, *Neptune and Shark River Hills*. Charleston: Arcadia Publishing, 1998.

Mazor, Barry, *Ralph Peer and the Making of Popular Roots Music*. Chicago: Chicago Review Press, 2015.

McKay, Lenora Walker, *The Blacks Of Monmouth County*. 1976.

Myers, Mark, *Why Jazz Happened*. Berkeley: University of California Press, 2019.

Peterson, Leif Bo, & Theo Rahak, *The Music And Life Of Theodore "Fats" Navarro: Infatuation*. Studies in Jazz, Book 59. Lanham, MD: Scarecrow Press, 2009.

Pike, Helen-Chantel, *Asbury Park's Glory Days.* New Brunswick, NJ: Rutgers University Press, 2005.

Pike, Helen-Chantel, ed., *Asbury Park Where Music Lives.* Asbury Park: Clayton Press, 2011.

Rust, Brian, and Malcolm Shaw, *Jazz and Ragtime Records (1897 - 1942) Vol. 1, A-K.* Denver, Mainspring Press, 2002.

Rust, Brian, and Malcolm Shaw, *Jazz and Ragtime Records (1897 - 1942) Vol. 2, L-Z.* Denver, Mainspring Press, 2002.

Snyder, Jeab R., *Harry T. Burleigh: From the Spiritual to the Harlem Renaissance.* Champaign: University of Illinois Press, 2016.

Southern, Eileen, *The Music of Black Americans.* New York: W. W. Norton & Co., , 1971).

Taylor, Frank C., and Gerald Cook, *Alberta Hunter: A Celebration In Blues.* New York: McGraw Hill Book Company, 1988.

Teachout, Terry, *Duke: A Life of Duke Ellington.* New York: Gotham Books, 2013.

Tucker, Mark, and Duke Ellington, *The Duke Ellington Reader.* New York: Oxford University Press, 1993.

Vache, Warren W. Sr., *Crazy Fingers: Claude Hopkins' Life In Jazz.* Washington, DC: Smithsonian Institution Press, 1992.

Van Rijn, Guido, *Roosevelt's Blues: African American Blues and Gospel Songs on FDR.* Jackson. MS, University Press of Mississippi, 1997.

Wade, Steven, *The Beautiful Music All Around Us.* Champaign, IL: University of Illinois Press, 2012.

Waller, Maurice, and Anthony Calabrese, *Fats Waller.* New York: Schirmer Books, 1977.

Ward, Geoffrey C., and Ken Burns, *Jazz: A History of America's Music.* New York: Alfred A. Knopp, 2000.

Whitburn, Joel, *Pop Memories 1890 - 1954.* Menomonee Falls WI: Record Research Inc., 1986.

Wolff, Daniel, *4th of July, Asbury Park.* New York: Bloomsbury Publications, 2005.

NEWSPAPERS and PERIODICALS

Asbury Park Journal

Asbury Park Press

Baltimore Afro American

Belleville Telescope (KS)

Billboard

Blues Research

Brooklyn Citizen Sun

Brooklyn Daily Eagle

Brooklyn Times Union

Buffalo Commercial

Chicago Defender

Cincinnati Enquirer

Coaster (Asbury Park, NJ)

Courier Post (NJ)

Detroit Free Press

Echoes of the Past

Indianapolis Freeman

Los Angeles Times

Monmouth Inquirer

New York Age

New York Times

Norfolk New Journal and Guide

Pennsylvania Gazette

Philadelphia Inquirer

Philadelphia Tribune

Pittsburgh Courier

Plain Speaker (Hazelton, PA)

Red Bank Register

Shore Press (Asbury Park, NJ)

Index

Hines, Earl, 174
Hippodrome Theatre, 63
Hite, Charles "Les," 71-72, 74-76
Holland, Dolores "Dee", 167, 169, 171
Holland, Eugene "Peggy", 85
"Honeysuckle Rose," 55
Hong Kong Inn, 95-97
Hopkins, Claude, 108-114, 121, 143
Hot Mikado, 133, 136
Hotel Brunswick, 5
Hotel Columbia, 5
Hotel Taylor, 106-107
Hunter, Alberta, 122. 135

I

Influenza Pandemic of 1918, 50
Ink Spots, 166

J

Jackie's Cotton Club, 116, 158-159, 169-170.
Jackson, Milt, 158
Johnson, Clifford, 134, 138, 157, 166-171, 177
Johnson, William, (*See also* Four Brothers Quartet), 166, 168, 177
Johnson, Douglas Jr., (See also Four Harmony Kings), 132-133
Johnson, James P., 51, 101, 146
Jones, Shrimp, 51
Jones, Sissieretta, (*See* Plack Patti)
Joplin, Scott, 30-31
Jubilee Songs, 16
Junior Harmony Kings, 132-133
"Junk Man Rag," 47-48

K

Kings of Syncopation (*See* Harry Richardson)
Kinmouth, Dr, Hugh S., 25-28
KKK (Ku Klux Klan), 8, 30, 95, 112
Knights of Pythias, 2, 31-38, 98

L

La Revue Negre, 110-111
Lafayette Hall, 120-121
Lambert, Donald "The Lamb", 51, 90-91, 102
Lopez, Henry O., (*See also* Cuba's), 156-158
Lopez, Minnie, (*See also* Cuba's), 156-158
Lord, George R., 9-10
Loudin, Frederick (*See also* Fisk University Jubilee Singers), 17
Lou's Tavern, 160
Lunceford, Jimmie, 176
Lyric Hall and Garden, 24-28, 34, 36-37, 43

M

Mack, Wilhelmina "Baby," 64-76
Madonna, Louis, 160,
Madonna, Ralph, (*See also* Club Madonna), 159-161
Madonna, Vince, 161
Magnolia Hotel, 107
Majestic Theatre, 43-44
Maraglia, Professor, 168
May, Butler "String Beans", 65-66
McLeod, Tommy, (*See also* Squires of Rhythm), 166-171
McGuire, Raymond, 87, 89
Methodist Camp Meeting Association, 3
Metropolitan Hotel, 44, 169
Miller Quartette Concert Company, 17
Mills Brothers, 130, 166
Monmouth Elk's Choir, 177
Morris, Annie Mae, (see also Willing Workers), 180
Morris, Arthur, (*See also* Harmony Singers), 176-179
Morris, Betty and Barbara, 180-181
Morris, Willie, 180, 181
Morrow's Hall, 15, 24, 33-35, 37-38, 50, 97

S

Sand Hill Indians, 1-2, 14-15, 24, 31, 38, 98-99, 143
Savoy Bar & Grill, 159, 171
Schiffman, Frank, 139
Scotty's Bar and Cabaret, 52
Scudder, Fillmore, 100
Second Baptist Church, 13-14, 17, 24, 105, 167, 179
Shockley's Hall, 36
"Shortnin' Bread," 119
Shuffle Along, 144-145
Singing Jane (chicken), 124
Smile-A-While Inn, 105-115
Smile-A-While Tavern, 116, 158
Smith, Bessie, 63
Smith, Clara, 66
Smith, Mamie, 66-67
Smith, Marie, 61
Smith, Willie "The Lion", 51
Sousa, John Philip. 18, 31, 41
Southernaires, 130
Springsteen, Bruce, 1
Squires of Rhythm, 157, 166--171, 177
St. Augustine Episcopal Church, 13-15, 24, 39, 97-99
St. Stephen AME Zion Church, 13, 17, 23, 36, 38, 99, 132, 134, 167, 176
State Ballroom, 158, 171, 174
Stetson's Uncle Tom's Cabin, 7
Stewart, Charles, 171
Stewart, Helen, 165,
Stride Piano, 23, 50, 51
String Beans, (*See* May, Butler)
Suarez, Julius, 105-106, 113
Sunset Lake Ice Carnival, 37
Swanee Inn (Los Angeles), 75

T

Taylor, Yack, 164
Te-Wan-Ka (Kate Patterson), 26-27
Theater Owners' Booking Association (TOBA), 62, 113
Thomas, Bobby 150

Thornton, Gladys (*See also* Willing Workers), 180
Tolbert, Skeets, 164-65
"Topsy," 151
Traveling Four Quartet, 132
Tribble, Andrew, 45
Turf Bar, 158
Turpin, Carie Williams, 52
Tuxedo Club, 121
2 Door Tavern, 156

U

Uncle Tom's Cabin, 6-7

V

Vanderveer, Leroy, 39, 143-147
Vanderveer, Eddie, 147-149
Versatile Glee Club, 13, 134
Vibranaires (vocal group), 150
Victor Orchestra, 37-38

W

Waller, Fats, 51-55, 101
Ward, Billy, 43-44
Water's Restaurant, 94
Watt, Eddie, 166
WCAP-AM, 130-132, 134, 177-178
WDWM, 130
Webb, Chick (Orchestra), 155
Wheeler, Alex F.(Band), 24, 36-38, 49-50
White, Britton, 2-3, 9
Whitman Sisters, 45
Williams, Clarence, 69
Williams, Cootie (Band), 176
Williams, Corky, 52-54, 89, 120
Williams, Courtney, 149-150
Williams, Elmer, 89, 94, 101-102, 109-111
Williams, Ike (See also, Four Kings of Harmony, Harmony Singers), 132, 177

About the Authors

Charles J. Horner Jr is a world-renown music historian, specializing in African American popular music. Born and raised in Philadelphia with a PhD from the University of Pennsylvania, Charlie's been totally immersed in black music since he began collecting records at age 11. That collection has now grown to over 55,000 records. From 1970 to 1995, Charlie hosted a popular weekly radio program out of Philadelphia on the history of R&B vocal groups. He's interviewed hundreds of singers and musicians. Charlie's produced and emceed over a hundred acappella stage shows and is largely credited for a resurgence in doo wop music in Philadelphia that began in the late 1970's and continues today. He's written liner notes for over fifty albums and published dozens of articles in magazines such as *Echoes of the Past, Goldmine, Bim Bam Boom, Record Exchanger, Harmony Tymes* and *Yesterdays Memories*.

Charlie's served on the board of directors of the United In Group Harmony Association's Hall of Fame and was president and co-founder of the Mills Brothers Society. He currently serves on the board of directors of the East Coast Music Hall of Fame and the Asbury Park Museum, where he is vice-president. He was awarded the Philadelphia Group Harmony Association's only Lifetime Achievement Award and received a Lifetime Achievement Award and a Doo Wop Preservation Award from the Philadelphia Doo Wop Festival. The Rock & Roll Hall of Fame & Museum in Cleveland has called Charlie, "one of the foremost authorities on early rhythm & blues and vocal group music."

Pamela Horner was born in Massachusetts and raised in Rhode Island. Pam earned a BS Degree from Rhode Island College and a MS Degree in Education from Queens College in NYC. She has more than 25 years experience as an educator and administrator in Connecticut, New York and Rhode Island. Pam's been a fan of r&b and doo wop vocal groups for many years. She's a skilled researcher in the fields of r&b, early r&r and doo wop vocal harmony. As a free lance writer and concert reviewer she's published articles in music periodicals like *Echoes of the Past* and *It's About the Music*. Pamela serves on the Board of Directors of the Asbury Park Museum and on the Advisory Council of the East Coast Music Hall of Fame.

Charlie and Pamela Horner jointly run Classic Urban Harmony LLC which promotes the legacy of African American music genres through multimedia presentations, workshops, courses, historical research, interviews, magazine articles, radio guest appearances, library and museum displays, producing and emceeing concerts, booking doo wop and acappella vocal groups, consulting for documentaries and books, a free Classic Urban Harmony email newsletter and the website, **www.ClassicUrbanHarmony.net.** The company's subsidiary, Classic Urban Harmony Press is active in writing and publishing books on popular music history. In 2019, the Horners were honored with the "Best Music Historians" award by the East Coast Music Hall of Fame and the "Distinguished Historians" award by the Asbury Park Historical Society.

Other Books by Classic Urban Harmony Press include:

- **"How D'Ya Like Me Now: The Story of Earl Lewis & the Channels"**
  by Earl Michael Lewis (2019). Available on Amazon.com

- **Springwood Avenue Harmony: The Unique Musical Legacy of**
  Asbury Park's West Side. Volume Two: 1946 - 1980.
  by Charles J Horner and Pamela Horner. Available soon.

Made in the USA
Middletown, DE
06 March 2020